ALSO BY DEBORAH KRASNER

Kitchens for Cooks: Planning Your Perfect Kitchen

Heirloom Skills and Country Pastimes:
Traditional Projects for the Kitchen, Home, Garden, and Family

From Celtic Hearths:
Baked Goods from Scotland, Ireland, and Wales

Celtic: Design and Style in Houses of Scotland, Ireland, and Wales

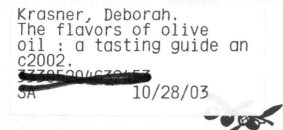

THE FLAVORS OF OLIVE OIL

A TASTING GUIDE AND COOKBOOK

Deborah Krasner

ILLUSTRATED BY ELIZABETH KRASNER

PHOTOGRAPHS BY ANN STRATTON

NEW YORK   LO   Y   SINGAPORE

SIMON & SCHUSTER
Rockefeller Center
1230 Avenue of the Americas
New York, NY 10020

For information about special discounts for bulk puchascs,
please contact Simon & Schuster Special Sales:
1-800-456-6798 or business@simonandschuster.com

Design by Vertigo Design, NYC

Manufactured in the United States of America

10 9 8 7 6 5 4 3 2 1

Library of Congress Cataloging-in-Publication Data

Krasner, Deborah.
    The flavors of olive oil: a tasting guide and cookbook / Deborah Krasner;
    illustrated by Elizabeth Krasner; photographs by Ann Stratton.
        p. cm.
    Includes bibliographical references and index.
    1. Cookery (olive oil). 2. Olive oil. I. Title.

TX819.O42 K73 2002
641.6'463—dc21   2002070744

ISBN 0-7432-1403-X

This book is dedicated to my dearest daughters,
Abby and Lizzie, who have grown up eating this food.

ACKNOWLEDGMENTS

For teaching me so much about olive oils and about other ingredients, I am deeply indebted to Diane Harris Brown, Wendy Lane, and the International Olive Oil Council, who sponsored trips to Greece, Spain, and Sicily, and seminars in Stresa, Italy, which educated me greatly. I am also profoundly grateful to Marina Thompson and to the cooks, food producers, and wine makers of Friuli and Umbria who hosted and taught our small groups of food and wine journalists about the foods and wines of their regions. Marina also arranged for me to spend two days with the great Italian cook Paola di Mauro, who furnished an unforgettable example of cooking with generous amounts of olive oil from her own olive grove.

Here in the United States, Beatrice Uggi of Esperya has been especially generous in teaching me about less well known ingredients and specialty products. Cindi Nicolson of The Olive Merchant was the first vendor to be excited about this project and to support it with tasting samples, and Karine Lefrere of Oliviers&Co, Ari Weinzweig of Zingermans, and David Tourville of the Olive Oil Club each contributed oils and insights. Ken Skovron, of Darien Cheese, awed me with his olive oil knowledge and was full of help. Manicaretti Imports sent me an extraordinary selection of outstanding oils, as did Corti Brothers and DeMedici Imports. Thank you too to Simpson and Vail, Foodmatch, Foods from Spain, Spirit of Provence, and A Cook's Wares for sending oils for tasting.

Thank you to Kathleen O'Neill of Culinary Inspirations in Turkey, who took me to the grill restaurant in Bodrum, where we both experienced vanilla-infused olive oil for the first time. Thank you too, Kathleen, for your help in deconstructing Turkish food, and thank you to the Turkish Tourist Board for bringing me to Turkey in the first place.

Kathy Gunst has been a true friend, source of inspiration, traveling companion, and a generous resource, honest critic, and recipe tester during the writing of this book; I am immensely grateful. I am deeply grateful too to food writer Michael McLaughlin, who offered ideas, emotional support, and extensive and helpful comments on the manuscript, and even tested recipes too. Food writers Nancy Verde Barr, Georgeanne Brennan, Paula Wolfert, and Nancy Harmon Jenkins offered information, encouragement, insights, help, and inspiration. Janice Easton was the first person to encourage me to consider this topic; she bought the book for Simon & Schuster, and she encouraged me to fly as high as I wanted to with the idea. Sydny Miner became the enthusiastic adoptive mother of this book, and she has done it as proudly as if she had birthed it. I am very grateful. My new hero, and the individual who is responsible for every bit of correct information in this book, is a man I've never met: Darrell Corti. He went through the manuscript line by line for three hours on the telephone, displaying not only his erudition, breadth of knowledge, and ability to correct spelling in three languages other than English, but also kindness. Any mistakes that remain are my own, but to the extent that any of the technical information is accurate, Darrell Corti is the man to thank for it. Two friends, Margaret Mikesell and Aliza Green, offered extraordinary acts of generosity and friendship by pre-editing language and recipes, respectively. I am deeply appreciative.

Friends and home cooks who tested recipes (thank you!) and commented include Maggie Cassidy, Ruth Clark, Linda Enright, Jessie Haas, Jill Hulme, Abby Jacobsen, Rebecca McBroom, Mary Oberly, and Connie Warren.

Heartfelt thanks also to: José Guerra, Trade Commission of Spain/Foods from Spain; Karen MacKenzie and Holly Hansen, The MacKenzie Agency; and Caitlin Connelly and Kim Yurio, Yurio/Connelly Public Relations, for their help in publicizing the book. Thanks too to Sur La Table stores and Cookworks for inviting me to teach.

I am thrilled that my daughter Lizzie was able to do the line illustrations of olive oil labels for this book. She is the third generation in my family to do illustrations, and she did these under considerable time pressure before leaving for a semester abroad. She was fifteen years old when Simon & Schuster approved her as an illustrator without knowing her age, identity, or relationship to me.

Finally, my husband, Michael, not only ate these dishes again and again, but even cooked many of them himself so that we could be sure that anyone could follow the recipes. For this, and much more, I thank him for his support and love.

CONTENTS

FOREWORD

At a time in my life when conformity meant everything, olive oil betrayed me. Sixth grade, Memorial School, Paramus, New Jersey. I'd managed a social coup; our class arbiter of popularity, Vicki S., came to my house to play and stayed for supper. It was our usual—meat cooked in wine with herbs and olive oil. Fresh vegetables, a quartet or quintet, seasoned with olive oil and vinegar, and a big salad that my mother dressed at the table. Mom's family is Tuscan. Each year the family sent oil from the farm in Italy. Olive oil in our house was like water and air . . . constant and necessary. It served as food, medicine, and cosmetic. It was part of who we were. In fact, it still is.

Mom measured her oil into the salad spoon, then tossed it with the greens. Already screwing up her nose at the unfamiliar tastes on her plate, Vicki asked, "What's that?"

The kindly reply: "Olive oil."

"Yuck!" was the comeback.

A deep freeze descended. In Italian my grandmother asked what was wrong. Mom explained (still in Italian) that our guest was an uncivilized little peasant. There was barely a drop of conversation after that. My dream of being one of the popular kids pretty much evaporated.

I'll bet right now Vicki S. has olive oil in her kitchen and she's none too secure about its quality. That's where Deborah Krasner and this book come in.

At last a gifted food writer and researcher has devoted a book to everyone who is trying olive oil but isn't sure of themselves (which, I believe, is 95 percent of us). Deborah has gone deep and wide, traveling to olive-producing regions from Greece to California, asking—and asking again—questions until she can distill the information with absolute clarity.

She is there for us at that moment when we stand in the market puzzling over which oil to buy, wondering about things like: What in heaven's name does "extra virgin" actually mean? What kind should I cook with? How do I store it? And then there is the greatest gift of this book: What do these different oils taste like?

Deborah's tasting of more than 200 oils provides us with lucid, intelligent descriptions. No one has done this before. They are invaluable; now we know.

For much of the world, olive oil is part of life, almost as vital and ubiquitous as air and water. Deborah reaches out to us with information and delight to gift us with that kind of familiarity. Yet she digs too into health issues, production methods, ways of keeping and not keeping oil, as well as providing a generous collection of delectable recipes. If Vicki's mom had had this book, who knows, it might have forestalled that fatal exclamation at our kitchen table all those years ago.

—Lynne Rossetto Kasper,
host, public radio's The Splendid Table,™ *St. Paul, May 2002*

THE FLAVORS OF OLIVE OIL
A TASTING GUIDE AND COOKBOOK

INTRODUCTION

As a food professional in a small town in rural Vermont, I'm frequently questioned by friends and acquaintances when I'm grocery shopping. Even in my local food coop, the proliferation of olive oils on the shelves over the past few years has been phenomenal. What is in all those alluring and beautiful bottles? How do the tastes differ? Which oils should I use for cooking, which for salads? Often the information on the labels doesn't offer much help. Given the confusion we were all experiencing, I decided to embark on this research and tasting project, describing and characterizing more than 150 of the most interesting extra virgin olive oils, creating a cohesive descriptive system, and providing recipes keyed to that system to showcase their special characteristics.

These guidelines for choosing and tasting a wide variety of oils have been designed to help you find the oils that most enhance the foods you eat. While we continue to receive conflicting messages about the healthiest diet plan to follow, it seems that olive oil plays an important and positive role in each of them. I hope *The Flavors of Olive Oil* will help you to eat more healthfully, deliciously, and simply.

In considering the questions posed by friends and family members, I began to see how to shape this book. The basic questions about how to know which oil to buy, or when to use what kind of oil, led me to try to characterize oils. If we can all choose wines based on simple ideas about flavor (white, red, dry, sweet), I think we can easily learn to do something similar for olive oils, which will allow us to reap the benefits of good matches for the food we serve. In its simplest form, the rule that guides my choices is this: *Use a delicate oil with delicate foods, and a robust and pungent oil with strongly flavored foods.*

You may think that you lack the palate to taste subtle or even obvious differences between olive oils. Think again. Although olive oils are as individual, complex, intriguing, and delightful as fine wine or great chocolate, I think you'll find that they're more accessible.

To discover the pleasures of olive oil, you don't need fancy equipment. You need only to taste a variety of oils with attention and focus. You don't need a specialized vocabulary; all that's required is interest, will, and some tips from this book.

How easy is it to learn to taste olive oil? My friend Jessie Haas is a good example. She's an adventurous home cook, but she doubted that she could taste the differences among oils. I invited her to my first olive oil tasting, and she's the only taster who has come to every single one since. As one of the most articulate tasters in our group, she's living proof that everyone can develop their sense of taste and refine their perception of flavors.

My own formal education in olive oil started with the International Olive Oil Council. The IOOC is dedicated to informing people about the benefits of olive oil, and they invite food journalists to learn firsthand how olive oil is made, how to taste it properly, and how to conserve oil at its best. Although I'd been cooking with olive oil for many years, that first trip taught me so much that it inspired this book. I've traveled extensively to olive oil regions since then, and on each journey I've learned more about olive oil production, about the foods of the Mediterranean, and about cooking. Now it's time to pass along what I've learned about a product that's delicious, beneficial to our health, and until recently, foreign to our North American food tradition.

A SHORT COURSE
ON OLIVE OIL

ONE OF THE MOST ANCIENT FOODS, olive oil has been a part of the human diet for thousands of years, and although the technologies for harvesting, hauling, and crushing have evolved, at its best olive oil remains essentially the same pure juice of the olive it has always been.

Today olive cultivation has spread around the world, though the Mediterranean region retains its central role. Spain leads the world in volume, followed by Italy and Greece. Other European producers include (in descending order by number of hectares of olives under cultivation) Portugal, Albania, Croatia, France, Yugoslavia, Slovenia, and Malta. In Africa, Tunisia leads the way, followed by Morocco, Algeria, Libya, Egypt, South Africa, and Angola. In the Americas, Argentina is the significant producer, followed by the United States, where our California olive oils are becoming notable. Mexico is the next largest grower of olives, though it produces little oil, followed by Peru, Chile, Uruguay, and Brazil. In the Mideast and Asia, olives are grown in Turkey, Syria, Jordan, Lebanon, Israel, Iraq, Cyprus, Iran, and China. In the South Pacific region, New Zealand and Australia have created outstanding olive oils.

Like wine grapes, olives respond strongly to variations in climate, soil, cultivation practices, harvesting methods and timing, processing, and age. While we can speak of Sicilian or Tuscan oils, just as we identify wines from these regions, we can also (again, like wines) talk about olive oil flavors. Although the tasting notes included here do allude to region, varieties of olives, and (occasionally) harvesting or processing methods, my focus is on broad flavor categories. Just as we can speak of fruity white wines, so can we identify a fruity olive oil. Similarly, a leafy green and grassy oil has the intensity of a full-bodied tannic red wine.

It's important to remember, however, that in fact there are many factors that account for the taste of an oil. Some obvious differences are accounted for by the variety of olive and by the climate (or microclimate) that the olive tree grows in. Every variety of olive has different flavor characteristics due in large part to differences in chemical composition and to the actual taste of the fruit. (It may be useful here to use apples as an analogy: Granny Smiths taste different from Red Delicious.) Like cider makers, olive oil producers frequently create a blend of oils from different varieties both to achieve a particular flavor profile and also to enhance the keeping ability of the oil, because some varieties of olives are more stable than others. Thus in Spain, producers often blend Arbequina olives (which have a delicate flavor) with Picual olives (which have a very distinctive flavor and high stability, prolonging shelf life) to make a longer-lasting oil with good flavor characteristics.

Less obvious factors that profoundly affect flavor include the difference between an oil made from underripe olives and one made from olives that are so ripe they've dropped from the tree. Very underripe olives are green, astringent, bitter, pungent, and intensely leafy-herbal and olive-fruity, whereas ripe olives tend to be sweet, low in antioxidants, light, flowery, and more nutty-fruity. The timing of the harvest is often a matter of regional tradition: In Italy, Tuscan oils, such as Laudemio, owe their pungency in large part to the fact that they are harvested early, while Ligurian oils, such as ROI, known for their delicate, light, and fruity flavors, are made from ripe olives.

Climate and cultivation practices affect the taste of an oil. Growers want a good rain (or the ability to irrigate) during critical growth periods, and then very little rain until just before harvest, because olives, like most fruits, acquire the most flavor when they are thirsty. Assuming a good climate and location for cultivation, the three most important factors in producing a good oil are the variety of olive, the age and vigor of the trees, and the quality of the soil. Olive farmers influence the acidity of the olives by their judicious use of fertilizer and water, and by their choice of the moment to harvest. While there is an influential movement in favor of organic oil production (and there are many organic oil producers), the majority of large producers practice nonorganic pest management in their groves to combat the olive moth, the olive fly, and black beetles, as well as a number of fungal diseases.

This brings us to the dark side of current olive production in countries of the European Union: According to the World Wildlife Fund and Birdlife International, European Union farm subsidies are creating an environmental problem. Because the subsidies are linked to production rather than providing flat-rate payments based on the area of cultivation, farmers are in effect subsidized to increase their production. According to the WWF, this policy "encourages the intensification of production, irrigation and the expansion of olive growing." It has led to an enormous increase in land

EARLY HARVEST
AND NEW OILS

Olive oil produced from the fruit of the first days of harvest is the most pungent because it is made from the least-ripe fruit. Like Beaujolais Nouveau wine, Early Harvest or New Oil olive oils are a seasonal delicacy, fleeting and short-lived. That's because olive oil improves after a rest in a tank, where the sediments can sink and the oil can settle. Oils that are immediately bottled, as are New Oils, inevitably suffer over time. New Oils are a wonderful taste treat when fresh, but they should be used up rapidly.

devoted to olive culture. The WWF estimates that up to 80 million tons of topsoil are being destroyed annually as a result of intensive olive cultivation in Spain, Italy, Portugal, and Greece. Further, the irrigation needs of increased olive production have led to serious water shortages in Crete, Puglia, and Andalucia. These subsidies have encouraged growers to clear both natural habitats and ancient olive groves to create intensive plantations in Greece, Spain, and Portugal. Today these subsidies amount to $1.9 billion per year. Reform in these policies is expected in 2003.[*]

However olives are grown, the speed with which they are harvested and pressed is one of the most important factors that affect taste. Olive oil producers are always aiming for a balance of sweetness and acidity, and because fresh olives are inedible before brining or curing, growers rely on practice, experience, and/or laboratories to do a chemical analysis to determine the precise moment to harvest. When the olives are judged to be ready, time is of the essence in getting those olives off the tree and to the mill, because olives oxidize and degrade rapidly. In order to make extra virgin olive oil of the required low acidity and perfect flavor characteristics, an olive has to be transported from the tree and through the mill in less than twenty-four hours. To visit an olive grove in the midst of harvest is to see many people working purposefully and ceaselessly until the harvest is done.

There are a number of harvesting methods, some antique and some brutally modern. Not surprisingly, many growers feel that the best oil comes from the most ancient method, hand-harvesting. (You'll see that many of the best oils have labels that indicate that the olives were picked by hand—it's a signal of artisanal production and pride in the product.) Other methods include spreading nets under the trees to collect either ripe olives

---

[*]Quoted in *Business Week,* July 16, 2001. More information can be found at http://europa.cu.int/comm/environment/agricultural/pdf/oliveoil.pdf. A summary can be found at http://europa.eu.int/comm/environment/agricultural/pdf/oliveoil_xs.pdf

that fall naturally or olives that fall as a result of manual beating of the branches, hand-held electric combs that strip the fruit from the branches, and tree-shaking machines. These machines look like Matchbox trucks, but they have a kind of brutality that belies their appearance when they are driven up to a tree and proceed to grip and shake the trunk vigorously, causing the olives to fall. These machines are loud, they belch harsh diesel fumes, and they seem discordant among the orderly rows of trees in full fruit. Growers who use such machines say they don't hurt the trees or affect their production, but seeing them in action can be disturbing.

As the olives are harvested, the varieties are kept separate. Each farmer delivers his own olives to the press or factory, where they are tagged according to grower and variety. Although many of us imagine an old mill with grinding stones to crush olives into paste, where the oil is hand-poured bottle by bottle (and indeed, some of these do still exist and are in use), many oils are extracted and bottled in spotless modern factories equipped with stainless steel machinery controlled by a computer and a single operator. Here's the process as I saw it in a number of large olive oil factories in central and southern Spain:

Once delivered to the factory, the olives are inspected for quality and cleaned of leaves and debris by blasts of air, and then (if necessary) by water. The containers of olives are weighed, and the farmer is paid accordingly. The olives then travel to the mill, which is actually a series of metallic hammers (a hammer mill) that crush the mass of olives and/or cut the olives with a series of parallel knives (the paste looks like tapenade at this point). Then the paste is pumped to a malaxator, where it goes through a fifteen- to thirty-minute four-stage mixing process, which agglomerates the oil globules. The paste then moves from the malaxator to a horizontal centrifuge, which separates the oil, water, and pomace from the sludgy paste in a two- or three-phase process. The oil is then sent through a vertical separator, which further separates oil from olive water, just as cream is separated from milk.

(There are several other methods for extracting olive oil: One is a method of selective filtration using Sinolea equipment, which uses the attraction of oil to metal to separate the oil; another is called the "flowering" of the oil [*affioranto* in Italian, or *lagrima* in Spanish], which extracts a very special oil by skimming off the oil that rises to the top of the malaxated paste.)

After the olive oil is extracted, it's given a chance to settle and then is drawn off to rest in large containers, often for months, before any further treatment (unless it is being sold as New Oil, in which case it will be

WHAT THOSE INITIALS MEAN

AOC: Appellation d'Origine Contrôlée (France)

DOC: Denominazione di Origine Controllata (Italy)

DO: Denominación de Origen (Spain)

DOP: Designation of Origin Protected (European Union)

All of these are official designations that cover foods and wines whose raw materials are (often traditionally) produced and manufactured within a specific geographical area, and have distinctive qualities due to the natural environment, manufacturing process, and/or aging methods.

bottled sooner). The oil may be filtered at the depository, or it may be sold as unfiltered oil. The leftover pomace is often sold to another producer, who then uses powerful chemical solvents to separate more oil from it to produce olive pomace oil. Sometimes on large olive estates such as those I saw in Jaen, the olive pomace stays on the property, where it is used as fertilizer; often it's returned to the groves it came from.

The depository is frequently in another building or in a wing of the same building. It too is filled with stainless steel pipes, and cases of clean bottles there await filling. After racking, the oil is pumped from the mill to the depository, where bottles (generally under gas pressure) are placed on a bottling line to be filled by machine. (The gas is inert and is used to create headroom in the bottles and to preserve the oil.) The bottles are sealed, labels are slapped on, and the bottles are packed by the dozen into cases to be shipped all over the world. Workers at a factory I visited in southern Spain said their prize-winning Estepa oil, sold under a variety of brand names, is shipped from their facility in Seville to Australia, the United States, Portugal, the United Kingdom, Sweden, France, Italy, Germany, Mexico, Puerto Rico, Brazil, Chile, Saudi Arabia, Jordan, and Israel.

THE GRADES OF OLIVE OIL

EXTRA VIRGIN OLIVE OIL. The highest class within the designation "Virgin Olive Oil." These oils must, by regulation, have less than 1% acidity. (Expect this standard to become even more stringent in the future; proposals are under way to reduce the acidity limit for extra virgin to 0.8%.) Many of the finest oils in this class already have less than 0.5% acidity

Because "cold pressed" and "mechanically pressed" mean the same thing, "cold pressed" is a marketing term that actually has no meaning today. In the old days, when a lot of hot water was added to the olive paste to maximize the extraction of oil, it meant that the oil was pressed without that added heat—and was thus superior. These days, most producers extract oil using a two- or three-phase system, the Sinolea method, or the "flowering" of the oil. Some labels still indicate "cold pressed," but it's meaningless. The important words are "Extra Virgin"—all the rest is window dressing.

(Siurana, a Spanish DOC oil, for instance, has 0.4%). Characterized by an extraordinary range of colors, flavors, and textures, these oils are never subjected to heat or chemicals in their production. They must be mechanically (not chemically) produced, and milling and extraction nearly always occur within twenty-four hours of the harvest; frequently the interval is shorter. They cannot have any smell or taste defects. *Extra virgin olive oil is the subject of this book.*

VIRGIN OLIVE OIL. These oils range in acidity from 1.5% up to 2%. Their less distinctive flavor makes them economical candidates for deep-frying and for baking.

OLIVE OIL. A blend of chemically refined oil with virgin or extra virgin oils. ("Refined" means that the oils have been treated with caustic chemicals to achieve a neutral taste.) It is sometimes labeled "Light" when the amount of extra virgin olive oil in the mix is low. Contrary to popular assumption, in this case "Light" does not mean lower in calories—it means lower in flavor!

LAMPANTE OIL. Any oil which has been sent for rectification (it may have been rancid or had extreme defects) or which has over 2% oleic acid. It must be refined before it can be used as a foodstuff. Its name refers to its function in antiquity, when it was used as lamp oil. Lampante Oil is the refined oil that forms the base of "Olive Oil" (see above).

OLIVE POMACE OIL. A by-product of the production of olive oil. The pomace—the pulp left after the oil is extracted—is dried and then heated, and more oil is extracted from it by means of evaporation and chemical solvents. This oil is then rectified to remove the solvents, and then further rectified to be rendered flavorless. It is blended with virgin olive oil to be sold as "fit for consumption" but must, by regulations, be labeled "Olive Pomace Oil" and *never* "Olive Oil."

EXTRA VIRGIN OLIVE OIL
AND HUMAN HEALTH

Our awareness of the benefits of olive oil in the diet dates from the famed Seven Country Study conducted by Ancel Keys and Francisco Grande Covian in the 1950s.[*] They looked at the diet, serum (blood) cholesterol, and incidence of coronary heart disease in twenty-two populations spread over seven countries. They found that populations that ate little saturated fat had low levels of serum cholesterol and a much lower incidence of coronary heart disease than did populations that ate high levels of saturated fat. Interestingly, they found that coronary health in a given population wasn't attributable to avoiding fat altogether, but varied according to which fat was consumed. (We now know that other vital elements include regular physical activity and a high intake of greens, other vegetables, whole grains, legumes, and fruits. In Crete, the area that had one of the most exemplary health profiles, second only to Japan, we have seen that as the Cretan lifestyle became more sedentary and the diet more "American" in terms of meat consumption, coronary health worsened even though Cretans still used olive oil as their primary fat.)

In the 1950s, populations that followed a traditional Mediterranean lifestyle and ate a traditional Mediterranean diet, in which their primary fat was in the form of olive oil (a source of monounsaturated fatty acids), had much lower cholesterol levels and a lower incidence of heart disease.

In the decades that followed, a number of different fats were touted by researchers and health authorities. As British nutritionist Rosemary

---

[*]Rosemary Stanton, "Overview of the Nutritional Benefits of Olive Oil," in *World Olive Encyclopedia* (Madrid: International Olive Oil Council, 1996).

Stanton portrays it, our thinking about what constitutes a "good" fat has changed nearly every twenty years, as our scientific research has become more sophisticated and focused. I think it's useful to look at her formulation decade by decade, because it helps to explain why it is that we are still confused on this issue.

In the 1950s and '60s, researchers began studies that looked at different types of fat, and reported that polyunsaturated fatty acids seemed to reduce serum cholesterol levels better than monounsaturated fats. Thus was the age of vegetable fats born in the United States. As Stanton says, "The result of this era was that polyunsaturated fats were praised, saturated fats (animal fats) were damned, and monounsaturated fats (like olive oil) were considered neutral." The effects of this research are still visible today if you look at the vast vegetable (mostly corn) oil display in any supermarket, along with the stacks of tubs of margarine in the refrigerated section.

FLAVOR CUES FOR ANTIOXIDANTS

Nutritionist and syndicated health columnist Ed Blonz, Ph.D., says that in his discussions with researchers, he's been told that you can actually taste the antioxidants in olive oil. Olive oil that is pungent, that burns in the throat, or that causes a cough is exhibiting the presence of tocopherols and other polyphenols. Since these antioxidants are affected by time and heat, make sure that you also enjoy such oils fresh from the bottle. Take it as folk wisdom that drizzling good olive oil over cooked food not only is a flavor enhancer, but may also be good for you.

Antioxidants in olive oil are so potent, they've also been used for *external* health care since antiquity and have a treasured place in folk medicine. If you treat a new sunburn with a good strong extra virgin olive oil, the antioxidants in the oil will hasten healing and perhaps prevent skin cancer in later life.

Removing makeup with pure extra virgin olive oil enhances skin texture and skin health. Olive oil has been used to treat diaper rash in olive oil–producing countries, and it has also been used, gently warmed, to soothe and treat ear infections. Widely available pure olive oil soap is soothing to the skin and safe enough for facial use. Dry skin heals and becomes velvety faster if you apply extra virgin olive oil to it regularly.

As a result, the 1970s and '80s marked huge shifts in fat intake, as health-conscious consumers switched from butter to margarine and used polyunsaturated vegetable oils in cooking. Researchers discovered, however, that cholesterol could be carried on two kinds of particles: high-density lipoproteins (HDL) and low-density lipoproteins (LDL). They further found that the cholesterol carried by HDL had a protective role in that the lipoproteins carried cholesterol fragments away from the arteries to the liver, whereas LDL cholesterol was the element that increased the risk of arterial plaque and accelerated the process of atherosclerosis.

Suddenly researchers told us that not only does saturated (animal) fat increase the level of "bad" LDL and decrease "good" HDL, but polyunsaturated (vegetable) fats, although they did decrease the "bad" LDL fraction, could also (if used in large quantity) reduce the "good" HDL fraction. Thus, by the end of the 1980s we were told to use polyunsaturated fats in small quantities, to continue to avoid dangerous saturated fats, and to value and use monounsaturated fats such as olive oil.

THE NUTRITIONAL COMPOSITION OF EXTRA VIRGIN OLIVE OIL*

VITAMIN E, at the rate of 15–17 mg/100 ml of oil. This antioxidizing vitamin is overwhelmingly in alpha form (the most biologically active form).

PHENOLIC COMPOUNDS, which also act as antioxidants.

PHYTOESTROGENS, which may have a role in preventing bone loss.

STEROLS, which counter intestinal absorption of dietary cholesterol.

HYDROCARBONS, which can inhibit cholesterol synthesis, and BETA-CAROTENE, which has both VITAMIN A and antioxidant properties.

TERPENIC ALCOHOLS, which assist in the fecal excretion of cholesterol

through increased bile acid secretion.

COLORING SUBSTANCES (naturally occurring), such as carotenoids and chlorophyll, which have antioxidant properties.

AROMATIC SUBSTANCES, which provide the characteristic taste and smell of good olive oil.

*Mark L. Wahlqvist and Antigone Kouris-Blazos, "Nutrition and Biological Value," in *World Olive Encyclopedia* (Madrid: International Olive Oil Council, 1996).

From the 1990s to the present, research has focused on the harmful effects of oxidized particles of LDL cholesterol, because they are more likely to cause arterial plaque than are other elements. Polyunsaturated fatty acids seem to be more susceptible to oxidation than monounsaturated fats, which is why we are currently so much more conscious of the importance of antioxidants.

Here's where olive oil becomes the hero of this health story: It naturally contains a great variety of antioxidants, and it's high in monounsaturated fatty acids. We know it's a safe and nutritious food—it's been in continual use in the human diet since antiquity. We know from the original Seven Country Study that populations that live a Mediterranean lifestyle and habitually use olive oil as their primary source of fat for cooking and dressing foods live longer, healthier lives.

Researchers are now beginning to focus on some of the other elements in olive oil, elements that are similar to anti-cancer compounds found in some fruits and vegetables. Olive oil does appear to have a role not only in combating heart disease, but also in the control of excess weight and diabetes and in protection against some kinds of cancer.

I've got to put in a caveat here, since we Americans tend to go overboard fast on health information. This does not mean that adding olive oil to a bad diet will make you healthy. Certainly cutting fat intake, limiting animal fats to special occasions, and using olive oil in moderation as your primary source of dietary fat, along with a diet rich in fruits, grains, legumes, and vegetables and accompanied by a consistent level of physical activity, will indeed enhance health. Pouring olive oil on a steak on a daily basis, and then watching television for many hours after dinner, will not.

Another warning is in order: Unscrupulous producers can sell oil as "extra virgin" as long as it successfully meets acidity standards, passes the rigorous taste panel test, and satisfies chemical analysis standards, without

SOME HEALTH BENEFITS OF OLIVE OIL

The International Olive Oil Council sponsors a wide variety of medical and epidemiological studies devoted to documenting the effects of extra virgin olive oil. According to recent studies:

- Olive oil has a protective effect against some types of malignant tumors: breast, prostate, colon, squamous cell, and esophageal.

- Olive oil has been shown to strengthen the immune system in mice.

- Olive oil helps prevent insulin resistance and contributes to better control of glucose in the blood, which is particularly important for people with Type II (non-insulin-dependent) diabetes.

informing consumers that some of the oil is chemically rectified or that it has been blended. Frauds include blending olive oil with nut or seed oils, as well as blending rectified oil with extra virgin olive oil. Naturally, such oils will not have the health benefits of a true extra virgin olive oil. The easiest way to be assured that you are buying a reliable product is to buy extra virgin olive oil from a merchant who knows he is selling a good product from a reliable producer. Many of those merchants can be found in the Resources section of this book.

We have a lot to learn from the elements of a traditional Mediterranean diet; there's also a great deal we can learn from the traditional Mediterranean lifestyle. First and foremost, in my view, is the central place of sharing food with family and friends. While what we eat does not have to be elaborate or terribly time-consuming to prepare, all meals are enhanced by the companionship of people we care about, when the food is consumed with pleasure, accompanied perhaps by a glass of wine, and with the leisure to enjoy it. I think that's the easy part, and I hope the recipes in this book will make it easy for you too. Much harder, at least for

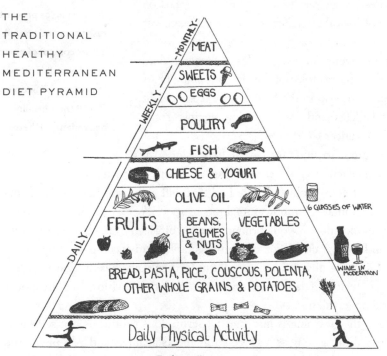

THE TRADITIONAL HEALTHY MEDITERRANEAN DIET PYRAMID

MONTHLY / MEAT

WEEKLY

SWEETS

OO EGGS OO

POULTRY

FISH

CHEESE & YOGURT

OLIVE OIL

6 GLASSES OF WATER

DAILY

FRUITS

BEANS, LEGUMES & NUTS

VEGETABLES

BREAD, PASTA, RICE, COUSCOUS, POLENTA, OTHER WHOLE GRAINS & POTATOES

WINE IN MODERATION

Daily Physical Activity

me, is integrating physical activity into daily life, along with time spent out of doors. If nothing else, researching and writing this book have increased my awareness about the whole range of factors that influence good health. I hope it does the same for you.

The Mediterranean Diet at a Glance

The Mediterranean diet—the cuisines of southern Italy, Spain, Morocco, Tunisia, Greece, and southern France—is based on the three primary fruits and grains of these regions and the products derived from them: olives, grapes, and wheat. Foods are generally plant-based, seasonal, and locally grown; they include grains, fruits and vegetables, beans and other legumes, nuts, and olive oil. As nutritionist Connie Guttersen characterizes the diet, "minimal processing, seasonal use, and freshness of these plant foods maximize their content of protective nutrients, such as phytochemicals, antioxidants, fiber, vitamins, and minerals."

It's instructive to look at the Mediterranean diet pyramid as portrayed by Oldways Preservation & Exchange Trust because it is different from the USDA food pyramid, particularly in regard to the consumption of dairy products (there is a lower consumption in the Mediterranean) as well as the consumption of olive oil. It's important to note that it is an accurate representation of the kind of diet eaten not only in Crete in the 1950s, but throughout the Mediterranean to some degree even to this day. Unlike the USDA pyramid, it was not devised under the influence of food industry lobbyists.

HOW TO READ A LABEL

You're not likely to find all of these elements on any single label, but as you begin to scrutinize olive oil containers, you are certain to find some of them. Here are important items to look for:

HARVEST/BOTTLING DATE: The most significant information is the date of harvest because unlike wine, olive oil loses fruitiness and flavor as it ages. The closer to harvest, the more flavorful the oil. Note that although harvest takes place from November through January all around the

NEI NOSTRI OLIVETA
SI PRATICA L'ANTICA
COLTURA TRADIZIONALE

Imbottigliato
L. il ___ 22-11-00

Da consumarsi
preferibilmente
entro il ___ 22-05-02

bottiglian ___ 122H

NON DISPERDERE NELL'AMBIENTE

Mediterranean, these oils take time to settle (the best oils rest for two months), and then to bottle and to ship. (A more useful harvest dating method would be to write the date like an academic year, for example "Winter 03-04".) In any case, under the best of circumstances this year's oil is usually not available in the United States until late winter or early spring. Plan on using up this year's oil within twelve to eighteen months, especially since it can come to you as much as six months after harvest. The rule of thumb is this: You have up to two years after the oil is bottled to use it up (or one year after opening), provided you keep it airtight and store it in a cool, dark place. If the label doesn't tell you the harvest date, it should have a "consume by" or "best before" date, another good indicator of freshness (although not of consumability, because although well-kept oils will mellow, they can be consumable for long periods). If neither of these indicators is present, ask the store if they know when the oil was bottled. If they can't supply a credible answer, be suspicious.

UNFILTERED MEANS JUST THAT: The oil is as it came out of the tank, with some solids that will sink to the bottom of the bottle. Unfiltered oils are frequently very special, but not all special oils are unfiltered; many great oils have been filtered for aesthetic reasons. However, in my experience, unfiltered oils often are more flavorful and are probably an artisanal product, sometimes organic.

ORGANIC: Organic oils are usually labeled as such. Sometimes a label will describe the process, for example "Grown without the use of pesticides or chemical fertilizers."

COUNTRY OF ORIGIN: Look for specific information on where the olives were grown, such as that found, for example, on bottles of Tenuta I Bonsi: "Produced and bottled at the estate I Bonsi by the owner Budini Gattai in Regello, Firenze, Italy." "Bottled in" or "product of," without the other information, is not adequate. "Product of Italy," for example, can mean the olives were grown and the oil extracted in Italy, or it can mean that the oil was grown and processed elsewhere and then bottled in Italy.

ESTATE BOTTLED means that the olives were grown, processed, and bottled on the same property.

MADE IN A COOPERATIVE means that a group of local growers pool their harvests to sell their oil under one brand. This means that the oil is grown and processed in the same region, and one can assume that it has been tasted by the people who grew the olives.

Single Variety or Blend?

While there are indeed oils that are labeled "single variety," even these may contain a small amount of other oils because olive trees require pollinators from different varieties. In general, knowledgeable olive oil tasters prefer blends of varieties for their ability to create complex flavor profiles and to enhance the stability of the oil. It's interesting to read the varietal notes on the labels—you'll see the same regional combinations of varieties over and over again. Again, the Tenuta I Bonsi label is instructive: "This oil is obtained from Frantoio, Moraiolo, Leccino and Pendolino variety olives picked from the olive trees on the property and pressed at the estate's olive press."

YOU CAN TELL AN OLIVE OIL FROM ITS PACKAGE

There are a number of clues that consumers can read in the packaging and presentation of any bottle of olive oil. Although they are not fail safe, they are frequently good indicators of the quality of the oil within because they demonstrate the care that the producer has taken to protect his product. In addition to the information on the label about where (and sometimes how) the olives are grown, where (and sometimes how) they are processed, and where the oil may have been bottled, there are some other important indicators of pride and quality.

COLOR OF THE BOTTLE/FOIL WRAPPING/PROTECTIVE BOX: A dark bottle, a bottle wrapped in foil, or a bottle packaged in a cardboard or wooden box indicates pride in production and concern for maintaining the oil at its best. While these are of course also marketing strategies that can make a product stand out on a shelf, they are more importantly to be seen as protective measures. Biolea Extra Virgin Olive Oil, from Greece, comes in a wooden box, which lets you know immediately that there's something special inside; Elea, also from Greece, is sold in a dark sealed bottle with a pour spout tied to the side. Ardoino Vallaurea olive oil, from Italy, is always sold with an eye-catching gold foil wrapping, which imparts a similar message. In this country, California-grown McEvoy Olio Nuovo is packaged in clear glass, protected by a well-made cardboard box.

BOTTLE VS. TIN: If you see an oil that is available in both a tin and a bottle, such as the Sicilian Don Luigi, I think it is always a better bet to buy the tin because metal protects oil better than glass. Some oil, such as Spain's

Nuñez de Prado Baena, is available not only in glass and in big five-liter tins, but also in a decorative bright yellow ceramic bottle. Clay is perhaps the best container for olive oil (terracotta amphoras were the traditional storage modes before metal or glass), although topping a ceramic container with a cork is not always the best method for maintaining an airtight seal. (Just as an aside, Podere di Pillore, an Italian oil, is stored in terra-cotta before being bottled. We were amazed to discover that we could taste the difference.)

HOW THE BOTTLE IS SEALED: A screw cap covering an internal plastic pouring spout shows that the producer is concerned about keeping the product airtight. Some bottles are packaged with a pour spout that's attached to the bottle by string so that the consumer can fit it to the bottle to use for controlled pours. I find such spouts very useful, particularly when they have a little plastic cap that keeps even the tiny spout covered (you can buy inexpensive pour spouts at Katz and Co.; see the Resources section).

HOW THE DATE IS EXPRESSED: I have to admit that when I see evidence of the human hand, I feel more confidence in the product. Thus, I'm utterly charmed by handwritten harvest and bottling dates. I also have confidence in stamped dates because, again, they're applied annually.

STORING OLIVE OIL

Every single expert I've consulted says the same thing: *Store olive oil in a cool dark place, and keep the bottle cap well screwed on.* A cool pantry, a low cupboard, or the coldest, darkest corner of the kitchen is a good spot. Because those who understand the value of keeping olive oil fresh devote thought to good storage, I shouldn't have been surprised several years ago when Marcella Hazan asked me, in designing her kitchen, to create a special cupboard just for olive oil that wouldn't be heated by the under-cabinet halogen lighting.

If you've bought oil in a clear glass bottle, do as a man I met in Friuli advised: Cover the bottle entirely with aluminum foil. Alternatively, you can decant some of the oil into an airtight ceramic or steel decanter, keeping the decanter on the counter and storing the rest of the oil in a cool place. Or you can do what they do all over the Mediterranean: Buy oil in bulk, whether in a five-liter tin or in a large tank that you keep in the cellar, and decant oil as needed into a clean dark wine bottle topped with a pour spout.

Here's where the experts disagreed: when I asked about storing olive oil in the refrigerator and in the freezer. Many experts forcefully disdain refrigerating olive oil because home refrigerators are inconsistent in temperature and oils can suffer from condensation, which makes water mix with the oil. Other experts say this is rarely a problem, but some believe

WHAT HAPPENS WHEN OIL IS EXPOSED TO LIGHT?

One merchant told me that in just eighty hours of close exposure to fluorescent light, olive oil packed in clear bottles turns brown and rancid. That's why it's important to look critically at where oils are stored when buying from nonspecialty stores. Recently I looked at a vast olive oil display in a well-known Italian market in New York City. Tins of oil were set in the window to entice customers into the store (it worked—I came in to look), but the oil was in direct sunlight and the tins were hot to my touch. The nearby shelves were also exposed to sunlight, and they were filled top to bottom with once-fabulous oils from all over the world.

that refrigerating "breaks" the flavor of the oil. In short, the majority of olive oil masters say: *Don't refrigerate.*

Things are different when it comes to the freezer. While one expert I spoke to said that olive oil "breaks" in extreme cold, most agreed that freezing was fine. "Look at Antinori's New Oil, which is sold frozen," they said. But one expert told me something that seemed to definitively discourage freezing, except in very small quantities. He said: "Freezing oil is fine, but when it thaws it oxidizes very rapidly. As little as ten days out of the freezer can spell the difference between good oil and bad."

TASTING OLIVE OIL

IN THINKING ABOUT OLIVE OILS in all their varieties, I wanted to create a classification system that would make sense of the differences between oils. I wanted to go beyond the straightforward classes of "robust" and "delicate" because I was looking for a way of characterizing oils that was precise and that (most important) would point the way to figuring out how to pair oils of particular character with foodstuffs of particular character. As anyone who may have read my book on kitchen design knows, I tend to think in fours, because four categories leave enough room for complex ideas to be expressed more simply. These categories, then, are the ones that made sense to me as I tasted oils. Fortunately they seem to have been useful for the people I've done tastings with ever since.

Here are the four categories, from the least to the most intense in olive flavor:

 DELICATE AND MILD oils have a subtle and ephemeral quality. They combine best with delicately flavored partners such as tender new lettuces, fresh peas, or mild cheeses. Don't confuse this category with flavorless oils—these oils have a definite and haunting appeal. (When you do find an oil with very little flavor, save it for baking, frying, and for infusing with vanilla or herbs.)

 FRUITY AND FRAGRANT oils have personality. Often a blend of many luscious smells and tastes, their flavor notes can be fruity like apples, or fragrant like green leafy vegetables, green apples, or peapods. I love these oils drizzled over pasta and mixed salads, over fruits such as oranges for a palate-cleansing salad, on dessert cheeses, and with mild meats such as chicken breast.

 OLIVE-Y AND PEPPERY oils are the Clark Kents of the olive world. They start off in the mouth tasting lusciously like olives, but then can catch your throat with a pungent finish. Within this category, the degree of pungency ranges dramatically from a little to a lot, and tends to diminish as time passes. (In Italy there's even a word for this throat-catching quality: *pizzicante.* It's considered extremely desirable by Tuscan producers and consumers of Tuscan oil, although olive oil producers from other parts of Italy don't always agree on its desirability. As Nancy Harmon Jenkins, author of *Flavors of Puglia,* says, "Other Italians think it's a weird quality to prize since they appreciate much more the smoothness of, e.g., Pugliese or Ligurian oils.") Olive-y and peppery oils work wonderfully to flavor bread, to dress whole grains such as farro or barley, as a dip for vegetables, to make full-flavored pasta sauces, and for roasting meats.

 LEAFY GREEN AND GRASSY oils are the strongest oils of all, with an immediate appeal. Often pungent, with a distinct herbal note, these oils taste green even if their color is yellow. Leafy green and grassy oils have a great range, from straightforward to subtle. Use these oils for bruschetta; for pasta dressed with nothing but oil, garlic, and cheese; for strong salad greens such as spinach and arugula and watercress; and as a garnish drizzled over bean soups. Because these oils can stand up to almost anything and retain their flavor notes, I consider them the divas of the olive world.

OUR TASTING PROCESS

We tasted well over 200 olive oils, at first monthly and then weekly over the course of about fourteen months. Aside from myself, we had a core group of tasters as well as occasional guests—all people who were deeply interested in olive oil but who were not professional olive oil experts or food professionals. I trained our group in the process and vocabulary of tastings; the group taught me that anyone can learn to taste well. We got to know each other's palates very well—noticing who was sensitive to different flavors and who felt pungency more than anyone else. We also noticed how we all immediately knew which were outstanding oils, and which were past their prime.

Professional olive oil tasters follow elaborate procedures. They gently warm a special blue glass (so that their sense of the oil is not influenced by its color) in a water bath to heat the oil to body temperature. The glass is covered by a lid to hold and control the release of volatile aromas. (Tastings I've attended, led by professional tasters for food writers, have offered a variation on this method: Olive oil was poured into cups or glasses that were first warmed by both our hands, and then the glass was cradled in one hand while we covered the top of the cup with our other hand to hold in the volatile aromas.) These procedures aim to bring out the quality of an oil and to discern any flaws.

In contrast, our tastings for this book were much simpler because they focused on classifying the oils into flavor categories, and on the pleasure of tasting great olive oils. Although you can replicate our tasting procedure at home (and I'll tell you just how we did it), I would recommend a slightly different method if we were to repeat the whole process.

We started tasting oils using plastic spoons (many French producers and retailers use this method), but then we changed to stainless steel soup-

TASTING AND JUDGING
THE QUALITY OF OLIVE OIL

The International Olive Oil Council has created a list of descriptors for use in the grading of olive oil by professional taste panels.* Panelists rate the intensity of each defect and each positive attribute, which are then scored to determine the grade of an oil. The process of judging olive oil taste is called *organoleptic* judging, because it relies on human taste organs.

PERCEPTION OF DEFECTS:
Fusty
Musty
Winey-Vinegary
Acid-Sour
Muddy sediment
Metallic
Rancid

PERCEPTION OF POSITIVE ATTRIBUTES:
Fruity
Bitter
Pungent

An oil is judged, by taste, to be:

Extra Virgin: when the average of the defects is 0 and the average "fruitiness" is more than 0.

Virgin: when the "defects" average is between 0 and 2.5 inclusive, and the average "fruitiness" is more than 0.

Ordinary Virgin: when the "defects" average is between 2.5 and 6.0 inclusive, or when the "defects" average is up to and including 2.5 and the average "fruitiness" is 0.

Lampante Virgin: when the "defects" average more than 6.0.

Olive oils that have undesirable taste characteristics, that are made from olives that may be overripe or spoiled, or that are too high in acid ever to qualify for extra-virgin status (less than 1% acidity) can be rectified or refined (via heat and/or chemicals) and blended with better oils to change their chemical and taste profiles. This makes them eligible to be labeled "olive oil."

*International Olive Oil Council, *The Olive Tree, the Oil, the Olive* (Madrid: IOOC, 1998).

spoons for a more neutral aroma and for increased heat conductivity. We cupped our hands around the bowl of the spoon and smelled each spoonful first before putting any oil on our tongues. When we tasted, we made sure that the oil had contact with every area of the tongue by swirling it around our mouths, and we sucked in a little air to oxygenate the oil before swallowing. We did this once or twice, as necessary, to get a clear sense of the oil. Then we made notes about flavors and sensations (such as a peppery finish) before having a general discussion about each oil. We cleared our palates with slices of green apple and drinks of plain water, and changed spoons with each oil.

Here's how I plan to change tastings in the future: Since cupping the bowl of a spoon with both hands is not an easy task, I'm going to use small opaque waxed paper pill cups to hold and warm the oil from now on. This will allow for more control of the warming process. When you taste oils at your house, I'd recommend little cups for just this reason, changing cups with each oil so that the flavor of one oil doesn't affect the next.

TASTING THE SAME OIL, NEW AND OLD

Because the work of researching and writing a book frequently takes more than a year, gathering olive oils for tasting meant that sometimes two different harvests were represented in our tastings. It was extremely interesting to taste the same oil when it was fresh and when it was a year old. Provided that the oil had been kept in a dark, cool cupboard, we could immediately recognize that the flavor notes of new and old oils were the same, but the older oil was softer and more subtle. It's like watching someone age—the colors become less vivid, but the face remains the same.

As a result of this long process of tasting many oils in the company of nonprofessional tasters, I am convinced that anyone can tell the difference between a leafy green and grassy oil and a delicate and mild oil, and that with only a little practice, anyone can further discern fruity and fragrant from olive-y and peppery. I also know that anyone with a chance to taste a variety of oils will never be confused as to whether an oil is good or rancid, fresh or aged. Tasting oils will also provide you with clues to using a particular oil to best advantage, and will help you decide which oils are good values.

You'll discover that olive oil can be dense with flavor and dizzy with scent. It can be fierce and strong, burning the back of the throat; or it can be flowery and elegant, with a perfume that lingers on the palate. The meals you serve will never be the same.

CONDUCTING
YOUR OWN TASTING

Finding a Good Source for Oil

First, look for a store that has knowledgeable buyers, that sells a lot of olive oil, and that stores it on lower shelves not exposed to bright light. These are all crucial criteria, since olive oil deteriorates after bottling, and exposure to heat and light (as well as air, after opening) can speed deterioration. Look first to see if the oil you are interested in comes in tins or dark glass, because oil in clear glass is more fragile and can more easily oxidize before purchase unless it's being stored and sold by a knowledgeable merchant. (On the other hand, if you are buying from a specialty merchant who knows olive oil, don't hesitate to buy oil in clear glass.) Look at the harvest date or "consume by" date to make sure you are buying the freshest oil. Price is not always a good indicator of quality—we've found wonderful oils at both high and low price points. Specialty merchants such as those listed in the Resources section are an unusually good bet for finding great oils—often, every oil they sell is noteworthy. But there are also fine oils in supermarkets and in wholesale price clubs such as Costco, and at discount specialty grocers such as Trader Joe's or New York's Fairway Market. As you explore olive oils, you'll discover your own good and often unlikely sources.

Choosing the Oils to Taste

An easy way to begin to understand the differences in olive oil flavors is to start tasting by nationality. Since each country grows different species of olives, the flavor contrasts will be most obvious when you compare a Greek oil with a French one, for example. Look for estate-bottled oils from four different nations, such as France, Greece, Italy, and Spain. (You want an estate-bottled oil in order to preclude the possibility that an oil from one country has been shipped and bottled to be sold as the "product" of a second country.) It doesn't matter whether these oils are a blend or single-variety oils—in either case, they will be good examples of a national product. Inevitably, you'll be able to taste that they are different from each other.

How to Conduct the Tasting

Assemble the oils, along with tiny opaque cups. Set out water and slices of green apple, as well as paper and pens. Start by pouring one oil for everyone to taste. Pour just a small amount in each cup—unlike wine tasting, you swallow the oil for the full flavor experience. Before you put the oil to your lips, hold the cup top and bottom between both hands to warm it slightly and to concentrate the aroma. Uncup your hands and take a good sniff. Does the oil smell herbal or grassy? Floral? Nutlike? Is it a strong smell, or a mild one?

Now take a teaspoon to a tablespoon's worth of oil into your mouth and let it make contact with your whole tongue. Swirl it around. With the tip of your tongue touching your upper palate, suck in air from both sides of your mouth to oxygenate the oil. Taste it some more, then swallow. Take notes on your impressions and sensations. Is the oil light or heavy? Does it increase in intensity of flavor as you hold it on your tongue? What happens when (and after) you swallow? Is it pungent, with a peppery burn? Is it intensely pungent, or is it a milder sensation?

Finally, using our four flavor categories, think about where this oil fits in, starting from the two extremes. Is it delicate and mild? Or is it leafy green and grassy? Then consider, is it mildly grassy? Perhaps it can be more accurately described as olive-y and peppery? Or is it more fruity and fragrant than a delicate and mild oil? Think about where this oil fits in the flavor spectrum. It's okay to be tentative—this is your first oil, and your first tasting. The important thing is that you are on your way to being more discerning about the flavors of olive oil, and that discernment will show in all the oils you use in the future.

Other Tasting Suggestions

CROSS-TASTING FROM ONE SMALL REGION:
You can also taste by local region, such as a cross-tasting of a number of, say, Tuscan oils. This kind of tasting focuses on the similarities and differ-

SMELL AND TASTE TIPS FOR OIL THAT IS NO LONGER GOOD

I've encountered two distinct odors that are immediate indicators that the oil is no longer good.

ODOR OF CUCUMBER:
This is a sign of a stagnant oil; it occurs when oil has been kept in a tin for too long (2 to 3 years).

ODOR OF BANANAS:
This sweet banana smell always means that the oil is spoiled, frequently as a result of exposure to light.

ences among similar oils, and it can be an eye-opening experience. You'll immediately begin to discern the flavor differences between filtered and unfiltered oils, and between those that are more artisanally produced and those that are more commercial.

CROSS-TASTING BY OLIVE VARIETIES: You could plan a tasting based on one variety of olives, such as Arbequina (a Spanish variety) or Kalamata (a Greek olive), or a typical blend such as Correggiolo, Leccino, Moraiolo, and Pendolino, a Tuscan blend. As part of such a tasting you could also include olive varieties that used to be limited to one region and that are now planted in others, such as the Tuscan varieties now grown in California to make Tuscan-style oils.

CROSS-TASTING BY FLAVOR CATEGORIES: Finally, you could do a tasting based on some of the oils described in the tasting notes, using the flavor categories as your guide. A tasting solely of one category, such as leafy green and grassy, would be an eye-opening experience, since you would very rapidly taste a range of flavors within this designation.

You could also create a tasting with one oil from each category, for a different kind of appreciation of the character of each flavor class.

TASTING NOTES

TO CONDUCT THE TASTINGS for this book, I solicited extra virgin olive oils directly from producers all over the world, from discriminating retailers, olive oil producer associations and councils, and from Internet sources. Many oils did not make the cut, and there are undoubtedly worthy oils that we didn't get a chance to taste. Olive oil producers range from large to small and are found in a great many regions of the world. While we tried to get a good cross-section of producers, representing as many regions as possible, one visit to almost any specialty store showed us new gaps in our sourcing. It's a huge subject, and while we followed up all the leads we could, it is a never-ending task to catalog all the great extra virgin olive oils available in the United States. When you encounter an oil that is not listed here, don't assume it's not a good oil—rather, assume it's one we may have missed. Taste it for yourself, and then decide. All of the olive oils listed here we thought worthy of attention, and each is available from specialty stores as well as from the sources who supplied samples for the book or (in the case of some wholesalers) their designated retailer. (You'll find more information about the suppliers in the Resources section.)

Outstanding oils are marked with an asterisk (*), and good values with a dollar sign ($). Mass-market blended oils are marked with a barrel symbol (⊖).

The symbols for the four categories appear with each recipe as well.

DELICATE AND MILD • FRUITY AND FRAGRANT •
OLIVE-Y AND PEPPERY • LEAFY GREEN AND GRASSY

FRANCE

A L'Olivier* DELICATE AND MILD

De Medici Imports (845/651-4400)
This oil has a profoundly nutty aroma, with deep flavor and a thick texture. Our tasters who are most partial to delicate oils declared this a favorite.

Alziari* FRUITY AND FRAGRANT

www.spiritofprovence.com
This famous oil from Nice has a delicate flavor with lots of fruit. It's intensely yellow, the flavor has a hint of hazelnuts, and it's very fragrant. It comes in a beautifully decorative round tin that also does a good job of preserving its flavor.

Castelas Huile d'Olive de la Vallée des Baux de Provence* FRUITY AND FRAGRANT

De Medici Imports (845/651-4400)
This DOC oil starts with a nutty aroma and finishes with a peppery flourish. "Perfectly

balanced," "light," and "round" were some of the words our tasters used to describe this outstanding oil.

Huile d'Olive Vierge d'Aix en Provence
DELICATE AND MILD

www.terroirsdeprovence.com
Full-flavored in spite of its delicacy, this AOC oil has notes of almond and of grapefruit. Click on the English flag to read this website in English, and be prepared to pay shipping from France.

Huile d'Olives des Tzeilles
LEAFY GREEN AND GRASSY

www.zingermans.com
Intense yellow/green, with a complex and balanced herbal flavor and a "long slow burn" peppery finish. Leccio, Ribier, Bouteillan, and Picholine olives.

Le Vieux Moulin Huile d'Olive Vierge de Mirabel DELICATE AND MILD

www.spiritofprovence.com
Traditionally crushed between stones, this oil is fragrant, nutty, and sweet.

L'Oulibo Cuvée Aglandau

DELICATE AND MILD

export@deelen.com
This cuvée, or single-variety oil, from a cooperative in Languedoc, has a "sweet fragrance" and a "velvet" texture." "A sensual oil," said another taster. Sent direct from France.

L'Oulibo Cuvée Lucques

DELICATE AND MILD

export@deelen.com
A single variety from an unusual species, this oil is both nutty and delicate, with a very mild finish.

L'Oulibo Cuvée Olivière

DELICATE AND MILD

export@deelen.com
Another unusual single-variety olive oil—very buttery, mildly herbal, sweet, with a slight burn.

Moulin de Bédarrides* DELICATE AND MILD

www.spiritofprovence.com
An AOC oil, yellow, with a great aroma with hints of almonds, a sweet flavor, and a very mild peppery finish, from the Vallée des Baux de Provence.

Moulin Jean-Marie Cornille

FRUITY AND FRAGRANT

www.spiritofprovence.com
This remarkable oil is vividly green, with a strong olive scent and flavor.

O&Co. Aix en Provence AOC Château Virant, vat II* OLIVE-Y AND PEPPERY

O&Co. stores
www.oliviersandco.com
Yellow/green, with strong herbal notes yet delicate in impact. One taster said, "Oil like this is practically a vegetable." It has a full-flavored, mildly peppery finish.

O&Co. Château de Montfrin*

DELICATE AND MILD

O&Co. stores
www.oliviersandco.com
An oil with exceptional flavor, it's complex, fragrant, and nutty with a powerful finish. Wonderful for desserts and for asparagus.

O&Co. Haute Provence Moulin des Pénitents, Coopérative des Mées, vat P7

DELICATE AND MILD

O&Co. stores
www.oliviersandco.com
This DOC oil is pale greenish gold, with a scent of ripe fruit. It's made from Aglandau and Bouteillan olives.

O&Co. Moulin de l'Olivette, Coopérative de Manosque, vat 3, Haute Provence

OLIVE-Y AND PEPPERY

O&Co. stores
www.oliviersandco.com
Bright yellow, with a strong olive scent, we loved this oil's complex flavor of nuts and blossoms. It's made from Aglandau and Bouteillan olives.

O&Co. Nyons, vat 12

DELICATE AND MILD

O&Co. stores
www.oliviersandco.com
Mildly bitter and pleasantly nutty, Nyons is pale yellow-green. It's a DOC oil made from Tanche olives.

O&Co. Vallée des Baux COD La Craneco vat E FRUITY AND FRAGRANT

O&Co. stores
www.oliviersandco.com
Pale intense yellow, fruity pear notes, toasted hazelnut and faintly flowery, this oil is light in a good way.

Vallée des Baux de Provence, Moulin Jean Marie Cornille, Coopérative Oléicole de la Vallée des Baux* FRUITY AND FRAGRANT

www.spiritofprovence.com

Unfiltered, artisanal, with a very fresh flavor of green olives and a haunting hazelnut and vanilla fragrance, this oil was described as tasting "like olive essence."

GREECE

Biojoy Kolymvari Chania Crete*
DELICATE AND MILD

Corti Bros. (916/736-3800)
DOP, organic, unfiltered "flower of the oil," this oil is smooth, with a flowery scent, and "a good texture that floats above your tongue."

Biolea* FRUITY AND FRAGRANT

Williams-Sonoma stores
www.biolea.gr
Certified organic, stone-ground, an estate-bottled artisanal oil of the highest quality, Biolea oil is deliciously fragrant, slightly herbal and fruity. Beautifully packaged, it would be a great gift as well as a pantry asset.

Elea* FRUITY AND FRAGRANT

www.eleaoliveoil.com
Golden-green in color, this organic estate-bottled olive oil is fragrant and complex. We all loved its underlying sweetness, with earthy, peppery, honey notes. A good dark bottle preserves flavor, and an airtight spout adds a touch of practical elegance.

Eleni DELICATE AND MILD

www.olivemerchant.com
www.elenigourmet.com
Eleni is pale in color but hauntingly fragrant, with fruity (berry) notes. It's made from Koroneiki olives from Kalamata.

Greek Gold FRUITY AND FRAGRANT

www.blauel.gr
This oil is handpicked, stone-crushed, and organic. It's from the Mani area of the Peloponnese.

Hellas "Special Selection"
OLIVE-Y AND PEPPERY

www.cookswares.com
From Lakonia, this is a very fragrant and strongly pungent oil.

Kotinos DELICATE AND MILD

www.kotinos.com
This organic oil from Crete has a surprisingly sweet first taste and then becomes slightly bitter and grassy. It has a lovely texture.

O&Co. Kalamata DELICATE AND MILD
O&Co. stores
www.oliviersandco.com
Pale green and delicately olive-flavored with notes of green bell pepper, fresh artichoke, and green apple, Kalamata oil is appealing. From the Peloponnese, it's made from Koroneiki olives. "Lovely fragrance."

Perito's OLIVE-Y AND PEPPERY

www.olivemerchant.com
"A little sweet, a little nutty," with a peppery finish.

Renieris Estate $ DELICATE AND MILD

www.svtea.com
This very special Cretan oil is 0.1% acidity, and has mild flavor notes of asparagus and butter. "Just lovely" said one taster.

ITALY

Ardoino Fructus Aureus
OLIVE-Y AND PEPPERY

Corti Bros. (916/736-3800)
Unfiltered, limited production—this oil is made from pitted olives, which is a more expensive process and produces an oil that tastes different from oil that is extracted from olives with pits. "Tastes warm and full of flavor" said one taster.

Ardoino Vall'Aurea*

FRUITY AND FRAGRANT

Corti Bros. (916/736-3800)
Wrapped in gold foil to protect the delicate contents, this is an oil I've bought in Italy but had never seen before in the United States. It's fruity and deeply fragrant, with a slightly bitter edge and a slightly pungent finish. An "elegant" oil.

Arkade   DELICATE AND MILD

www.esperya.com
Clearly dated, from the Marches region, this oil is made from Leccino, Frantoio, Carboncella, and Sargana olives. It tastes mildly sweet, with notes of grass and hay.

Badalucco*   OLIVE-Y AND PEPPERY

www.svtea.com
Stone-crushed, this outstanding oil is slightly bitter, intensely fruity, strongly pungent, and "really good."

Badia a Coltibuono*

LEAFY GREEN AND GRASSY

De Medici Imports (845/651-4400)
With 0.25% acidity, and with harvest and bottling dates clearly marked, this outstanding oil is strongly and pleasantly bitter, with a pronounced burn. "Almost raw" said one taster, while another said, "It made my face scrunch up." Very green and grassy, this is an oil made for drizzling.

NOVEMBER HARVEST PARTY
AT A SICILIAN MILL

While traveling through Sicily to learn about olive oil, we arrived at an olive mill at dusk. We parked among trucks and farm vehicles, then walked the rough path through a field of sweet-smelling flowers. We'd been told that the mill was owned by a group of women (unusual in Sicily), and that this evening's party was the end-of-harvest celebration. Glinting white through the trees was a low square building that enclosed a cobbled courtyard. As we entered the court through the gate, lanterns hanging from the eaves of an inner arcade illuminated a single ancient tree, and a band of musicians struck up a song.

Looking through open doorways on all sides of the courtyard, we saw lit rooms, each filled with people talking and eating. One room held a wood-fired oven, with several cooks working in turns to toast piles of bread and drizzle them with new oil. Long wooden tables held platters of grilled vegetables, fish, and meats, with cruets of oil lined up along the table's center. There were young children and old people, men and women with sun-dark faces, music and convivial noise, fragrant smoke. New oil anointed every dish, giving us not only the flavor of the harvest but also the flavor of a way of life.

Badia a Coltibuono Albereto

OLIVE-Y AND PEPPERY

De Medici Imports (845/651-4400)
This unfiltered, single-estate, organic, limited-production Tuscan oil comes protected by both a dark bottle and a box; both are clearly harvest-dated and informative. Made from Frantoio, Leccino, and Pendolino olives, the oil has a well-rounded, complex flavor and some finish.

Bertolli Extra Virgin Olive Oil ☺

FRUITY AND FRAGRANT

supermarkets
Golden green, slightly bitter, not too intense, this oil has a pleasant fragrance and mild olive-y taste, making it a good all-purpose oil, especially for frying and sautéing.

Bucci dei Castelli di Jesi

FRUITY AND FRAGRANT

www.esperya.com
Estate-bottled, harvest-dated, with a rich flavor that hints of walnuts. One taster said, "This oil is almost resinous."

Buon Delmonte FRUITY AND FRAGRANT

www.esperya.com
From Tuscany, this estate-bottled oil is a little leafy, with a soft texture and rich aromas; best used raw over salads, vegetables, and soups.

Capezzana* LEAFY GREEN AND GRASSY

Market Hall Foods (888/952-4005)
"So complex," marveled one taster, while another said, "One of the best we've ever tasted." Capezzana comes in a clear glass bottle, harvest-dated. It's an estate-bottled gem that also elicited the comment "I'd drink this for breakfast."

Caricato* FRUITY AND FRAGRANT

www.zingermans.com
Estate-bottled, unfiltered, organic, and stone-pressed, this intense, green-yellow oil from Puglia is thick and complex, with fruity notes and a peppery finish.

Carpineto FRUITY AND FRAGRANT

www.carpineto.com
From Greve in Chianti, this oil starts with a strong grassy and bitter beginning with pepper in back. It rounds further into complex herbal notes with a floral scent. Pure sunny gold in color, with 0.8% maximum acidity.

Casetta d'Ulisse*

LEAFY GREEN AND GRASSY

www.esperya.com
From an "Indicazione Geografica Protetta" in the Maremma, in Tuscany, this outstanding oil has a strong, bitter start, an intense pungency, and a strong finish. "A really assertive oil."

Castellare di Ugnana*

FRUITY AND FRAGRANT

www.frantoio.com
From Greve in Chianti, unfiltered and estate-bottled, this limited-production oil is intense and fruity, and tastes of walnuts and herbs. It's complex and bold, with a bitter afterglow and a peppery finish. One taster said, "It's got lots up front," while another praised the "fresh bright taste."

Castello di Cacchiano*

DELICATE AND MILD

www.zingermans.com
Intense yellow, with nut, fruit, and vegetal notes; unctuous texture; fabulous on bread.

Castello di Mongiovino*

OLIVE-Y AND PEPPERY

Market Hall Foods (888/952-4005)
Intense color, very pleasing bitterness, mild burn, with an outstanding flavor and a delicate texture one taster described as "milky."

Ciro Federico Intenso*

OLIVE-Y AND PEPPERY

www.esperya.com
Unfiltered, harvest-dated, this intensely fruity and pungent oil has a winning underlying sweetness. A favorite.

Colavita Extra Virgin Olive Oil $ ⊜

OLIVE-Y AND PEPPERY

supermarkets
We cross-tasted all of the major mass-market
blends of Italian olive oils widely available in
grocery stores, and this one emerged the
clear winner—it's slightly bitter, with a nice
burn. "A real olive oil," concluded one
taster, and a very good value.

Colonna Extra Virgin   DELICATE AND MILD

De Medici Imports (845/651-4400)
Characterized as "light-tasting" by one of our
panel, this olive oil has an attractive strong
olive-y scent and a very mild pungency.

Come Una Volta   DELICATE AND MILD

www.esperya.com
Handpicked, with an intense aroma and
a smooth texture, this oil has a delicate flavor and haunting mild bitterness. It's just
wonderful drizzled on fish and vegetables.
From Montegridolfo, clearly harvest- and
bottling-dated.

Costa dei Rosmarini*   DELICATE AND MILD

www.esperya.com
This handpicked oil has flavor notes of
almonds and artichokes; it's fruity and
sweet, with a mild finish. The gold foil
wrapper further protects a dark bottle.

Don Luigi $ FRUITY AND FRAGRANT

800/850-7055
www.tcitelbros.com
Available in a tin (best) or clear glass bottle,
this very fragrant Sicilian oil is unfiltered,
with flavor notes of nuts and artichokes,
ending in a peppery finish. It's a terrific oil,
and a great value.

Filippo Berio Organic Extra Virgin Olive Oil $ ⊜

FRUITY AND FRAGRANT

supermarkets
A very good value for a mass-market organic
oil. We found this pleasantly bitter, leafy,
with a "good cough" and a "mild burn."

Frantoia*   OLIVE-Y AND PEPPERY

www.olivemerchant.com
Green/gold in color, with a hint of garlic in
taste, this Sicilian oil hits the back of the
throat with a strong peppery finish.

Frantoio di Sommaia N.H. Martini-Bernardi

LEAFY GREEN AND GRASSY

Market Hall Foods (888/952-4005)
From Florence, this oil is pleasantly herbal
and bitter.

Fini*   OLIVE-Y AND PEPPERY

www.svtea.com
From Umbria, this pleasantly bitter and
fruity oil is pungent, with a strong vibrant
flavor that persists for a long time.
"Fabulous with good bread and great salt."

Gabro*   FRUITY AND FRAGRANT

www.olivemerchant.com
Organic oil, handpicked from groves in the
Calabrian hills, filled with fruity, olive-y,
flowery flavors that start off sweet and end
with a very strong peppery finish. We all
loved this oil.

Gaziello   DELICATE AND MILD

www.esperya.com
From Ventimiglia, this Ligurian oil is
famously delicate. It's made from Taggiasca
olives, and is estate-bottled and unfiltered.
"Late and mild finish."

Gelsemani Grand Cru*

LEAFY GREEN AND GRASSY

Market Hall Foods (888/952-4005)
A single-variety oil made from the "wild"
species, the *olivastro* or oleaster, which is the
ancestor of cultivated olives. This oil from
Abruzzo is intensely yellow-gold, with a
strong fragrance of olives. Pleasant bitter
and herbal notes. One taster said, "It's got
finish right at the start," while another said,
"Lots of character." Features a good dark
bottle with a pour spout.

I Lecci* DELICATE AND MILD

www.zingermans.com
A DOP oil from the "riviera dei lecci" on Lake Garda, this delicate oil has flavor notes of hazelnuts and grass, with a slightly peppery finish. One taster said, "I'd drink this like wine in a tiny glass," while another described it as having a "divine texture—light and cloudlike."

IANVS* LEAFY GREEN AND GRASSY

Corti Bros. (916/736-3800)
From Umbria, this extraordinary oil is pungent, fruity, and full of olive flavor. It made one taster's eyes tear (!), while another characterized it as "big flavor, complex and robust." Another called it "Rambo oil."

Il Nobile di Puglia OLIVE-Y AND PEPPERY

www.minervausa.com
One of Primoli's regional oils, this one from Puglia is balanced after an initial bitterness. It's peppery, with green herbal notes.

Il Signore di Toscana
LEAFY GREEN AND GRASSY

www.minervausa.com
Another of Primoli's regional oils, this Tuscan oil is exemplary, right down to the dark bottle with harvest date. It's intensely yellow, with a strong fragrance, a nice bitter flavor, and the *pizzica* peppery finish that Tuscans love.

Il Torrione* LEAFY GREEN AND GRASSY

www.esperya.com
A DOP oil from Spoleto, Umbria, this bottle is clearly harvest-dated. The oil is made mostly from Moraiolo olives, and is organic and handpicked. This is a deliciously assertive oil, one characterized as "a big boy" by one gasping taster. We loved it.

Kirkland Signature Extra Virgin Toscano $
LEAFY GREEN AND GRASSY

Costco Price Clubs
This is one of the great bargains in olive oil, labeled "new harvest" in some stores but always sold as a store-brand olive oil. It's pungent, filled with ripe olive flavor, and has a long slow finish.

La Giara FRUITY AND FRAGRANT

www.oliveoilclub.com
From Calabria, this fruity and rich-tasting oil is made from two varieties of olive—Carolea and Dolce di Rossano.

La Mola Fruttato OLIVE-Y AND PEPPERY

www.esperya.com
A DOC oil made from Frantoio and Leccino olives, the bottle is clearly harvest-dated, and the oil is unfiltered. We liked its intense flavor and nice peppery finish.

La Spineta DELICATE AND MILD

www.zingermans.com
Stone-pressed Coratina olives contribute a mild yet full-flavored oil with hazelnut notes.

Laudemio* LEAFY GREEN AND GRASSY

www.olivemerchant.com
Exceptionally fragrant, with a peppery mouth-feel, Laudemio is bottled with a great spout for slow dripping or drizzling over food. A gorgeous green color, it's estate-bottled by Conti Guicciardini at Castello di Poppiano.

Leopardo FRUITY AND FRAGRANT

www.olivemerchant.com
Full of flavors that range from flowers to hay, this estate-bottled oil has a pleasant bitter finish that adds to its charms. "Fabulous," said one taster.

Lucini* $ LEAFY GREEN AND GRASSY

supermarkets
Lucini is available in supermarkets across the U.S.; I've found it in my local Hannafords. While relatively expensive for a supermarket olive oil (about $12 per bottle), it remains a very good value on the wider scale of olive oils. It's pleasantly bitter and peppery, with a great aroma.

Manca del Bosco*

LEAFY GREEN AND GRASSY

www.esperya.com
This outstanding organic oil from Calabria is limited in production, unfiltered, and intensely flavored. It's a single-variety oil, made from Carolea olives. We found it dense, sweet, and bold, with a "very nice bitter flavor and warm finish." The bottle is clearly labeled with the year of production and the number of bottles produced, and each bottle is also numbered.

Mancianti Affiorato*

LEAFY GREEN AND GRASSY

Corti Bros. (916/736-3800)
Produced in limited quantity by the "flowering of the oil" method, this is an outstanding "big oil," with big bitter flavor and a gorgeous color. "This oil will be wonderful with food," said one taster.

Mancianti Umbria Collie del Trasimeno

DOP FRUITY AND FRAGRANT

Corti Bros. (916/736 3800)
Made from a blend of Frantoio, Leccino, Agogia, and Moraiolo olives, this oil has a rich aroma and flavor, some pungency, a delicious fruity taste, and a light texture.

Marfuga Affiorante*

LEAFY GREEN AND GRASSY

www.olivemerchant.com
This special "flowering of the oil" from Umbria is incredibly strong and peppery, with bold flavor. "Clears your sinuses," said one taster. We characterized it as an "oil with legs." Vibrantly yellow, fragrant and elegant, it has a "gorgeous taste." Unfiltered and clearly harvest-dated.

Masserie di Sant'Eramo Delicate

DELICATE AND MILD

www.svtea.com
From Bari, made with Ogliarola olives, this complex and subtle oil has a nutty aroma, smooth texture, and some pungency.

Masserie di Sant'Eramo Flavorful

OLIVE-Y AND PEPPERY

www.olivemerchant.com
Made in Bari mostly from Coratina olives, with less than .05% acidity, this seemingly delicate olive-y and fruity oil is daffodil-yellow in color. Although it has a slow start, it surprised us with a long, intensely piquant finish that tasters described variously as "flame-thrower" and "wasabi."

Molini di Valdolce FRUITY AND FRAGRANT

www.minervausa.com
This soft and fruity oil is made from ripe olives and has a delicacy that stronger oils may lack. It's one of Primoli's line of regional Italian olive oils.

Monte Pollino DELICATE AND MILD

www.olivemerchant.com
Made in Calabria, with a pale yellow color and a mild green flavor. All of us liked Monte Pollino's pleasant texture.

Montiferru* OLIVE-Y AND PEPPERY

www.esperya.com
An outstanding Sardinian oil with good body and a lovely aroma—"almost perfume." Both delicate and pleasantly bitter, it has a warm, slow, peppery finish.

O&Co. Azienda Olearia Clemente

LEAFY GREEN AND GRASSY

O&Co. stores
www.oliviersandco.com
Medium yellow in color, with herbal notes and a bitter-edgy finish, this grassy oil is a good match for grilled vegetables, meat, and fish. Made in Puglia from Ogliarola, Nostrana, and Paranzana olives.

O&Co. Disisa, vat 1

OLIVE-Y AND PEPPERY

O&Co. stores
www.oliviersandco.com
A Sicilian oil made from Cerasuola, Biancolilla, and Nocellara del Belice olives,

it's yellow-green in color, with a strong herbal scent, a mild start, and a warm, spreading finish.

O&Co. Fattorie di Galiga e Vetrice*

DELICATE AND MILD

O&Co. stores.
www.oliviersandco.com
Intensely yellow, with a grassy, almond scent and flavor. We all loved this oil made from Frantoio, Pendolino, and Morinello olives.

O&Co. Fontana San Giovanni, vats 1-3-4

DELICATE AND MILD

O&Co. stores
www.oliviersandco.com
Fruity and mild, a beautiful subtle oil with a delicate finish, made from Leccino, Pendolino, Picholine, and Coratina olives blended to O&Co.'s specifications. This is a great salad oil.

O&Co. Mulino Frantoio del Trasimeno

OLIVE-Y AND PEPPERY

O&Co. stores
www.oliviersandco.com.
Bitter edge, with a green and peppery finish. Made in Umbria from Frantoiano, Moraiolo, and Leccino olives.

O&Co. Ravidá (Azienda Agricola Ravida)

LEAFY GREEN AND GRASSY

O&Co. stores
www.oliviersandco.com.
Yellow-green in color, with a pronounced fragrance. Made from Biancolilla and Cerasuola olives.

Olio della Cilestra   DELICATE AND MILD

www.esperya.com
Stone-crushed and fruity, with 0.15% acidity, this oil from the Marches is herbaceous and delicate. "Very flavorful."

BUYING A YEAR'S WORTH OF OIL AT ONCE

In Sicily, one man I met described his olive oil purchasing process:

Each year he and his wife scrub out their big stainless-steel olive oil tank, available at any hardware store. The tank preserves the flavor of olive oil by means of an inner diaphragm that hugs the surface of the oil, creating a tight seal. As the oil is drawn off by a spigot near the bottom of the tank, this inner lid descends to protect the remaining oil. The tank rests in a cool cellar. A liter at a time, oil is drawn into an empty wine bottle and capped with a pour spout.

Every year in November, my acquaintance and his wife go to their local olive oil cooperative with their clean tank and, after tasting the oil, fill the tank. They know from experience that the oil that tastes green and peppery at harvest will mellow over the course of the year, but will not alter its essential character. This oil serves for frying, sautéing, dressing salads, and passing at the table.

Olio Trevi Umbro OLIVE-Y AND PEPPERY

www.olivemerchant.com
Deep green and unfiltered-looking, this oil is
nutlike in aroma and green apple–flavored.
Curiously, half of the tasters experienced an
extremely peppery finish, while the other
half got no finish!

Olio Verde* OLIVE-Y AND PEPPERY

Market Hall Foods (888/952-4005)
This beautifully colored and winsome estate-
grown artisanal oil from Sicily is nutty and
herbal, with complex taste nuances.

Petraia Organic OLIVE-Y AND PEPPERY

www.zingermans.com
Fragrant, slightly bitter, this intense yellow
oil has a dense and pleasing texture.

Pianogrillo* FRUITY AND FRAGRANT

www.esperya.com
Organic, from Sicily, made from Tonda Iblea
and Moresca olives, this oil has 0.5% acidity.
Its intense and attractive aroma leads into an
oil with some pleasing bitterness and a
round mouth-feel.

Podere di Pillore*

LEAFY GREEN AND GRASSY

www.zingermans.com
Estate-bottled and artisanal in quality, this
outstanding Tuscan oil is fresh-tasting. It's
pressed and then decanted into antique
terra-cotta jars, and tasters said they could
"immediately sense something different
about this oil." One said, "It felt like cold in
my mouth."

Podere Pornanino OLIVE-Y AND PEPPERY

www.chiantionline.com
Golden yellow and fragrant, with olive
and almond notes, Podere Pornanino is
harvested by hand from Correggiolo,
Leccino, Moraiolo, and Pendolino olive
trees. We loved this oil even though we
were tasting the previous year's harvest.

Rasna LEAFY GREEN AND GRASSY

www.rasna.com
A Tuscan new-harvest oil, Rasna is green-
gold, herbal, and peppery. A great typical
Tuscan oil, with all the high-flavor characteristics one would look for.

Ravidá* LEAFY GREEN AND GRASSY

De Medici Imports (845/651-4400)
This outstanding Sicilian oil is DOP and
estate-bottled, and is made from Cerasuola,
Biancolilla, and Nocellara olives. It's strong,
pungent, green, and pleasantly bitter. "A
gorgeous big strong oil," said one taster,
while another suggested it would be "wonderful on a lentil salad."

ROI Olio Extra Vergine d'Oliva
DELICATE AND MILD

www.zingermans.com
From a single variety (Taggiasca) and
organic, this yellow nutty, delicate, and
elegant oil from Liguria has the flavor of
artichokes. Very special.

San Vito* OLIVE-Y AND PEPPERY

www.zingermans.com
Stone-crushed, with a lovely texture and a
delicate sweet almond and herbaceous flavor.

Santa Casa (Azienda Agricola) Fruttato
OLIVE-Y AND PEPPERY

www.esperya.com
Good flavor, warm burn, very fruity and
olive-y, it has a round texture without spikes
of flavor. "A very enjoyable oil."

Sauvignola Paolina OLIVE-Y AND PEPPERY

www.zingermans.com
From Greve in Chianti, it mixes subtle
melon notes with herbaceous flavors,
making for a complex oil.

Sempre FRUITY AND FRAGRANT

www.oliveoilclub.com
Made from a blend of oils from four regions
of southern Italy, this unfiltered oil is richly
fruity and fragrant.

Sinolea Il Gualdo*

LEAFY GREEN AND GRASSY

jane@nywines.com
From the Chianti region, this outstanding oil
has an intense green-gold color, a strong,
attractive fragrance, an herbal, well-rounded
texture, and a nice piquancy. "A really great
oil," said one taster, noting that it would be
good on vegetables, bread, salad greens, or
on soup. The "Sinolea" refers to the extraction method.

Soliana* LEAFY GREEN AND GRASSY

Corti Bros. (916/736-3800)
Made in Sardinia from Bosana and Nera di
Oliena olives, this outstanding oil is bitter,
full-flavored, and pungent. "Grass stems
and dandelions," said one taster, while
another just said "delicious." Handwritten
harvest-dating emphasizes the artisanal
nature of this product.

Stupor Mundi LEAFY GREEN AND GRASSY

www.olivemerchant.com
From Sicily, this oil may well be "world-
stunning": it's peppery and nicely bitter,
with a beautiful buttery body and lots
of flavor undertones. It's unfiltered and
stone-crushed.

Tenuta Del Numerouno*

LEAFY GREEN AND GRASSY

De Medici Imports (845/651-4400)
Estate-bottled and unfiltered, this outstanding Tuscan oil is bitter, pungent, and grassy.
One taster said, "This oil *started* with a
finish."

Tenuta di Valgiano FRUITY AND
FRAGRANT

www.zingermans.com
An estate-bottled oil from Lucca that is
yellow-green with a nutlike fragrance, with
flavor notes of artichokes, grass, and
almonds.

Tenuta I Bonsi* LEAFY GREEN AND GRASSY

Corti Bros. (916/736-3800)
From Firenze, this oil is pungent, with a
long hot finish. "A gorgeous oil."

Tenuta San Guido Sassicaia* LEAFY GREEN
AND GRASSY

jane@nywines.com
From a very special estate in Tuscany that
produces some of the best wines of Italy,
this oil has a strong olive fragrance, is vivid
green in color, and has a peppery finish.
"Tastes like a fresh vegetable."

Tigliano* OLIVE-Y AND PEPPERY

www.esperya.com
From Pontassieve, this oil is made from a
blend of Leccino, Moraiolo, and Pendolino
olives, making it a great Tuscan poster-child
of an oil. It has all the Tuscan characteristics:
a rich and complex flavor, with notes of nuts
and artichokes, and a haunting fragrance.

Trader Joe's Organic Extra Virgin $

OLIVE-Y AND PEPPERY

Trader Joe's stores (see www.traderjoe.com
for locations)
This is another great olive oil bargain. The
oil is green, slightly bitter, with a long slow
burn at the back of the throat.

U Trappitu* Delicato OLIVE-Y AND PEPPERY

www.esperya.com
Although this oil is Sicilian, it's a subtle oil
with complex flavors (nuts, artichokes) and
aromas.

U Trappitu* Intenso

FRUITY AND FRAGRANT

www.esperya.com
Another version of this great Sicilian oil, the
intense version is complex and powerful,
with a grassy fragrance and a nice warm
finish. "Orchard grass" was one taster's
comment, trying to coin a word that would
combine fruit and hay fragrances.

Vicopisano OLIVE-Y AND PEPPERY

www.esperya.com
Organic, estate-bottled, handpicked, and
stone-crushed. We found this oil had a
"nice bitter burn."

MOROCCO

Mustapha's Moroccan $
DELICATE AND MILD

Haddouch Gourmet Imports
(206/382-1706)
www.olivemerchant.com
With a pale straw color, strong olive
fragrance, and slight bitter notes, this oil has
a lovely flavor with a hint of hibiscus and a
little pepper. Made from Picholine olives
from the Atlas Mountains; grown without
fertilizer or pesticides.

Nomads $ LEAFY GREEN AND GRASSY
www.nomads.com
A slightly harsh olive taste that works well to
spark food flavors, especially when drizzled
over hot dishes such as rice and vegetables,
or pasta.

NEW ZEALAND

Moutere Grove* FRUITY AND FRAGRANT
www.zingermans.com
Certified organic, a blend of Leccino and
Pendolino oils with an acidity of less than
0.2%. This gold-green oil has great depth
of flavor, with a fragrance of apricots and
almonds.

PORTUGAL

"Gallo" Azeite Novo $
LEAFY GREEN AND GRASSY

Triunfo Imports (973/491-0399)
Seabra's Supermarkets, Newark, NJ
Strong and pungent, this oil is sweet.
Long finish with a slow fade.

Romeu* $ LEAFY GREEN AND GRASSY

www.olivetree.cc
Certified organic, single-estate, unfiltered,
and stone-ground, this exemplary oil has a
DOP designation and a strong aroma, with
peppery, herbal, and pleasantly bitter notes.

Victor Guedes Extra Virgin $
OLIVE-Y AND PEPPERY

Triunfo Imports (973/491-0399)
"Nice bitterness," strong pungency. "It
looks like a supermarket bottle, but the taste
is surprising."

SPAIN

Almazara Luis Herrera*
LEAFY GREEN AND GRASSY

www.oliveoilclub.com
inq@classicalwines.com
Uniquely made, "Aceite de lagrima," or
"Tears of the olive," is the stone-crushed unpressed "flowering" juice of Manzanilla and
Cornicabra olives, grown in the province of
Murcia in the high, remote Valle La Jimena.
Limited production. This is a full-flavored
olive-fruity and pungent oil, great to dress
strong-flavored greens, to drizzle on bean
soups, to wake up grilled vegetables.

Baena Nuñez de Prado*
LEAFY GREEN AND GRASSY

www.rogersintl.com
One of the great olive oils of Spain, available
in glass or ceramic bottles as well as large
tins. This is an oil that has been blended to
create great subtlety and élan. Unfiltered,
"flower of the oil" extraction method.

Columela $ FRUITY AND FRAGRANT
www.zingermans.com
Made from Picual and Hojiblanca olives,
this oil is unfiltered and is described as "true
cold extraction"—the oil is extracted with
frictionless stainless steel blades (the Sinolea
system). It has great depth of flavor and a
warm finish.

Dauro de Aubocassa*

DELICATE AND MILD

inq@classicalwines.com
Unfiltered, marked with a well-dated label, with a maximum of 0.1% acidity, this outstanding oil was described as "sweetly green, like hay would taste." Complex flavors, unctuous texture. Made in Mallorca from Arbequina olives.

Dauro de L'Emporda *

FRUITY AND FRAGRANT

inq@classicalwines.com
Unfiltered with a maximum acidity of 0.1%. Made from Arbequina olives grown in Girona, this oil has notes of hay, artichokes, and apple, and was described as "sweet grass with a little pepper." A nice dark bottle helps to preserve oil, and the label is well dated.

Hacienda Fuencubierta

DELICATE AND MILD

Corti Bros. (916/736-3800)
Made from Hojiblanca, Picual, Ocal, and Arbequina olives in Córdoba, this oil is pleasingly bitter, "really nice and mild," with a rounded flavor and "nice texture."

L'Estornal Organic   OLIVE-Y AND PEPPERY

De Medici Imports (845/651-4400)
The organic version of Arbequina olive oil, this version has a nice pungency and an aroma of almonds.

L'Estornell   OLIVE-Y AND PEPPERY

De Medici Imports (845/651-4400)
Very peppery finish in this single-variety Arbequina oil. Acidity is 0.5%.

Mas Portell Organic   OLIVE-Y AND PEPPERY

www.olivemerchant.com
Organic, intensely gold in color, this special oil has a good mouth-feel and a peppery finish. Nice body—a great all-purpose oil.

Miguel & Valentino Arbequina D.O. Siurana $

DELICATE AND MILD

www.svtea.com
Sweet, light, delicate, and soft

O&Co. Baena*, vat 26

LEAFY GREEN AND GRASSY

O&Co. stores
www.oliviersandco.com
Grapefruit, almond, and bay leaf flavors with a peppery finish. Made by the Cooperative Nuestra Señora de Guadalupe, this DOC oil is a great example of a quintessential Andalusian blended olive oil; it's made from Picado, Hojiblanca, Picudo, and Lecchin olives.

Pons Early Harvest*

FRUITY AND FRAGRANT

www.casaponsusa.com
Made from Arbequina olives, stone-crushed, unfiltered. From the Garrigues region of Catalonia, in northern Spain, this vibrant yellow-gold oil has pungency along with a little sweetness and a hint of vegetal/herbal notes. "Just lovely," said one taster.

Pons Extra Virgin   DELICATE AND MILD

www.casaponsusa.com
Made from Arbequina olives, stone-crushed. Nice delicate olive flavor.

Spectrum Naturals Organic Olive Oil
Arbequina   DELICATE AND MILD

www.spectrum.com
Available also in natural foods stores, this is the fullest-tasting of the Spectrum Naturals line of oils. We found the others to be nearly flavorless, but we loved this Arbequina version. It's nutty, mild, and delicate, with an intense yellow color.

Teresa Arroja   FRUITY AND FRAGRANT

www.zingermans.com
A beautiful unfiltered, organic, artisanal oil that's made from Manzanilla Cacerena olives. It's fruity and aromatic. The attractive clear glass bottle offers no protection to the precious oil within.

Unio Siurana $ OLIVE-Y AND PEPPERY

Darien Cheese (203/655-4344)
One of the greatest values in good olive oil;
try to buy this oil in the tin rather than the
clear glass bottle, as one of our samples in
glass was oxidized (one tip-off to oxidation
was the pronounced banana flavor; the
other was the pale brown color). This is
a fruity oil with a nutty aroma. It's got a
mild flavor and a soft peppery finish. Made
from Arbequina olives in a cooperative
production.

Ybarra $ DELICATE AND MILD

www.tienda.com
Mild, sweet, and slightly fruity with a pleasing bitter finish, this oil was characterized as
"nice and light" and "well made."

TUNISIA

Miriam LEAFY GREEN AND GRASSY

www.oliveoilclub.com
Pale, slightly bitter, herbal and peppery, this
oil gets more vivid as it is swallowed.

Moulin Mahjoub* $

LEAFY GREEN AND GRASSY

www.olivemerchant.com
www.moulinmahjoub.com
Organic, unfiltered, a good bitter bite with
strong herbal notes. This is a strong oil,
great on food but not as wonderful by itself.
It's an outstanding oil for dressing foods
with strong flavors because it holds its own.

TURKEY

Laleli Early Harvest* DELICATE AND MILD

www.zeytinim.com
Pale yellow with a burn and taste of nuts.
One taster said it was very pleasing, "like
sunshine."

Laleli "From the Wild"

OLIVE-Y AND PEPPERY

www.zeytinim.com
A sunny yellow oil with nice bitter notes,
this has such a grassy herbal quality that one
taster approvingly said it was "like sucking a
dandelion stem." A special oil, good for
grilled bread and grilled vegetables.

Olive Farm Early Harvest $

OLIVE-Y AND PEPPERY

www.olivefarm.com
Available only on the Internet, this limited-
edition oil is a beautiful pale green color,
with a delicate, nutty taste that closes with a
peppery finish. Price includes shipping from
their U.S. facility.

U.S.A.: CALIFORNIA

B. R. Cohn Organic Calaveros*

LEAFY GREEN AND GRASSY

www.olivemerchant.com
Very pale in color, with fragrant grass notes
and a peppery finish. We also tasted it at one
year, and found that the oil mellows beautifully, with an aroma of olives that faded
slightly over the course of the year. The oil is
also available direct from B. R. Cohn.

B. R. Cohn Sonora Gold

DELICATE AND MILD

www.olivemerchant.com
A very mild oil, pale gold in color with hints
of green.

Calaveras LEAFY GREEN AND GRASSY

Calaveras (209/785-1000)
With an admirable, clearly dated harvest
label, this oil has layers of flavor that
includes nuts, herbs, a bitter note, and a
strong burning finish. "Perfect for dipping
bread," said one taster.

Corsica* LEAFY GREEN AND GRASSY

Darien Cheese (203/655-4344)
A blend designed by Ken Skovron, owner
of Darien Cheese, this outstanding oil is
dense and unfiltered, pleasantly bitter and
herbal tasting. It has a robust flavor, and the
peppery mouth-feel grows and warms the
throat. "Well balanced and delicious,"
commented several tasters.

DaVero* OLIVE-Y AND PEPPERY

www.katzandco.com
www.davero.com
Made in California from transplanted
Tuscan varieties, this outstanding oil has
flavor notes of fennel and artichoke. It's
lightly peppery and mildly pungent, making
it an exceptionally food-friendly oil to serve
dizzled over vegetables or good bread. A
great favorite.

Frantoio California Unfiltered*

OLIVE-Y AND PEPPERY

www.katzandco.com
Stone-crushed, unfiltered, richly flavored,
with a buttery texture, this outstanding oil is
complex and rounded, with "green stem"
notes that are pleasantly bitter and peppery.
It is actually cold-pressed, in that it's made
in a hydraulic press.

Frantoio Proprietor's Select*

OLIVE-Y AND PEPPERY

www.frantoio.com
Made from a single variety, Sevillano, this
outstanding California-Tuscan oil is pleasantly bitter at first taste and then rounds to
a balanced, complex flavor with apple notes.
A wonderful oil that, like the oil above, is
actually cold-pressed.

McEvoy Olio Nuovo*

LEAFY GREEN AND GRASSY

www.mcevoyranch.com
Certified organic, presented in a beautiful
bottle protected by a cardboard box, this
intensely fragrant, slightly bitter New Oil
has a mellow herbal edge, with a powerful
peppery finish. "You can almost taste the

dandelions," said one taster. This oil is
an extraordinary example of the best of
California, and can hold its own with
Italian oils.

McEvoy Olive Oil* OLIVE-Y AND PEPPERY

www.mcevoyranch.com
This dense yellow oil tastes of grass and hay,
with a peppery finish that "comes crawling
up your throat after swallowing." Arguably
the best producer of California olive oils,
McEvoy oils are extracted by the Sinolea
method.

Olio del Le Colline di Santa Cruz*

FRUITY AND FRAGRANT

Valencia Creek Farm (831/662-2345)
Fabulous pea-green color; fruity, mild, and
sweet with flavor notes of asparagus, nuts,
and figs. Made from a blend of Frantoio,
Leccino, and Pendolino olives.

Prato Lungo Extra Virgin Napa Valley*

OLIVE-Y AND PEPPERY

877-NAPA-OIL
www.longmeadowranch.com
This elegant and full-flavored oil has a
hauntingly rich olive flavor and a mild pungency. It is beautifully packaged in a unique
diamond-shaped bottle, protected by a cus-
tom box. It's organically grown and
estate-bottled.

Santa Barbara Olive Oil Co.*

FRUITY AND FRAGRANT

www.olivemerchant.com
Richly olive-flavored, yet delicate, with a
mild finish; greenish yellow.

**St. Helena Olive Oil Co. 100% Napa Valley,
Pedregal Estate*** OLIVE-Y AND PEPPERY

St. Helena Olive Oil Co. (800/939-9880)
A blend of Leccino, Sevillano, Pendolino,
Frantoio, Manzanillo, and Coratina olives.
These six varieties produce a sunshine-
yellow, intensely aromatic and perfumed
oil with an elegant peppery finish.
"Harmonious" was one description.

St. Helena Olive Oil Co. Single Variety:
Sevillano DELICATE AND MILD

St. Helena Olive Oil Co. (800/939-9880)
Aromatic, with a nice round olive flavor
and mild pepper.

St. Pierre California Tuscan Style
OLIVE-Y AND PEPPERY

John Addleman (797/585-9955)
www.stpierreproducts.com
This yellow-green oil is herbal, slightly
bitter, and slightly peppery, with hints of
almonds and artichokes.

St. Pierre Five Star Series
OLIVE-Y AND PEPPERY

John Addleman (797/585-9955)
www.stpierreproducts.com
This oil is yellow, with an herbal aroma and
flavor notes of hay and green pepper.

Stella Cadente OLIVE-Y AND PEPPERY

www.olivemerchant.com
Made by a new producer and distributed
only by olivemerchant.com. We tasted
the first press ever and found the pale
sunshine-yellow oil to be grassy and herbal,
with a slightly metallic note and a pleasing
peppery finish.

Storm Olive Ranch DELICATE AND MILD

www.katzandco.com
Greenish-gold in color, with a full-flavored
middle and a strong finish.

Villa Mille Rose FRUITY AND FRAGRANT

www.katzandco.com
From the Napa Valley, this blend of Tuscan
varieties (Frantoio, Leccino, and Pendolino)
is stone-crushed to yield a delicate yet full-
flavored oil with almond notes and a fruity
mouth-feel.

Wente Vineyards "Oro Fino"*
OLIVE-Y AND PEPPERY

Wente (925/456-2300)
A certified organic, unfiltered blend of six
varietals—Luque, Manzanillo, Picholine,
Ascolano, Mission, and Sevillano. Smooth at
first taste, slightly bitter; then notes of green
apple and bell pepper emerge along with an
herbal aroma and a long finish.

INTERNATIONAL BLENDS

Balzana FRUITY AND FRAGRANT

www.olivemerchant.com
A blend of Tuscan and California oils, this
limited-production oil is rightly called
"the best of both worlds."

Los Olivas FRUITY AND FRAGRANT

www.olivemerchant.com
A limited-edition oil, blended from an international array of olive varieties and bottled
in a good dark bottle with a pour spout, this
has an attractive olive aroma and a balanced
round taste, finishing with a mild bite.

O Olive Oil OLIVE-Y AND PEPPERY

www.ooliveoil.com
An international blend that includes oils
from Italy, Greece, Tunisia, and California.
This olive oil is colorful and fragrant, with
a satisfying flavor and a mild finish. Our
tasters characterized it as "really good"
and "lively."

When citrus fruits are pressed with olives, oils like these are the result. Originally done in Italy as a way of improving oil that might have flavor defects, citrus oils made with good olive oil have more recently become a tradition both in Italy and in California. The actual citrus juice is removed at the same time as the olive water—all that remains are the oils from the citrus zest mixed with the oil extracted from the olives. These oils are never used for cooking—rather, they're made for drizzling over cooked foods, and for dressing salads and vegetables.

COLONNA OILS

De Medici Imports
(845/651-4400)

Colonna Granverde is made with lemons pressed with olives, and it's very special because Italian lemons have such a unique and intense flavor. Especially wonderful on fish and on salads.

Colonna Arancio is made the same way but with oranges; it's a wonderful dessert oil, and can also be used in baking. **Colonna Mandarino** is made with Mandarin tangerines. It's lovely on fatty fish such as salmon, as well as on salads.

DAVERO MEYER LEMON OLIVE OIL

www.davero.com
www.katzandco.com

DaVero uses mild sweet California Meyer lemons and takes this tradition to new heights. Use this oil on salads, to dress fish or poultry, or on sliced fruit. It's just wonderful.

LALELI BERGAMOT

www.zeytinim.com

This unusual oil, pressed with bergamot, is a flavor revelation. Slightly orange in flavor, with the taste of Earl Grey tea, this oil is a great match for a melon-and-goat-cheese salad, or on fish.

O OLIVE OILS

www.ooliveoil.com

This California company has made a specialty of citrus oils. **O Ruby Grapefruit Olive Oil** is intensely flavored, and good on strong greens like spinach or endive salads. **O Blood Orange Olive Oil** is made with sweet blood oranges, and pairs well with pork dishes, salads containing walnuts or pecans, and fatty fish such as salmon. **O Meyer Lemon Olive Oil** was the first Meyer lemon olive oil to gain prominence, and it is brilliant on white fish such as trout, pasta with asparagus and other green vegetables, and side vegetable dishes. **O Tahitian Lime Olive Oil** is vibrant and zesty; it adds pizazz to salmon and tuna, to feta cheese, and to ears of grilled corn.

OLIVE OIL CUISINE

MONTE POLLINO

PRODOTTO ITALIANO

EXTRA VIRGIN
OLIVE OIL

(Net wt.500ml 16.9 fl.oz.)

ALTHOUGH I GREW UP MAINLY IN NEW YORK, my very earliest food memories are Italian. My family lived in Rome for two years when I was quite young, and I remember vividly the dishes that I loved. In Rome, our dinners were cooked by an Italian woman who cared for the house, and they had tastes and smells I'd never before experienced. My favorite dinner was white and intensely aromatic; I remember asking my mother for years after we returned to the United States to make it for me. I never was able to describe it well enough for her to know what it was, and I spent much of my childhood yearning for this lost dish. It was only as a young restaurant-going adult that I tasted Risotto with Four Cheeses, and recognized with great delight the lost flavors of my early years.

Cooking as an adult, I have instinctively followed the most basic Italian culinary principle: Let the quality of the ingredients make the dish. However, it has taken me another twenty years to discover a second key: *Use great olive oil to enhance flavor.* Many of us may have started our cooking lives with the idea that oils contribute neutral flavor. Corn oil, canola oil, and many industrial olive oils add little to the final taste of a dish. Instead, they provide a kind of lubricating medium that prevents food from sticking to the pan. Great olive oils, on the other hand, make a positive impact on flavor.

SHOULD YOU USE GREAT OILS FOR COOKING?

Conventional wisdom (in this country) says that you shouldn't expose great oils to heat, because heat destroys the volatile elements that contribute so much to flavor. In contrast, on farms and estates where olive oil is produced, or when families buy a year's supply of olive oil from a farmer or cooperative press, a single oil is used for every cooking and dressing need.

Before starting work on this book, I used a mass-produced extra virgin olive oil for cooking and reserved special, artisanal oils for dressing and drizzling. This economical system ensured that we ate only good extra virgin olive oil. However, once I began researching this book, I found that I had lots of wonderful oils in the house that wouldn't last forever. I started using great oils for cooking, and my food has never tasted better. Of course heat destroys some of the oil's character, but enough flavor remains to enrich the food. I know now that I'll always search for the best-tasting oils.

The point of all these recipes is good food. While olive oil has extraordinary health benefits, I want to showcase the flavors that olive oil enhances. These are my favorite dishes—simple enough for everyday cooking, but good enough for company. Every recipe has been tested exhaustively, and none made the final cut unless several cooks thought they were worth adding to our regular repertoires. You'll find the names of all the other testers in the acknowledgments; many are "regular people," not highly skilled or deeply knowledgeable food professionals. I'm lucky, though, to have generous friends in the professional food community as well, and some of them also tested recipes and made valuable suggestions. All these testers made sure that anyone can follow these recipes, and they told me whether or not they'd ever cook these dishes again.

I've written fairly extensive notes for each recipe, offering ideas for serving and emphasizing a number of options for each dish. As someone who cooks for vegetarians, I can often suggest ways to make a dish palatable for those who disdain meat. Sidebars offer further tips, tricks, or variations, and they're designed to provide you with ideas to carry into your everyday cooking.

Another thing you may notice is that almost any category of recipe—soup, salad, small dish, rice—can be a meal. I've written the recipes that way because that's the way we eat: In winter our dinners are frequently soup, or pasta, or a rice or potato dish accompanied by a simple green salad; while in summer we tend to revel in fresh vegetables on the grill or in salad meals. Flexibility is key, I think, when trying to find a way to have real home-cooked from-scratch food for family meals under time constraints. These recipes are a record of how we do it in our house, and I hope they'll give you some useful ideas for meals at your place too.

As long as we're on the subject of family meals, let me say clearly that I have had the same problems getting my kids to eat healthy, well-balanced meals as anyone else. I've lived with a vegetarian child for about fifteen years, and another who won't eat most vegetables, disdains most meats and fish, and dislikes spices. In the last few years, the erstwhile vegetarian has declared herself open to and appreciative of everything except shellfish and pork. The vegetable-hater is still partial to a diet consisting of pasta, cheese, and fruit, with the occasional salad. Striking some kind of balance and still pleasing adult palates is a challenge, but I'm happy to say that most of these recipes passed the family review board with gusto.

You'll also see that in some cases, headnotes for recipes include suggestions for other recipes. Some examples include the Oven-Roasted Asparagus recipe (page 176), which also has directions for making Pasta

One of the great pleasures of cooking, for me, is the way it engages all the senses. When I first started teaching my family to cook, I noticed that they needed to be reminded to pay attention to those sensual cues.

The sound of food sizzling in the pan tells you immediately about the degree of heat, and can serve as a reminder to lower the heat, add more food, or stir the contents of the pan. The smells that emanate from the pan can tell you that something is about to burn, or that the heat is too high (for example, if all the spice smells are in the air, you know they're no longer in the food). Similarly, when the fragrance of a cake or bread starts to fill the house, that's the signal that it's almost cooked through.

Visual cues (and good light to see them in) are even more essential, showing when a food is ready to be turned or removed from the pan. Touch is as useful as any other sense. You can feel when meat, poultry, or fish is cooked by pressing lightly on the flesh with your fingertips and judging the degree of resistance. You can hold a piece of pasta between two fingers and know how close it is to al dente.

You may find you enjoy cooking more when you deliberately pay attention to these sensual clues. You'll also find that your cooking will be the better for it.

with Oven-Roasted Asparagus and Cheese, and the recipe for Tapenade (page 72), which has a headnote suggestion about using Tapenade as a pasta sauce with farfalle.

Many of the recipes here use ingredients common to the Mediterranean. When it's possible to substitute more American ingredients, I do (as in the White Bean Puree using navy beans). When, on the other hand, a unique ingredient adds an extraordinary touch to a recipe, I'll suggest mail-order sources (as in Flash-Roasted Salmon with Saba) or a homemade substitute that has some of the attributes of that ingredient (in this case, it's Fig "Balsamico"). Please know too that even if you don't have saba and aren't planning to make Fig "Balsamico," Flash-Roasted Salmon is a great-tasting dish with nothing more than a squeeze of lemon and a drizzle of oil as a sauce. In other words, don't feel you have to outfit your pantry with the delicacies of the Mediterranean before starting to cook from this book—there will be good options and clear alternatives for most recipes and they'll still taste terrific. I do hope you'll be willing to read through and consider the ingredients section, however, because even the simplest dish tastes best when all the elements are as good as they can be. If you don't want to invest in Italian tuna packed in olive oil, or specialty vinegar, that's fine. But do please consider buying the best coarse sea salt, olive oils with pure clean flavors, real hunks of Parmigiano-Reggiano (and a good cheese grater), and the freshest, ripest vegetables available to you. You'll taste the difference, I promise.

EQUIPMENT

BLACK CAST-IRON FRYING PAN. I used to think that everyone had a black (raw rather than enameled) cast-iron frying pan, but listening to testers has taught me that I am wrong. If you don't have one, please do buy one, because they are invaluable for flash-roasting in the oven and for stovetop use. Look for one at a tag sale, or go to Kmart or similar stores and buy one made by Lodge, an inexpensive brand that's available nationally. A large 12-inch pan is extremely useful and costs around $10. These pans last forever—the one I use was given to me, already well used, nearly thirty years ago—but they must be cured before you use them.

To cure raw cast iron, wash the pan with hot water and soap, dry it well, and coat it lightly with any vegetable oil inside and out, using a paper towel. Put the pan in a 250°F oven and cook it until dry (2 to 3 hours), checking every hour. If you see that the oil has been absorbed when you check the pan, wipe the pan with more oil and repeat the process. The cured pan will look darker and will have a slight sheen. This coating of oil creates a natural nonstick finish that will improve over time as long as you make sure to preheat the pan well before adding food to it. If you do have a problem and food sticks to the pan, scrub it out with all the steel wool and soap you need, and then repeat the curing process. While most people say never to use soap on a cast-iron pan, I find it makes no difference as long as the pan is well cured and is dried immediately. If the pan seems dry, give it another thin coating of oil before putting it away, wiping it out well with a dry paper towel. You'll know your pan is well seasoned when you wash it and water beads up on the surface—that's a sure sign that it's well impregnated with oil.

Do note that cast-iron reacts badly to acid foods, such as tomatoes, lemons, and vinegar—choose a nonreactive pan for recipes that call for such foods.

ENAMELED CAST-IRON DUTCH OVEN. The French manufacturer Le Creuset makes a large selection of Dutch ovens in many colors and shapes; they are available from cookware stores and specialty catalogs such as Williams-Sonoma. If you treat it with care and always use a wooden spoon to avoid scratching, an enameled cast-iron pan will last you for many years.

The weight of enameled cast-iron pans, and the manner in which they conduct heat, profoundly affects the way food cooks in them. I tried cooking the Slow-Cooked Boneless Pork Spareribs in Tomato, Rosemary, and Juniper Sauce (page 170) in an anodized aluminum braising pan and

RESPECTING A RECIPE, RESPECTING FOOD

Having friends try out recipes has taught me a lot about what can sometimes go wrong when people cook from books. The biggest problem, I find, is substituting ingredients. Of course we all run out of ingredients from time to time, and are forced to make substitutions. The real issue is how to do this in a way that will work.

Let me give you a real-life example: One friend was anxious to try the Honey-Glazed Rolled Turkey Breast recipe (page 162), but only had a chicken breast and fresh tarragon on hand. She substituted the skinless chicken breast (which weighed about a pound) for the much larger skin-on turkey breast, and used ½ cup of tarragon for the mixed herb paste. She did not adjust the recipe's timing, which was worked out for a 6- to 8½-pound bone-in turkey breast. She also didn't reduce the amount of fresh herbs needed to stuff the meat, nor did she pay attention to the fact that the recipe called for an herb mix. In the end, her dish was inedible—"dry, overcooked and bitter from the intensity of the herbs."

How could my friend have dealt with this situation? First of all, if she'd thought about the relative weight of the meat she had on hand vs. the recipe's requirements, she would have realized that she'd need less time to cook it (since meat cooks by weight), as well as fewer herbs (because her piece of meat was much smaller). A skinless piece of meat cooks differently from one with a skin to protect it; she might have put more olive oil on the surface to provide some of that shield. She also needed to think about why the recipe called for a mix of herbs—in this case, because any single herb would be too strong, particularly an intense herb

in an enameled cast-iron Dutch oven, and the results and timing were entirely different. The Dutch oven was by far the better pot for this cooking method.

SAUTE PANS. Although a cast-iron frying pan will brown food extremely well (and can serve if you don't want to buy a sauté pan), a sauté pan has higher, straighter sides and is available in large sizes. A really large unlined sauté pan, for instance a hard-anodized dark pan like those manufactured by Calphalon, makes it easy to cook Caramelized Cauliflower (page 178), for example, because you can brown a great many pieces at

such as rosemary or tarragon. A few simple adjustments would have made the difference between failure and success.

Another friend made the Flash-Roasted Salmon (page 150) using a Corning Ware casserole as the pan. Naturally the fish cooked differently than it would have when seared on hot metal. The high sides of the ceramic held in the heat, and the fish steamed more than roasted, completely changing the texture of the dish. He also ignored the suggestion for dressing the fish with olive oil and lemon if saba wasn't

available, and instead poured brandy over the salmon. Although he said it was still a good dinner, it was entirely different from the dinner he would have been able to try if he'd followed the recipe more closely.

In writing the recipes, I've tried to incorporate the feedback and reports I've gotten from testers so that the most important elements are emphasized. Where ingredients can be substituted, I try to suggest alternatives; and where things are essential, such as an herb blend, or a heavy and well-conducting metal pan, I've done my

best to let you know what those things are.

The rule I follow when cooking from other people's cookbooks is this: At least the first time around, follow the recipe exactly. Then, if I've got ideas for improvements or amendments, I may depart from the recipe the next time I cook. I write in my cookbooks, noting changes I've made, and commenting on whether or not I think a recipe is worth doing again. It's been very useful to have those comments when I go to look for something good to cook later on.

once. Large sauté pans are also very useful in other instances, such as when cooking a pasta in its sauce. Alternatively, a wide, shallow, curved braising pan (it looks like a flat-bottomed wok) is also very good for this purpose. You can also always cook a pasta in its sauce in an enameled cast-iron Dutch oven.

NONSTICK PANS. Nonstick pans can be marvelous, letting you cook sticky foods without fear. Many people don't know, however, that they are much less useful when browning food, because the nonstick surface actually insulates food from the heat. If you want your food to brown, don't use a nonstick pan. Also know that a nonstick surface is not made to withstand high heat, and can emit an odorless gas that can make you unwell when the pan is heated over 500°F. Don't preheat nonstick pans; instead, add olive oil when you put the pan on the heat, and then heat it gently.

ROASTING PANS. From my perspective, there are two kinds of roasting pans: regular "real" rectangular or oval roasting pans like those you use at Thanksgiving, and then all the other pans one can use to roast in, depending on the food to be cooked. For instance, I frequently roast whole chicken or flash-roast fish in a black cast-iron frying pan with a heatproof handle. I also find an enameled cast-iron lasagna pan from Le Creuset immensely useful for roasted vegetables, baked pastas, and large roasting chickens ringed with potatoes and root vegetables, because the cast iron holds the heat well and contributes to the caramelization of the food surfaces.

PASTA POT. A big pot is invaluable for cooking dried pasta. I use an 8- or 10-quart pot for a pound of pasta. Look for a pot that is highly conductive; I like hard-anodized aluminum (such as Calphalon) because water boils faster in such a pot than it does in an all stainless steel pot of the same size. (I know this because in the process of writing about cookware for a magazine, I set two such pots side by side with the same amount of water and "raced" them against each other to see what the difference would be in terms of boiling speed; it was significant!)

TRADITIONAL EARTHENWARE CERAMIC COOKWARE. I'll admit it—I'm a sucker for traditional earthenware (terra-cotta or red clay) cooking pots. I particularly like the way rice cooks in shallow round Spanish *cazuelas,* which are uncovered pots made for cooking rice. I urge you to buy one (they cost about $15) from one of the Spanish specialty merchants listed in the Resources section or from an ethnic market in your town. They will last forever when treated properly, have a beautiful rusticity, and look as good on the table as they do on the stove. Never bring them quickly from one extreme of temperature to another (hot to cold or cold to hot), but rather allow them to change temperature gradually. Although most people say to use a flame tamer on top of the stove with such a pot, I find this is necessary only when cooking on an electric burner. Do not worry about lead glazes—EU standards have made them illegal and obsolete. Of course, if you see glaze flaking off the inner surface of a cooking pot, it's not food-safe and should not be used for either cooking or serving.

GRILL PAN. While certainly not essential, a ridged grill pan does allow you to create the look and achieve some of the flavor attributes of outdoor grilling in your kitchen. I prefer cast-iron or anodized aluminum grill pans because of the way they conduct and hold heat. Inexpensive cast-iron grill pans are made by Lodge and are available at Kmart (about $13) and housewares stores; anodized aluminum grill pans are made by Calphalon and are available at specialty stores. Do not buy a nonstick grill pan; they don't brown as well.

SAUCEPANS. These single-handle pots range from 1 quart to 3 or 4 quarts in size, and they are the workhorses of any kitchen. I use a small saucepan for heating water to add to polenta, while I cook the polenta itself in a bigger saucepan. It's easier to see the contents when the pan is lined with stainless steel; I like the All-Clad line.

CHEESE GRATER. Since grating Parmesan cheese is a daily necessity, I love the Microplane cheese grater, available at specialty stores and from www.cookingbythebook.com. It grates almost effortlessly, producing a shower of airy and fluffy cheese shreds. (The Microplane citrus zester is also a "must have" in my kitchen for lemons, limes, and oranges.)

FOOD PROCESSOR. I find my food processor immensely useful, but of course you can do by hand everything a food processor does with its motor. In fact, one of the recipe testers for this book lives "off the grid," without electricity. She had no problems following these recipes without recourse to a machine.

MORTAR AND PESTLE. I've recently started using my mortar and pestle, and I am impressed with the difference it makes in the taste of some pastes and sauces. You can buy inexpensive stone mortar and pestles at Thai grocery stores, since they are a traditional and essential part of any Thai kitchen.

IMMERSION BLENDER. These "stick" blenders are great for pureeing soups right in the pot they were cooked in. You can also use a rotary food mill if you prefer a low-tech alternative.

STAND MIXER. Again, anything you can do in a stand mixer, you can do with more effort by hand. It is not essential, but can make baking easier.

SALTCELLAR/SALT MILL. I keep salt in a covered sugar bowl next to the stove for cooking, and in a pretty little saltcellar on the table. When I want the texture of the salt to be fine, I either pound it in a mortar or use one of William Bound's salt mills to grind the salt to a powder.

PEPPERMILL(S). Ideally, you should have two of these: one with a big grinding knob that's easy for greasy hands to control to keep next to the stove or on the food preparation counter. The second peppermill can be a more domestic model for the dining table. Do buy good black peppercorns from a spice merchant and grind the pepper fresh.

WOODEN SPOONS. I use wooden spoons and wooden spatulas to stir and scrape up browned bits of food. I like them because they don't scratch cookware and don't conduct heat (or melt) if I leave them balanced on a pot rim.

TONGS. These inexpensive tools make it easy to turn foods as they are cooking without piercing the skin. I find tongs indispensable, and keep a couple of pairs near the stove.

FAT-SEPARATING PITCHER. Made of plastic or glass, with a long low spout, these pitchers allow you to pour pan juices into the pitcher and then pour off the good stuff (which sinks to the spout level), while leaving the fat (which rises) behind in the pitcher.

INGREDIENTS

If you can't find any of these locally, refer to the Resources section for mail-order sources.

ANCHOVIES. The fattest, most flavorful, whole anchovies are usually salt-packed in huge tins. If you buy them, you'll need to repackage the contents after opening, and you'll need to clean and rinse the whole anchovies before using them. If you love the flavor they contribute to food, you'll probably find this well worth doing. If you're not sure about anchovies, do try the good Spanish ones packed in glass jars—they are much more flavorful than those in tins. Tins, however, are very convenient, in that you can find them at almost any supermarket. If that's what's available to you, don't hesitate to try them; they'll add a subtle flavor to your dishes.

CAPERS. I prefer capers packed in salt, and I buy a huge jar of them annually and use them, rinsed, as needed. (You can get these big containers of salt-packed capers from Tienda.) You can also get the most intensely flavored capers from Pantelleria (an island near Sicily) from Esperya, a real treat. They offer them both packed in salt and packed in olive oil. If you prefer to buy your capers at a grocery store, you're more likely to find them packed in brine, a less flavorful method. Specialty food stores stock capers packed in salt as well as brined, and may offer the salt-packed version in smaller containers.

COARSE SEA SALT. Great salt is an affordable luxury! Let me encourage you to be extravagant in your salt purchases: Even if you buy the best salt in the world, you won't spend a great deal of money. I love coarse regional sea salts; my two favorites are Maldon, from the south coast of England, and Guérande, from Brittany, in northwestern France. Maldon is white and has thin pyramid-shaped crystal shards that melt on the tongue; Guérande sea salt is gray and has larger crystals. Both have a pleasing crunch and an essential minerality. One of the things I like most about the salt from Guérande is that it contains a tiny amount of seawater. This means that when you scatter this salt on a hot cast-iron pan (as you do when pan-broiling meat), it actually crackles and pops! Both of these natural salts taste wonderful with olive oil and with the foods cooked in it. *Fleur de sel,* another extraordinary sea salt from Brittany, is the most precious salt of all.

It's made like "the flowering of the oil" olive oil—that is, it's extracted from the ponds used to harvest Guérande salt by skimming off the finest salt crystals that come to the top. It's a wonderful condiment (yes, you can taste the difference), but it's too precious to cook with.

DRIED PASTA. There are lots of good brands of dried pasta on the market. Among my favorites are Latini, which is slow-dried and still made with brass dies that date from the Renaissance, and which offers an irregular surface to catch sauce in (available from Esperya, as are other slow-dried artisanal brands, including Rustichella and Pasta Morelli). Bionaturae, an organic pasta company, produces unusual shapes and a wonderful whole wheat pasta called Gobbetti (found at health-food stores). DeCecco is widely available in grocery stores here in the United States, as is Luigi Vitelli's organic pasta. Everywhere I went in Italy, whenever I got a look into a kitchen, I saw Barilla pasta, which is also widely and inexpensively available in supermarkets here. When shopping, I look for pasta that's made in Italy. I prefer artisanal pasta when I can find it, and I buy organic when I can.

FLOUR. Nearly all the baked goods in this book were made with King Arthur unbleached all-purpose flour, available in many supermarkets and by mail from www.kingarthur.com.

FRESH NUTS. It's appallingly easy to buy rancid nuts, and the off-flavor comes through in your cooking. Buy nuts from merchants who sell a lot of them, so there's a good turnover, and when you find a merchant who keeps nuts in the cooler, patronize his store. I recently was given some cashews that were just brought back from India, and their freshness was a revelation—I've never tasted cashews that good. To preserve them at their best, I store nuts in the freezer.

GARLIC. I buy local organically grown garlic whenever I can. Look for fat, healthy heads; if you find a little green sprout when you slice open a clove, pick it out and discard it, since it will be bitter. I use the side of a chef's knife to smash the garlic flat before chopping it.

GOOD BREAD. In my view, good bread is made from slow-risen dough, and if it has been made of a wet dough (like ciabatta), it often has big irregular holes and a little shimmer of shininess in the strands when you look closely at a slice in good light. It is usually available whole rather than sliced; it's frequently in a shape made by the hand rather than a pan—big *boules,* or rounds, flat ovals (ciabatta), long baguettes or *batons,* or fat ovals dusted with flour. It's always made by a baker or other individual rather than on an assembly line in a factory, and it's made from dough that was mixed on the premises, not brought in by truck from a central commissary. There is an artisanal bread revolution happening in this country, and I believe there are good bakers in every major city and not a few smaller ones. If there's no good bread in your area, bring back bags full to freeze whenever you travel, or learn to make your own. There are a couple of very good bread cookbooks on the market; look for one that talks about "retarding the dough," making a *levain* or *biga* (starter), and using a baking stone for hearth breads. Good bread is a delight with good olive oil; it's valuable even when old and stale, for bread crumbs and croutons and for layering under soups. If there is no good bread baker near you, you can order bread from Zingermans.

PARMESAN CHEESE. There's a lesson that one can hear over and over before it finally sinks in: Good quality is not expensive. When you buy the best quality of anything, whether it's olive oil or real Parmigiano-Reggiano, the flavor is so intense and true that you'll use less of it than you would an imitation of a lesser quality. Go for the real Parmigiano-Reggiano, with the name pricked out in dots on the rind. Double- or triple-wrap a wedge with waxed paper, and then place it in a plastic bag if necessary. Keep it stocked in your refrigerator, and you'll always be able to make dinner with nothing but dried pasta, good olive oil, and cheese. Get a good grater and grate it fresh whenever you need it for soup or pasta; shave it with a vegetable peeler for salads. Esperya sells the greatest Parmesan from red cows (Vacco Rosso); it has an unbelievably rich flavor (see the Resources section).

PIQUILLO PEPPERS. These Spanish fire-roasted smoky red peppers are sold in jars and cans. They are similar to marinated red peppers except that they are usually whole peppers rather than slices, and they have a distinctive full flavor.

SAFFRON. Again, saffron is one of those expensive items that are so good that a little goes a long way. I buy Italian or Spanish saffron and keep it airtight and cool to prolong its life. A good pinch, dissolved in hot water, is enough to flavor any dish. You can buy saffron from the spice sources or the Spanish specialty food retailers in this book, if you can't find good-quality saffron locally. Esperya has good-quality powdered saffron in packets.

SPICES. Many people don't know that spices get stale; take a sniff and throw out any old or musty spices. I buy spices from Penzey's or from Vann's (available from A Cook's Wares). Dean and DeLuca and Martha-By-Mail (www.marthabymail.com) also sell Vann's spices under their own labels.

VANILLA. Like anything else, there are tremendous variations in the quality of vanilla extract you can buy. I prefer the Nielsen-Massey brand for both the extract and the whole beans because their quality is consistently high. You can buy them in specialty stores and by mail from many merchants, including A Cook's Wares. Avoid using alcohol-free extracts because the alcohol releases flavors that would otherwise never emerge (see page 145). Keep vanilla extract in a cool dark cupboard.

PAN-TOASTED NUTS

MAKES 1 TO 2 CUPS

TOASTING IS A WAY to get more flavor out of nuts—it draws out the oil and caramelizes the surface sugars. It's a very easy technique, but it does require that you pay close attention because nuts can burn easily. Although you can toast nuts in the oven, I prefer the control of a pan on the cooktop. Toasted nuts can be used immediately, or they can be frozen for later use.

1 to 2 cups nuts, such as walnuts, pine nuts, almonds, or pecans

PREHEAT a cast-iron frying pan over high heat for 2 to 3 minutes, until the rim of the pan feels hot to the touch (the pan may even begin to smoke). Turn the heat down immediately to medium-low, and pour in the nuts (they must be in a single layer, so don't overcrowd the pan). Shake the pan to move the nuts around, and then, using a wooden spoon, stir the nuts every 30 seconds or so while they begin to toast. After 3 to 4 minutes, the nuts will begin to smell toasty and fragrant, and develop some dark spots. Remove the pan from the heat and put the nuts on a plate to cool (if you leave them in the pan, they will continue to cook in the residual heat).

USE these nuts whole or chopped.

OVEN-DRIED TOMATOES

MAKES ENOUGH TO
PARTIALLY FILL ABOUT
7 PINT FREEZER BAGS

OVEN-DRIED TOMATOES have intense color and flavor that are much more vivid than commercial sun-dried tomatoes. I buy whole trays or half bushels of tomatoes from the farmer's market several times during the summer in order to make batches of these tomatoes. I freeze them in pint self-seal freezer bags and use them all winter long, chopped up and added to soups and pasta sauces, and in stews. You can use cherry tomatoes (they dry the fastest), plum tomatoes, or cluster tomatoes. Just be aware that the bigger the tomatoes, the longer it takes to dry them. I've dried cherry tomatoes overnight in a low oven, while cluster tomatoes can take three or four days. Since they are going into the freezer, they don't have to be completely dry. I aim for the pliant consistency of a human ear!

As many of one kind (and size) of (perfect, unflawed, dead ripe) tomatoes as will fit, cut in half, on 2 cookie sheets (6 pints cherry tomatoes)

Coarse sea salt

WASH and dry the tomatoes, discarding any with holes, rotten areas, or cracks. Cut each tomato in half, and place the halves, cut side up, on a parchment paper–lined cookie sheet, filling it from edge to edge. Do this for as many cookie sheets as your oven will accommodate. Sprinkle the cut sides of the tomatoes with sea salt. Set the trays in the oven.

SET your oven to its lowest temperature—150°F is best; 200°F is acceptable. If you have a typical airtight oven, prop the door open a little with a wooden spoon to allow moisture to evaporate. If, on the other hand, you have a convection oven that has a direct exhaust, you don't need to prop the door open as the exhaust will draw out any moisture.

KEEP the oven on for at least 4 hours, checking periodically to see how dry the tomatoes are getting. If they need more time and you have a gas oven with a pilot light, you can close the door and continue drying the tomatoes with the heat from the pilot light. If you have an electric oven, you can alternate turning it on to its lowest setting for 20 minutes every couple of hours, and then turning it off, allowing the heat to stay in the oven, or turn off the oven

ALMAZARA

luis herrera

January Harvest
2001

Extra Virgin Olive Oil
Aceite de Lágrima

Stone-crushed unpressed freerun juice of Manzanilla and Cornicabra olives from familial groves located in Murcia provinces high, remote Valle La Jimena

Product of Spain
Cont.500ml. (17 Fl. Oz)

and leave it closed overnight. In any case, you don't need to prop the door open after the initial 4 hours. Use your own judgment about the timing and how often to keep turning the oven on and off. If you've got big, juicy cluster tomatoes, it can take up to 3 or even 4 days and nights of on-again, off-again oven settings before they are dried.

WHEN they're dry but still pliant, pack the tomatoes loosely in self-seal freezer bags (make sure they are freezer bags and not just storage bags). Push as much air out of the bag as possible before sealing. Store in the freezer for as long as a year.

FIG "BALSAMICO" AGRODOLCE

MAKES ABOUT 2 CUPS

LET'S BE CLEAR HERE—real *balsamico* is made in a labor-intensive process that involves progressively moving aged evaporated grape must from one variety of wooden barrel to a smaller barrel made of another over a period of at least ten years. The precious liquid draws flavor from each type of wood and is decanted into the next barrel annually until it's blended with the contents of all the other smallest barrels for a final year. Only then is it poured into tiny bottles to be savored. If you are ready to spend the money ($85 and up), it's an extraordinary condiment (available from Corti Brothers, Zingermans, and Esperya). In contrast, most of the balsamic vinegar we buy is a young, relatively sharp wine vinegar that has been blended with sugar to offer some of the flavor notes of aged *balsamico*. This recipe for "balsamico" takes young commercial balsamic vinegar a little further toward the flavor of the real thing, but it remains essentially a fake, since sugar and cooking are still standing in for time, weather, and wood.

1 cup sugar

¼ cup water

1 cup ordinary balsamic vinegar

1½ cups Concord or other grape juice

½ cup Marsala

5 dried figs, finely chopped

IN a deep, heavy nonreactive saucepan over medium heat, melt the sugar in the water without stirring, and cook the sugar until the color deepens to a rich brown, 5 to 10 minutes. Slowly add the vinegar, standing back because the mixture will foam and spit. Add the grape juice, Marsala, and dried figs, stirring well. Let the mixture cook down until it is reduced by half and is slightly syrupy, at least 30 minutes.

COOL, strain, and pour into a sterilized bottle. Allow the "balsamico" to set for a week or two before using. Keep refrigerated.

Note: If you want the flavor of this condiment but don't want to make this recipe, you can buy several products that are similar for $8 to $12 a bottle. These include, in order of sweetness, saba, which is reduced grape must, and fig vinegar, which will need to have a little brown sugar added to it to make it as sweet as the other alternatives.

When Trebbiano grape juice is cooked down and greatly reduced in volume (which concentrates the sweetness), the result is called *boiled must*. When boiled-down must is reduced by 30% to 50% of its original volume, it's called *saba*. (Saba is very ancient—it was used by the Romans as a sweetener.) When saba is poured into a series of barrels made from different aromatic woods, allowed to acetify and evaporate naturally for at least 10 years while exposed to extremes of temperature, it's called *aceto balsamico tradizionale.*

LEMON MAYONNAISE

MAKES ½ PINT

FOOD PROCESSORS make it easy to make your own mayonnaise, and it tastes much better than anything you can buy in a store. Do note that this recipe uses a raw egg, so if you don't have access to salmonella-free eggs, use pasteurized eggs or an egg substitute like Egg Beaters instead.

Check to see if your food processor has a tiny pinhole in the bottom of the feed tube pusher; if it does, it will be even easier to slow-drip the oil into the bowl. As long as you are careful to slow-drip every drop of oil, I have never known this recipe to fail or break. This mayonnaise makes the basis for the world's best BLT.

1 egg (see headnote)

½ teaspoon Dijon mustard

Coarse sea salt and freshly ground black pepper, to taste

Grated zest of 1 lemon

2 tablespoons fresh lemon juice

1 cup delicate and mild olive oil

IN the bowl of a food processor, combine the egg, mustard, salt and pepper, lemon zest and juice, and ¼ cup of the olive oil. Process. Keeping the machine running, either pour the remaining oil into the feed tube pusher to slowly drip it into the bowl, or very slowly pour the oil into the feed tube itself so that it enters drop by drop. You'll be able to see the mayonnaise thickening. The whole process of adding the oil will take about 5 minutes.

TRANSFER the mayonnaise to a clean glass jar and refrigerate for up to a week.

Variations

GARLIC MAYONNAISE: Add 3 cloves peeled garlic to the processor bowl with the other ingredients. A classic addition to fish soups and a delicious dip for raw vegetables.

ANCHOVY MAYONNAISE: Add 2 rinsed anchovy fillets to the processor bowl with the other ingredients. Use as a dip for raw vegetables.

HERB MAYONNAISE: Add ¼ to ½ cup fresh chopped herbs such as parsley, basil, or chives, or about ⅛ cup very strong herbs such as tarragon or rosemary to the processor bowl with the other ingredients. Use as a coating for chicken or fish as it roasts, or as a sauce for cooked fish or fowl, diluted with cream.

MUSTARD MAYONNAISE: Substitute 1 tablespoon grainy mustard for the Dijon mustard. Use as a coating for a leg of lamb that has been studded with garlic slivers.

SAUCE REMOULADE: Stir 1 tablespoon drained finely chopped capers, 1 tablespoon finely chopped fresh herbs, and 1 tablespoon finely chopped cornichons into the finished Lemon Mayonnaise.

PEPPERY SAUCE VERTE: Stir 1 tablespoon finely minced fresh watercress leaves, 1 tablespoon minced fresh chervil, and 1 tablespoon minced fresh tarragon into the Lemon Mayonnaise.

Carpineto

Olio
ExtraVergine
di Oliva
EXTRA VIRGIN
OLIVE OIL

FIRST COLD PRESSED

PRODUCED AND BOTTLED BY
Carpineto s.n.c.
VIA DUDDA 17/B
GREVE IN CHIANTI
ITALY

PRODUCT OF ITALY

NET CONT. 500 ML (16.9 FL OZ)

FIRE-ROASTED RED PEPPERS

MAKES ¾ CUP
¼-INCH STRIPS

WHEN WE LIVED IN PARIS, every night around suppertime, the appetizing smell of red peppers being roasted would waft through our kitchen window from the kitchens below. It's a wonderful smell, and one that now evokes Paris for all of us. Roasted red peppers are terrific to have on hand for salads, for making tapas and other little appetizers (strips of roasted red pepper on goat cheese, for instance), to puree into a pasta sauce (pureed roasted red pepper mixed with ricotta), or to use as a soup enrichment (shreds of red pepper on top of white bean soup). If you have an electric stove, you can do this under the broiler, putting the pepper as close as possible to the broiler element and using tongs to turn the pepper.

1 whole red bell pepper, washed and dried

STICK a fork into the red pepper at the stem end, and roast it over a gas burner on the stove by resting the pepper on the burner grate. Allow the side touching the flame to become completely charred, about 30 seconds. Using the fork as a handle, turn the pepper so that another area is exposed to the flame. Continue around the pepper, turning it every 30 seconds or whenever each area is charred, until the whole pepper is scorched. Still using the fork as a handle, remove the pepper from the stove and inspect it for any little live embers or flames. Blow out any fire! Immediately pop the charred pepper into a small brown paper bag (I use brown lunch bags) and seal the top by folding it over a few times. Let the pepper rest in the bag for about 10 minutes.

REMOVE the cooled pepper from the bag and flatten the bag. Using a small paring knife, scrape the charred skin off the whole pepper, working around the pepper and wiping the charred bits on the knife onto the bag. When the pepper is all scraped, cut down through the stem end to remove the core. Pull out and discard the ribs and seeds. (Don't be tempted to rinse the pepper—the juices hold lots of flavor.) Cut down one side of the fruit to lay it flat, and cut the pepper into strips (I like ¼-inch strips, but if you are pureeing the pepper, they can be wider and less regular).

IF you are using the pepper for salad or for appetizers, it is ready to be used immediately. If you are preparing it ahead, you can put the strips in a sterile glass jar and cover them with olive oil. This is like money in the bank for meals all week, as you can pull out pieces as needed. Use it up within a week.

Appetizers, small dishes, and sandwiches

CHICKEN "FOIE GRAS" CROSTINI

MAKES 1½ CUPS

LOOK FOR ORGANIC chicken livers for this dish; the difference is noticeable. Organic livers are a rich deep red; they're larger than conventional chicken livers; and they're better for you, since one function of the liver is to filter toxins, and organically grown chickens are exposed to fewer toxins.

You can easily halve or double this recipe, depending on the size of the crowd. This makes about one baguette's worth of topping, and it works especially well on a whole-wheat walnut baguette. Adding the capers enlivens the flavor, but feel free to leave them out.

Note that the livers can be cooked earlier in the day and brought to room temperature before spreading.

---

2 tablespoons delicate and mild olive oil

1 teaspoon unsalted butter

1 teaspoon chopped fresh sage leaves, *or* **½ teaspoon dried sage**

2 large shallots *or* **1 medium onion, sweet if possible, coarsely chopped**

½ pound chicken livers, cleaned and drained

1 tablespoon dry Marsala or red wine

Coarse sea salt and freshly ground black pepper, to taste

1 teaspoon capers, drained (rinsed if salt-packed)

1 baguette, preferably whole-wheat walnut (page 120)

HEAT a large frying pan, add the olive oil and butter, and reduce the heat to low. Add the sage and chopped shallots. Cook, stirring occasionally, for 3 to 4 minutes, until the shallots begin to look translucent.

INCREASE the heat to high and add the chicken livers, stirring to make sure each liver is in contact with the pan. Cook, stirring as necessary, to brown all sides and cook to a slightly pink interior, 8 to 10 minutes.

WHEN the livers are nearly done and slightly pink, add the Marsala and cook for another 3 minutes, until the alcohol evaporates. Salt generously and pepper to taste, and let cool.

CHOP the livers by hand or in a food processor, adding the capers if using. If you use a food processor, pulse no more than six times to make a coarse-textured paste.

SLICE the baguette diagonally into ¼- to ½-inch-thick slices. Arrange these on a baking sheet and broil (or use a grill pan on top of the stove, or a wood- or gas-fired grill), watching carefully to avoid burning. Spread the liver mixture over the toasted bread, and serve.

BREAD-DIPPING OIL

Good bread dipped into great olive oil is a time-honored and delicious appetizer. Unfortunately, here in the United States, our tendency to gild the lily has brought forth a plethora of "dipping oils." Many of these dipping oils are made from undistinguished olive oils that need the enhancement to be palatable. The fact is, you don't need infusions of herbs or spice blends to make a good dipping oil. A great olive oil is perfect on its own, with a little coarse sea salt to bring out its natural sweetness.

Here's how an Italian mixes bread and oil: First sprinkle the morsel of bread with some excellent coarse sea salt, and then pour on the olive oil, so that the oil helps the salt to penetrate the bread. Enjoy.

TAPENADE

MAKES ABOUT 2¹/₂ CUPS

THIS INTENSELY FLAVORFUL olive paste, my version of a classic, is a refrigerator staple in our house. Spread it on grilled bread or crackers as an appetizer, or stir it into a mild-flavored soup, such as the white bean on page 180, to vary the flavor. You can also spread it on top of a grilled chicken breast, or stuff it beneath the skin of a whole chicken before you roast it. Tapenade will keep, tightly sealed and with a layer of olive oil covering the top, in the coldest part of your refrigerator for up to a week.

To make *Farfalle with Tapenade Sauce,* thin 1¼ cups of this tapenade with ¼ cup hot pasta water, and toss with just-cooked-to-perfection bow-tie pasta. Serve either warm or at room temperature, dusted with freshly grated Parmesan and drizzled with a little more oil if necessary.

1 pound wrinkled strong-flavored black olives, preferably oil-cured

5 cloves garlic, peeled, split, green sprout removed if present

One 2-ounce tin anchovies, drained, *or* 1 fat salt-packed whole anchovy, cleaned and rinsed

2 tablespoons capers, drained (rinsed if salt-packed)

2 tablespoons herbes de Provence

¹/₃ cup leafy green and grassy olive oil

Grated zest of 1 lemon

Juice of 1 lemon, or more to taste

Coarse sea salt and freshly ground black pepper, to taste

PIT the olives: Using a sharp paring knife, slit each olive to expose the pit. Squeeze it out and discard.

COMBINE the garlic, anchovies, capers, and herbes de Provence in the bowl of a food processor, and process to make a rough and chunky paste. Add the olive oil, lemon zest and juice, and salt and pepper. Pulse briefly to blend, taking care to leave the paste with some texture. Taste for seasoning, and add a little more salt or lemon juice as needed.

POUR the tapenade into a clean jar, and pour a little more olive oil on top to seal it. Cover first with plastic wrap and then the lid, and refrigerate. Bring the tapenade to room temperature before serving.

PUREED CAULIFLOWER WITH TRUFFLE OLIVE OIL ON GRILLED BREAD

MAKES ABOUT
1 1/4 CUPS PUREE

ALTHOUGH THIS LOOKS LIKE an innocent little spread, it has a great aroma and sensuality, thanks to the truffle oil. I prefer Mas Portel's truffle oil because it has a visible truffle shaving in the bottle and the olive oil is of great quality, but I've also made this successfully using 1 tablespoon of a lesser truffle oil blended with 1 tablespoon leafy green and grassy olive oil. If you don't have any truffle oil, substituting a strong leafy green and grassy olive oil entirely will work, although the flavor will of course be different.

1 long baguette, cut diagonally into 1/2-inch-thick slices

1 small head white, unblemished cauliflower

2 tablespoons truffle olive oil or leafy green and grassy olive oil

1/2 teaspoon coarse sea salt

1 to 2 tablespoons heavy cream

Freshly ground black pepper, to taste

PREHEAT a broiler or grill, and when it is hot, toast the bread slices.

CUT off the outer leaves and lower stalks of the cauliflower, and cut the head into quarters. Steam the cauliflower in a vegetable steamer set over boiling water until it is soft but not mushy, 10 to 15 minutes for a small fresh head.

PLACE the cauliflower pieces in the bowl of a food processor, and add the truffle oil, salt, and 1 tablespoon of the cream. Puree until very smooth, about 3 minutes. Taste, and add the pepper. If the puree seems too thick, add more cream as needed.

MOUND the puree in a bowl surrounded by the toasts, or spread it directly on the toasts, and serve.

EGGPLANT CAVIAR

MAKES 1½ CUPS

I LOVE THE BRIGHT TASTE of this spread on grilled bread for an appetizer, and for sandwiches. I like to use Japanese eggplants, which are small and skinny and mild; if you can't find them, regular eggplant will do just as well. I use Barbara Kafka's microwaving method to roast eggplant— it's fast and very easy, and the kitchen stays cool. If you don't have a microwave, prick the eggplant all over and roast it on a baking sheet in a conventional oven for about 45 minutes at 375°F.

2 small Japanese eggplants *or* 1 medium eggplant (1½ to 2 pounds total)

1 red onion, roughly chopped

2 cloves garlic, peeled

3 tablespoons fruity and fragrant olive oil

Juice of ½ lemon (3 to 4 tablespoons)

½ cup fresh flat-leaf parsley leaves, washed and dried

¼ cup fresh basil leaves, washed and dried

1 teaspoon coarse sea salt

Generous grinding of black pepper

PRICK the eggplant all over with a fork, and set it on a double layer of paper towels in a microwave oven. Cook on full power for 10 minutes. Check to see if the eggplant is collapsed and cooked through. If it isn't, cook for an additional 5 minutes or until done. It should be wrinkled, deflated, and soft.

LET the eggplant cool, then peel away the skin. Use a spoon to scrape the pulp into the bowl of a food processor. Add the rest of the ingredients and process until smooth.

TRANSFER to a bowl if serving immediately, or store, well covered, in the refrigrator for up to a week. Serve at room temperature.

GRILLED PORTOBELLO, WHITE BEAN, AND ARUGULA SANDWICH

SERVES 1

HEARING JACK BISHOP describe this sandwich on NPR'S *Fresh Air*, I was delighted to find that I had all the ingredients in the house. After the making and the eating, I felt even happier. It's a terrific supper sandwich.

To make a platter of *Grilled Portobello, White Bean, and Arugula Bruschetta* for a party, follow the procedure as described below, using a baguette as your bread and using more of every ingredient.

These are best at room temperature, so don't hesitate to make them an hour or so ahead of time.

1 thick slice good country bread

1 clove garlic, peeled, sliced in half lengthwise

1 to 2 tablespoons leafy green and grassy olive oil

1 large fresh Portobello mushroom cap

2 to 3 tablespoons White Bean Puree with Sage and Garlic (page 180) *or* one 19-ounce can white beans, rinsed and drained, pureed with 1 garlic clove and 2 chopped fresh sage leaves

½ cup arugula leaves, washed

Coarse sea salt and freshly ground black pepper, to taste

GRILL or toast the bread until dark. Rub it vigorously with the cut side of the garlic, as if the bread were sandpaper. The garlic halves will get considerably smaller or disappear altogether. Drizzle a thin film of olive oil over the bread.

BRUSH the Portobello cap with a little of the olive oil, and grill it under the broiler, as close to the heat as you can manage, for 12 minutes, or until cooked, juicy, and fragrant. Cut into strips.

AT the same time, gently heat the White Bean Puree in a double boiler on the stove, or in a microwave for 1 minute on high power.

ASSEMBLE the sandwich by spreading the puree on the oiled and garlicked bread, then adding arugula, and then the grilled mushroom strips. Add salt and pepper, and enjoy.

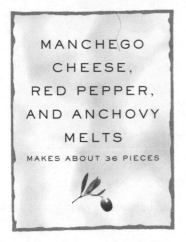

MANCHEGO CHEESE, RED PEPPER, AND ANCHOVY MELTS

MAKES ABOUT 36 PIECES

I'VE BEEN MAKING these tapas at home ever since I first tasted them in Spain. Manchego cheese isn't always easy to find locally; sometimes I order it from La Tienda (who also carry all of the other ingredients in this recipe). Alternatively, you can use any good melting cheese, such as Gruyère. I always make a couple of tapas without anchovies for my children, who wouldn't dream of touching the tiny fish. But really, even if you think you hate anchovies, try these with good Spanish anchovy fillets packed in olive oil, or with rinsed salt-cured anchovies, because those little shreds pack tremendous flavor.

1 baguette

About ¼ cup leafy green and grassy olive oil

1 or 2 bottled or canned grilled red peppers or piquillo peppers, or 1 or 2 Fire-Roasted Red Peppers (page 68)

2 anchovy fillets packed in olive oil

About 36 thin slices Manchego cheese

Coarse sea salt and freshly ground black pepper, to taste

SLICE the bread on the diagonal, aiming for slices that are ¼ to ½ inch thick. Heat a large griddle or grill pan over medium-high heat, and then heat 2 tablespoons of the olive oil in it until it shimmers and smells fragrant. Put as many pieces of bread as can fit in the pan in a single layer. (They should sizzle as they hit the oil—if they don't, the oil isn't hot enough.) Fry the bread until golden, turning the slices once to cook on both sides. Place the fried bread on paper towels. Continue until all the bread is fried, adding more oil to the pan between batches as necessary and being careful to heat it well before adding the bread.

SLICE the red pepper into long pieces, and slice the anchovies into shreds.

PREHEAT the broiler. Lay the fried bread out on a cookie sheet. Place a thin slice of cheese on each piece of bread, and top it with a slice or two of red pepper and a shred or two of anchovy. When all the bread is covered, place the cookie sheet under the broiler and broil for about 2 minutes, or until the cheese is melted.

ARRANGE the tapas on a large platter. This can be made several hours ahead and served at room temperature.

TOMATO TOAST

YIELDS 10 OR MORE
SERVINGS, DEPENDING
ON HOW YOU CUT THE
TOAST SLICES

THESE AMAZING TOASTS are a breakfast staple in Spain—I first encountered them at a hotel breakfast buffet in Valencia. They make such an excellent start to the day that now they're my first choice for breakfast during tomato season. But because these are so delicious, give those who don't have breakfast with you a chance to taste them by serving them as a first course for dinner: Arrange them on a platter, and stand back while guests enjoy them. They can be made an hour or so ahead, but if you don't have great tomatoes and great oil, wait to make them until you do—this is a completely ingredient-driven recipe. Although this is always best when freshly made, I sometimes make a batch of tomato puree and keep it in the refrigerator for a few days' worth of breakfasts.

2 pounds (6 to 8) red, ripe, juicy fresh tomatoes

10 or more toasted slices of superb country bread, such as a five-grain, semolina, or Overnight Country Bread (page 116)

Leafy green and grassy olive oil

1 to 2 teaspoons coarse sea salt

Freshly ground black pepper, to taste

GRATE fresh tomatoes on a box grater to form a coarse pulp.

TRANSFER the tomatoes to a pitcher or a bowl.

TOAST the bread slices (or grill them on a grill pan) to medium-dark, and then cut them into serving size—for breakfast I like a whole or half slice, but for appetizers I cut the toast into fat fingers.

FOR each slice of toast, drizzle on a thin film of olive oil and then spoon on a good coating of fresh tomato puree. Top with grains of sea salt and freshly ground pepper.

TOMATO, BASIL, MOZZARELLA, AND OLIVE OIL ON A BAGUETTE

SERVES 2

WE LIVED IN PARIS for half a year while our children were young, and this became our favorite sandwich there. We used to make half a baguette's worth per person, and then carry them along to picnic on after visiting a museum or far-away park. Now that the children are almost grown, it remains a favorite for car trips because the flavors only grow better as they blend.

1 baguette

Leafy green and grassy olive oil

2 very ripe tomatoes

1 cup fresh basil leaves, washed and dried

1 pound mozzarella cheese, thinly sliced

Coarse sea salt and freshly ground black pepper

SPLIT the baguette in half lengthwise. Drizzle some olive oil over the cut sides of the bread.

ON one half, layer slices of tomato, then basil leaves, and then mozzarella. Sprinkle with coarse sea salt and freshly ground black pepper to taste. Put the other half of the baguette on top, and press down.

CUT the baguette in half crosswise, to form two long sandwiches. Wrap each sandwich in waxed paper and let age for at least 1 hour at room temperature before eating.

TOMATO, BASIL, AND MOZZARELLA BRUSCHETTA

The combination of tomato, basil, mozzarella, olive oil, and garlic is a classic bruschetta topping. To make the bruschetta, toast or grill slices of baguette, cut on the diagonal. Rub each slice with the cut side of a garlic clove, drizzle with olive oil, and add a slice of tomato, a basil leaf, and a slice of mozzarella. Serve as is, or run briefly under the broiler to melt the cheese.

FRESH TOMATO TART

SERVES 6 TO 8 AS
AN APPETIZER OR
4 AS A MAIN COURSE

FOR A SUMMER LUNCH, an appetizer for a more formal dinner, or a simple supper dish paired with a hearty salad, this tart is a versatile addition to anyone's repertoire. Because the crust is made with purchased puff pastry dough, it's extremely easy to make, even for crust-phobics. Since I prefer the taste of fresh tomatoes, I make this like a savory version of a fruit custard tart, arranging the raw sliced tomatoes on top just after the baked tart comes out of the oven, which heats the tomatoes but doesn't cook them. If you prefer the flavor of cooked tomatoes, arrange the sliced tomatoes on the dough, pour the custard filling over them, and bake. Although you can make this tart early in the day if you put the tomatoes in first and then cook them, this is not a recipe to make ahead if you're topping it with raw tomatoes—once you've put the tomatoes on top of the custard, it should be served within an hour or two.

PREHEAT the oven to 400°F. Line a 9-inch porcelain or metal tart pan with the pastry. Do not grease the pan. Put the whole square sheet in the pan, cutting and patching as necessary to make it fit.

1 puff pastry sheet, thawed according to the package directions

1 cup fresh basil leaves, washed and dried

1 cup heavy cream

3 tablespoons fruity and fragrant olive oil

3 extra-large eggs

Coarse sea salt and freshly ground black pepper, to taste

2 large ripe tomatoes

COMBINE the basil, cream, 2½ tablespoons of the olive oil, eggs, and salt and pepper in the bowl of a food processor, and process until the basil is very finely chopped. Pour this mixture into the pastry-lined pan, and bake for 30 to 40 minutes, until cooked through, golden, and fragrant. The tart will puff up in the oven, but will immediately deflate when it starts to cool.

WHILE the tart is baking, use a sharp serrated knife to thinly slice the tomatoes. As soon as you remove the tart from the oven, arrange the tomato slices on top, working in a spiral from the outer edge to the center, overlapping the slices. Use the smallest pieces of tomato for the center. Drizzle the remaining ½ tablespoon olive oil over the tomatoes. Serve slightly warm.

POTATO GALETTE

SERVES 12 TO 14
AS AN APPETIZER

THIS RECIPE makes two giant potato pancakes, which is enough in our house for a main course for four to six when followed by salad. It's also good, however, as an appetizer, in which case the two pancakes, cut into smaller wedges, will easily serve a dozen people or more. This recipe can be divided in half to make only one pancake, which would serve four as a generous first course. I use a big frying pan and a shallow griddle to make the two giant pancakes.

10 Yukon Gold potatoes

1 onion

2 eggs, beaten

1 teaspoon coarse sea salt

½ teaspoon freshly ground black pepper

1 cup unbleached all-purpose flour

4 tablespoons fruity and fragrant olive oil

For the topping

Sour cream

Applesauce

WASH and peel the potatoes. Using the coarse grating disk of a food processor, shred them along with the onion. Pour the potato-onion mixture into a large mixing bowl and add the beaten eggs, salt, and pepper. Using your hands or a large spatula, combine all the ingredients. Sprinkle in the flour and mix again. The mixture should be fairly wet but not soupy; it should be slightly sticky as well.

HEAT two frying pans (or your largest griddle and a frying pan). Divide the olive oil between the two pans and heat it over medium heat. When the oil is hot, divide the potato mixture between the two pans, patting the potatoes to form a thin pancake that covers the pan from edge to edge.

COOK, uncovered, over medium heat until the underside is browned and has crisp bits, about 10 minutes. Using a plate that's bigger than the skillet (or a pizza pan, or the pan's cover), carefully invert each half-cooked pancake onto a plate. Now slide the pancakes back into the pans, cooked side up, and cook the other side, 5 to 7 minutes.

INVERT the pancakes onto serving dishes and cut them into wedges. Garnish each wedge with a dollop of sour cream and a dollop of applesauce.

WATERMELON, FETA, AND LIME PARFAIT

SERVES 4 TO 6

5 pounds watermelon

1 cup loosely packed crumbled feta cheese

2 teaspoons lime olive oil *or* 2 teaspoons fruity and fragrant olive oil combined with the grated zest of 1 lime and the juice of 1 lime

½ teaspoon coarse sea salt

ICED SWEET CHUNKS of watermelon contrast with the creamy saltiness of feta in this cooling summer first course. You can use O Olive Oil's O Tahitian Lime Olive Oil, or you can use a fruity and fragrant oil and add some lime zest and juice. Either way, this is a summer dish you'll want to include in your hot-weather repertoire.

CUT the watermelon into 1-inch-thick slices. Cut off the rind, and pick out the seeds with the point of a knife. Cut each slice into ½-inch dice, and put the pieces in a large bowl; you should have 4 cups diced melon.

SCATTER the crumbled feta over the watermelon pieces, and add the olive oil and salt. Gently toss to mix.

SERVE at once in martini glasses, goblets, glass bowls, or teacups.

Salads, salad dressings, and salad meals

DIONE LUCAS'S FRENCH DRESSING

MAKES ABOUT 1¼ CUPS

SO RETRO IN STYLE that I had to increase the garlic to make it taste right, this is a culinary souvenir from the early 1970s, when I worked at The Brasserie, a restaurant run by the late Dione Lucas in Bennington, Vermont. I've met people who remember this dressing more than twenty years later, so you know I'm not exaggerating when I say it is a winner. Keep a jar of this in your refrigerator (it lasts a week or two) and you'll be ready to make a salad at the drop of a hat. Note that this recipe contains a raw egg, so if you don't have salmonella-free eggs in your area, substitute Egg Beaters or pasteurized eggs for safety's sake.

1 teaspoon coarse sea salt

1½ teaspoons freshly cracked black pepper

¼ teaspoon sugar

½ teaspoon dry mustard

1 teaspoon Dijon mustard

1 teaspoon fresh lemon juice

2 cloves garlic, peeled and finely minced

1 tablespoon tarragon vinegar, white wine vinegar, or cider vinegar

1 egg, beaten (see headnote)

½ cup light cream

¾ cup fruity and fragrant olive oil

PLACE the salt, pepper, sugar, both mustards, lemon juice, garlic, and vinegar in the bowl of a food processor, and process until the garlic is very finely minced and integrated. Add the egg and the cream, and process again. Add the olive oil and process until blended. Pour the dressing into a clean 1-pint screw-top jar, and refrigerate until needed.

BASIC VINAIGRETTE, MADE THREE WAYS

YOU CAN MAKE a vinaigrette fresh with each salad, whisking it in the salad bowl or in a glass or a little jar; or you can make a bigger batch in a jar and have salad dressing on hand whenever you need it.

CLASSIC FRENCH WOODEN BOWL METHOD

MAKES ABOUT ¼ CUP

1 clove garlic, peeled

1 teaspoon Dijon or grainy mustard

1 tablespoon fresh lemon juice or wine vinegar, sherry vinegar, or balsamic vinegar

3 tablespoons olive-y and peppery olive oil

Coarse sea salt and freshly ground black pepper, to taste

FOR delicate greens.

IMPALE the garlic clove on a fork and rub it vigoroulsy around the inside of a wooden salad bowl. Either discard the garlic (if you think garlic will be too strong a flavor in your salad composition), or mash and mince it before adding it with the rest of the ingredients. Put the mustard in the bowl, and mix in the lemon juice or vinegar. Slowly pour in the oil, whisking as you pour. Add salt and pepper and taste. Add chilled greens and toss very well to coat each leaf with dressing. Serve at once.

WHICH OILS FOR WHICH SALADS?

In general, olive-y and peppery oils are the best all-around oils for salads of mixed greens. Use delicate and mild oils for salads made of tender greens such as Bibb lettuces, and leafy green and grassy oils for strong greens such as spinach, arugula, and watercress. Fruity and fragrant oils are the best choice for salads that have fruit as a main ingredient, such as oranges, apples, strawberries, mangoes, or sweet tomatoes.

ONE-SALAD'S LITTLE JAR OR GLASS METHOD

MAKES ABOUT ¼ CUP

1 clove garlic, peeled, mashed, and finely chopped (or put through a garlic press)

1 heaping teaspoon grainy mustard

¼ teaspoon coarse sea salt

Freshly ground black pepper

1 tablespoon balsamic vinegar, sherry vinegar, or wine vinegar

3 tablespoons olive-y and peppery or leafy green and grassy olive oil

FOR mixed and sturdy greens.

USING a fork (in a glass) or by shaking (in a screw-top jar), combine all the ingredients. Pour over the greens and toss well.

SCREW-TOP JAR OR MINI FOOD PROCESSOR METHOD

MAKES 1 CUP

3 cloves garlic, peeled and chopped very fine (or put through a garlic press)

1 tablespoon Dijon or grainy mustard

Scant ¼ cup sherry vinegar, wine vinegar, or balsamic vinegar

½ teaspoon coarse sea salt

½ teaspoon freshly ground black pepper

¾ cup olive-y and peppery olive oil, or more as desired

FOR a dressing to keep in the refrigerator as a bottled dressing.

PLACE all the ingredients except the olive oil in a jar or in the bowl of a small food processor, and shake vigorously or process. If using a jar, add the olive oil and shake very well. If using a small food processor, add the oil slowly while the machine is running, pouring the oil slowly through the feed tube or the little hole in the lid. Keep the dressing chilled, and use as needed.

Variations To make this a blue cheese dressing, add about ½ cup blue cheese to the processor before adding the olive oil. Herbs such as tarragon, chives, basil, or thyme can also be added to the processor bowl.

ORANGE, ONION, AND OLIVE SALAD

SERVES 4

NOT SURPRISINGLY, this wonderful-tasting combination is a traditional Mediterranean dish. Especially good served before a rich, meaty entrée, the salad also works well alongside fish.

1 mild onion, such as Vidalia or Walla Walla, peeled and thinly sliced

4 navel oranges, peeled and sliced paper-thin

¾ cup oil-cured black olives

¼ cup olive-y and peppery olive oil

1½ tablespoons white balsamic vinegar or white wine vinegar

Coarse sea salt and freshly ground black pepper, to taste

SOAK the onion slices in three changes of cold water over the course of 10 to 15 minutes. Drain and pat dry.

COMBINE the orange slices, the onion slices, and the olives in a serving bowl or on individual plates. Mix together the olive oil and vinegar, and drizzle this dressing over the salad. Season to taste with salt and pepper.

SERVE immediately.

ORANGES AND OLIVE OIL

The Nuñez de Prado family, makers of one of the world's great olive oils, serves a similar salad as a palate cleanser, using only peeled sliced oranges and a generous drizzle of their oil. It's so refreshing, it's practically dessert.

One of the testers for this book tried this with thinly sliced Ruby Red grapefruit and said it was also a winner.

WHITE PEACH, CORN, AND TOASTED ALMOND SALAD

SERVES 4 AS AN APPETIZER

I CAN FIND delicate white peaches only in August, but this salad could also be made with yellow Georgia peaches. The important thing is that the corn must be fresh. When the weather is really hot, a salad like this (plain, or served over cottage cheese or yogurt) can be the whole meal. It's also a good side dish with grilled chicken.

½ cup whole almonds, skin on

1 ear fresh corn

4 white peaches

1½ teaspoons fruity and fragrant olive oil

Grated zest of 1 lime

1 teaspoon fresh lime juice

Coarse sea salt and freshly ground black pepper, to taste

TOAST the almonds in an ungreased cast-iron pan over medium heat, stirring constantly. When they are fragrant and golden, immediately dump them onto a dinner plate to cool. Chop by hand or pulse in a food processor to make small crunchy bits.

HAVE ready a large bowl of ice and cold water.

STEAM the ear of corn for 10 minutes in a vegetable steamer until the kernels are bright yellow and cooked through. Remove the corn from the steamer and immediately plunge it into the ice water to cool completely. Remove the cooked corn and let it drain, reserving the ice water. (Add more ice if necessary to keep the water cold.) Standing the ear of corn on end, cut off the kernels with a sharp knife and place them in a mixing bowl. You should have about ½ cup.

BLANCH the peaches in a pot of boiling water for 2 minutes, or until the skin breaks. Remove the peaches from the pot and plunge them into the ice water to chill them. When they are cooled enough to handle easily, gently peel off and discard the skin. Cut the peach flesh into ½-inch dice over the mixing bowl with the corn (to catch the juices). You should have about 1½ cups diced peaches. Drizzle with the olive oil, sprinkle with the lime zest and lime juice, and gently blend. Season with salt and pepper to taste.

SPOON the mixture into small glass bowls or wineglasses, and sprinkle the chopped toasted almonds on top. Serve immediately.

WHITE BEAN, TUNA, AND RED ONION SALAD

SERVES 4

THIS SALAD-AS-MEAL makes a great lunch and a terrific light dinner. Because the ingredients determine the success of the dish, select each with care. The quality of the canned tuna, the flavor and freshness of the beans, and the unctuousness of the olive oil matter most. For instance, oil-packed albacore tuna will be tasty, but Italian, Spanish, or Portuguese tuna packed in olive oil will be even better. Use the artisanal canned Sicilian belly tuna offered by Esperya, and you will have duplicated the authentic taste of Italy.

Substituting canned white beans will allow you to keep all the ingredients ready on your pantry shelf, but do try the dish at least once with the best dried beans you can find. (Note that the beans soak overnight and then cook for 2½ hours.) The difference will amaze you.

For the beans

2 cups dried white beans, such as navy beans or cannellini

¼ cup fruity and fragrant olive oil

4 fresh sage leaves

2 sprigs fresh rosemary

2 cloves garlic, peeled

1 tablespoon sea salt

One 19-ounce can cannellini or navy beans

For the rest of the salad

¼ cup fruity and fragrant olive oil

TO cook the beans: Place the beans in a large bowl, cover with cold water by 1 inch, and soak for 4 to 6 hours or overnight.

DRAIN the beans and put them in a heavy cooking pot such as a Dutch oven. Add fresh water to cover the beans by 4 inches, and then the olive oil, herbs, and garlic. Bring to a simmer; then cover and cook for 30 minutes. Add the salt and cook, covered, for 2 hours more, or until the beans are tender. Allow them to cool in the broth until they are warm to the touch. Then drain the beans (you can reserve the flavorful bean broth and use it as a base for a vegetable soup if you wish), and discard the herbs and garlic.

PUT the beans in a wide serving bowl or a deep platter, and immediately toss them with the olive oil. (At this point, the beans can sit at room tem-

Two 6-ounce or one 12-ounce can tuna, preferably good quality, packed in olive oil

1 red onion, peeled and thinly sliced

Freshly ground black pepper

Coarse sea salt, to taste

perature for a few hours, if desired.) Taste and smell the tuna olive oil. If it is good, add it along with the tuna, breaking the fish into flakes with a fork. Add the onion slices, toss, and taste. Add more olive oil if desired, along with a generous grinding of black pepper and salt if needed. Serve immediately.

RULES FOR GREAT SALADS

- Consider using an assortment of greens—tender and crisp, mild and strong.

- Wash greens scrupulously, and dry them perfectly.

- Tear greens rather than cut them.

- Keep greens (and salad bowl and salad plates) chilled.

- Use a huge bowl to toss the salad and dressing in just before transferring it to a serving bowl, to be sure the greens and dressing are well mixed.

- Never dress a salad until you are ready to serve it.

SALADE À CHÈVRE CHAUD

SERVES 4

4 slices good country bread

1 small (5½-ounce) log goat cheese (chèvre), plain or herb

6 or more cups mesclun salad mix, washed and dried

6 tablespoons leafy green and grassy olive oil

2 tablespoons white wine vinegar with tarragon, or other white wine vinegar

Coarse sea salt and freshly ground black pepper

LONG A STAPLE of French bistros, warm goat cheese salad now ranks high in our home lunch repertoire. Here's another example of a "meal in a salad," requiring nothing more than good bread and perhaps a glass of wine.

PREHEAT the broiler.

TOAST the bread under the broiler or in a toaster until golden brown. Cut off the crusts and spread the goat cheese thickly over each piece. Arrange the toast on a broiler tray, and cook close to the broiler element until the melted cheese is flecked with brown spots.

MEANWHILE, arrange the mesclun mix on four chilled wide soup bowls or dinner plates. Mix the oil and vinegar in a small jar or glass.

WHEN the cheese toasts are ready, cut each piece into strips. Arrange the cheese toast strips over the mesclun on each plate, drizzle with the salad dressing, and serve immediately, passing the pepper grinder and sea salt at the table.

CRISP FRIED PROSCIUTTO, PEAR, AND PARMESAN ON ARUGULA

SERVES 4

THIS SALAD HAS CRUNCH thanks to the prosciutto (you could use a mild bacon instead), sweetness from the fruit, and pepper thanks to the arugula (a similar green would be watercress).

Shaving a wedge of Parmesan with a vegetable peeler yields pretty shards of creamy cheese. I recently started to make this salad and discovered that the end-of-the-season arugula I'd bought was bitter. So I blanched it in boiling water and made this as a cooked greens salad, eliminating the pear. It was delicious.

4 slices prosciutto (about ¼ pound)

¼ cup leafy green and grassy olive oil

2 ripe pears

1 teaspoon fresh lemon juice

½ pound arugula

Dressing

3 tablespoons green and grassy olive oil

1 tablespoon balsamic vinegar

Sea salt and freshly ground black pepper, to taste

Wedge of Parmesan cheese

CUT the prosciutto into ¼-inch pieces. Heat a frying pan; then heat the olive oil in the pan until it sizzles when you drop in a piece of meat. Fry the prosciutto in batches until crisp. Drain finished pieces in a sieve set over a paper towel; set aside.

PEEL, core, and slice the pears. Pour the lemon juice over the slices.

WASH and dry the arugula leaves and place them in a mixing bowl. In a small bowl, combine the oil, vinegar, and salt and pepper. Pour the dressing over the arugula, and toss. Divide the arugula among four plates. Arrange the pear slices on top, then scatter the crisp pieces of prosciutto over each plate. Shave a pile of Parmesan shards over the top, and serve at once.

SPANISH FRIED EGG AND ARUGULA SALAD WITH CROUTONS

SERVES 1

FRYING AN EGG in a quarter inch of very hot olive oil is magic—the edges of the egg get bacony-crisp while the yolk remains liquid. When you put that egg on a bed of greens, the heat from the egg wilts the greens. Then, when you cut the egg, the liquid yolk further enriches the salad and creates a memorable dish. I've written this recipe for one person, since each dish requires its own egg.

I first tried frying the egg in a nonstick omelet pan, and it was fine. Then I tried it in a 7-inch copper skillet, where 2 or 3 tablespoons of oil make a ¼-inch-deep pool, and it was superb. Copper's ability to conduct heat fast improved the texture of the egg significantly. Since little copper frying pans are often sold in cookware stores as a loss leader, you might consider buying one just for this recipe.

About 1 cup loosely packed arugula, watercress, or torn spinach leaves, washed and dried

One ½-inch-thick slice peasant bread, crusts removed, cut into cubes

3 tablespoons leafy green and grassy olive oil, or enough to create a ¼-inch-deep pool in your pan, plus 2 teaspoons oilve oil

1 egg

½ teaspoon sherry vinegar

Coarse sea salt and freshly ground black pepper, to taste

ARRANGE the arugula leaves or other greens on a dinner plate or in a wide shallow soup bowl, and place it near the stove. Have the bread cubes ready near the stove also.

HEAT a 7-inch frying pan over medium heat, and then heat the oil in it until it's fragrant and shimmery. Test to make sure the oil is hot enough by throwing a bread crumb in the pan—if it immediately sizzles, the oil is ready. Lower the heat to ensure that you won't be spattered. Break the egg into the pan, and cook it until the edges crisp. Flip the egg to briefly cook the other side, taking care not to overcook the yolk.

WHEN the egg is cooked, lift it out of the pan with a slotted spatula and place it on the greens. Immediately toss the bread cubes into the hot oil, and fry them until golden brown on all sides. Add these to the salad, along with 2 teaspoons fresh olive oil. Immediately drizzle the vinegar over the salad, and add salt and pepper. Using a sharp knife, cut the fried egg into strips. Toss the salad so that the yolk mixes with the dressing. Serve at once.

SPAGHETTI WITH FRIED EGG AND GREENS

The elements in the Spanish Fried Egg and Arugula Salad can be adapted to create *Spaghetti with Fried Egg and Greens,* a pasta supper that serves four to six. Eliminate the vinegar and change the size of the croutons—either make tiny cubes, or grind the fried croutons in a food processor to make coarse crumbs just before serving. Cook ¼ pound of spaghetti per diner while you fry 1 egg per diner. Toss the greens with the hot drained pasta to wilt them, then add the eggs and cut them into strips while they rest on the pasta. Add the croutons and oil, and toss again with good coarse salt and a generous grinding of black pepper. The yolks will break and form part of the sauce, blending with the salt and pepper. Pass a wedge of Parmesan cheese and a grater at the table.

There's a lot of confusion about frying. It's not the same as sautéing, which is done, usually stirring, in a small amount of fat over medium heat.

Although frying uses generous amounts of fat, when done correctly, it adds less fat to the food than sautéing would. That's because the hot fat seals the outside of the food so that no additional fat can enter. An advantage of frying with olive oil is that it doesn't smell bad or create lingering aromas in the house.

You can prove this to yourself by following the rules below. Measure the fat in the pan before and after cooking. You'll see that when you fry correctly, nearly all the fat stays in the pan.

Olive oil has a higher smoke point than do nut or seed oils, which makes it a wonderful oil for frying. For the best results, choose an olive oil that is filtered and mild in taste, since olive sediments could lower the smoke point.

Use a deep and relatively heavy pan.

Never fill a pot more than halfway with oil— 2 to 3 inches deep is almost always enough.

Use a thermometer to keep the oil at 365°F, adjusting the heat as necessary.

Make sure all the food is the same size.

Add food a few pieces at a time rather than all at once to aid in maintaining the temperature, and remove each piece in the order it was added. Lay each piece into the oil— don't drop, as the oil will splatter.

Don't overcrowd the pot. Turn the food over once only.

Listen to the sizzle— food should sizzle when you put it in the pan, and it should be removed before the sizzle stops.

Use the right tool for removing food from the oil—a slotted spoon, a Chinese flat basket skimmer, a soup strainer, or a wire sieve.

Use a wire rack or sieve to drain foods of oil as they cool, and set it over, but not on, a wad of paper towels.

Drain the food completely when it's done.

SEARED SIRLOIN STEAK ON A BED OF WATERCRESS WITH PARMESAN SHAVINGS

SERVES 1

HERE'S ANOTHER DINNER SALAD that's a favorite at our house. Let the number of eaters determine the amount of watercress and the size of your steak. This is also good on a bed of spinach in early summer and early fall. In the heat of summer, I serve this salad ringed with ripe tomato wedges, with piles of good bread and saucers of good olive oil. I start the dinner with a cold soup and end with a Torta di Noci (page 201).

1 big bunch watercress, washed, stemmed, and dried

About 1 teaspoon coarse sea salt

¼ to ½ pound sirloin steak, trimmed of fat, about ¾ inch thick

Wedge of Parmesan cheese

2 tablespoons olive-y and peppery olive oil

Freshly ground black pepper

¼ teaspoon commercial balsamic vinegar *or* 2 drops artisanal *balsamico*

ARRANGE the watercress leaves on a plate.

TURN on the exhaust fan. Heat a heavy cast-iron frying pan until the rim is hot to a brief touch. Sprinkle the pan with coarse salt, heat for another minute (the salt may crackle and pop), and then add the steak. Cook the steak for 2 or 3 minutes per side (for medium-rare on a very hot burner), or until done as desired.

PLACE the hot steak on top of the watercress and let it rest for 5 minutes to slightly wilt and cook it, and to mix the steak's juices with the greens.

REMOVE the steak to a cutting board and cut it into thin slices. Return these to the watercress, arranging them on top, and then garnish with shavings of cheese (run a vegetable peeler along the surface of the cheese to make shavings). Drizzle the olive oil over the salad, add a grinding of fresh pepper, drizzle the balsamic over it, and finally add a little salt.

CHICKPEA, TUNA, OLIVE, AND GOAT CHEESE SALAD

SERVES 4 TO 6

THIS MAIN-COURSE SALAD contains all the flavors of the Mediterranean. A great light dinner or hearty lunch, it can be dressed up or down, depending on the accompaniments. For a warm-weather buffet, add platters of Caramelized Cauliflower (page 178), Orange, Onion, and Olive Salad (page 86), an assortment of breads, pizzas, and bread sticks, and a knock-your-socks-off dessert like "Hot" Chocolate Cake (page 204).

Soaking the sliced onion in ice water makes it mild tasting and more digestible.

3 cups loosely packed mesclun (mixed baby lettuces)

One 19-ounce can garbanzo beans (chickpeas), drained and rinsed

One 12-ounce can albacore tuna or imported fine tuna, drained

½ cup flavorful black olives cured in olive oil, pitted and halved

1 small mild or red onion, very thinly sliced and soaked in cold water for 10 minutes

2 tablespoons capers, drained (rinsed if salt-packed)

1 small log (about 4 tablespoons) goat cheese

6 to 8 small Yukon Gold potatoes or new potatoes, washed, peeled, and cut into chunks

WASH and dry the mesclun, and arrange it on a serving platter or in a shallow bowl. Scatter the garbanzo beans over the greens. Layer on the tuna, flaking it with a fork, then the olives, the drained onion rings, and the capers.

CUT or crumble the goat cheese into teaspoon-size pieces and scatter over all.

COOK the potatoes: To do this in a microwave, place about ⅛ cup of the olive oil and the garlic cloves in a microwavable dish. Add the potatoes, stir, and cook, covered, for 10 minutes on high power. To do this on the stovetop, steam the potatoes in a vegetable steamer until tender, about 25 minutes. In a small saucepan, heat the garlic cloves in ⅛ cup of the olive oil until the oil is the temperature of hot tap water, remove the pan from the heat, and let the garlic infuse the oil.

¼ cup leafy green and grassy olive oil

3 cloves garlic, peeled

Freshly ground black pepper

Coarse sea salt

Juice of ½ lemon

3 tablespoons chopped flat-leaf parsley

PUT the hot cooked potatoes, along with the garlic cloves and the garlic-infused olive oil, on top of the salad, gently mashing the garlic cloves. Generously grind black pepper and salt over all. Pour on the remaining ⅛ cup olive oil, and add the lemon juice and the chopped parsley. Toss and serve.

SALAD ADD-INS

- Finely chopped fresh herbs such as mint, marjoram, basil, or thyme.

- Fat curls of Parmesan made with a vegetable peeler, or crumbled feta cheese.

- Crisp-fried shallot pieces.

- Olive-oil-fried bread cut into croutons.

- Toasted nuts or sunflower seeds.

- Drained fresh-cooked or rinsed canned beans.

- Thinly sliced shallots or onions that have been soaked in ice water for 15 minutes and drained (this takes away their bite).

- Sliced, drained rendered cracklings from chicken, duck, or goose.

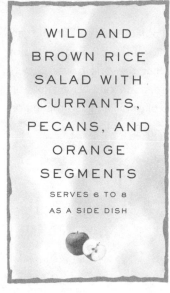

WILD AND BROWN RICE SALAD WITH CURRANTS, PECANS, AND ORANGE SEGMENTS

SERVES 6 TO 8
AS A SIDE DISH

SUMMERY RICE SALADS are refreshing on hot days; this version with crunchy nuts and wild rice is especially good. Arrange it on beds of tender mixed lettuces, stuff it into hollowed-out ripe tomatoes, or serve it proudly as a side dish (consider this for Thanksgiving). It's good either cold or at room temperature, and it keeps well in the refrigerator for a few days, especially if you don't add the orange until just before serving. Cooking the brown rice separately from the wild rice ensures that each will be perfectly cooked. This recipe can be doubled for a crowd.

For the wild rice

2 cups water

½ cup wild rice, washed and drained

½ teaspoon sea salt

¼ cup fruity and fragrant olive oil

For the brown rice

1 cup long-grain brown rice

3 cups water

½ teaspoon sea salt

¼ cup fruity and fragrant olive oil

For the salad

1 cup pecan halves (about ¼ pound)

1 navel orange

8 scallions, white part only, chopped

COOK the wild rice: Combine the water, wild rice, and salt in a saucepan and bring to a boil, stirring once. Cover the pot and cook over low heat for about 35 minutes, or until some of the grains are split and fluffy. The rice should have some crunch. If there is any water remaining, pour it off. Pour the olive oil over the rice and set it aside to cool a little.

WHILE the wild rice is cooking, prepare the brown rice: Put the brown rice in a saucepan, and add the water and salt. Bring to a boil, reduce the heat to low, and cook the rice for about 30 minutes, or until it is dry, fragrant, and soft. If there is any water left, drain the rice. Pour the olive oil over the rice and set it aside to cool.

HEAT a heavy frying pan, such as a cast-iron skillet, and then add the pecans and reduce the heat. Watch closely, stirring, until the nuts are fragrant and toasted. Immediately remove the nuts from the pan to stop them from overcooking, and let them cool on a plate.

½ cup dried currants

2 stalks celery, chopped

2 tablespoons chopped fresh mint leaves

Juice of 1 lemon

Juice of 1 orange

GRATE the orange zest into a large bowl. Add the brown rice, wild rice, toasted nuts, scallions, currants, celery, and mint. Gently stir in the lemon and orange juices. Just before serving, section the orange (remove all the white pith) over the bowl, so it catches the juices, and add the sections to the salad.

SERVE immediately.

Note: This salad can be kept at room temperature for several hours before adding the orange segments. Refrigerate if storing for longer than part of a day.

STRAWBERRY AND SPINACH SPRING SALAD

SERVES 4

I FIRST ENCOUNTERED this salad years ago in *Eating Well* magazine, where it was billed as an "antioxidant salad." While the subtitle wasn't appetizing, the salad was a smash hit in my household, and it has been a springtime staple ever since. If it sounds weird to you, remember that tomatoes are fruits too; the strawberries in this salad act like sweet tomatoes. My children like this salad so much that they eat it for dessert as well as dinner (if you knew them, you'd know this is the highest praise). It should go without saying that if you can find organic produce, use it.

1 pound young fresh spinach

½ pint fresh strawberries

¼ cup white sesame seeds

3 tablespoons fruity and fragrant olive oil

1 tablespoon balsamic vinegar or Fig "Balsamico" Agrodolce (page 64)

Coarse sea salt and freshly ground black pepper, to taste

TEAR the spinach into bite-size pieces, discarding the stems. Wash the torn leaves in as many changes of water as necessary to make sure they're clean. (I use a large bowl that I keep dumping and refilling.) Spin the leaves dry in a salad spinner, and place them in a salad bowl or on a shallow platter.

WASH the strawberries and drain them before removing the hulls. Cut the berries in half, and set them on top of the spinach leaves.

HEAT a cast-iron or other sturdy frying pan, and dry-toast the sesame seeds until they become slightly golden and fragrant, about 3 minutes. Use a long wooden spoon to move them around the pan; they'll pop like tiny popcorn as they toast. Pour the toasted sesame seeds onto a plate to cool.

MIX the oil and vinegar together, and pour the dressing over the strawberries and spinach. Sprinkle the toasted sesame seeds over all, along with salt and pepper, and serve.

OLIO EXTRA VERGINE DI OLIVA

SOUPS

CAPEZZANA

Conte Contini Bonacossi

FAVA BEAN SOUP

SERVES 6 TO 8

THIS HEARTY SOUP, a variation on a Tuscan classic, uses two kinds of olive oil—a delicate and mild olive oil for cooking the onion at the beginning, and a flavorful leafy green and grassy oil to pass at the table for drizzling over the hot soup. Dried fava beans are available in the international section of most supermarkets, packaged by Goya, and in health food stores in bulk. The health food variety is often shelled, or peeled, and is much preferable for ease of cooking. In fact, it's so much easier that I'd go to a lot of trouble to be sure I was buying the shelled kind. (You can order peeled favas from Global Food Market.) Here's how to tell the difference: An unshelled fava has a dark brown exterior with a black smile at one end; a shelled fava is a more uniform pale green-brown. If you do buy unshelled favas, be prepared to take the time to peel them as indicated in the recipe below. If you are using fava beans that have already been shelled, all you need to do is rinse them off—skip the second step below. And if you're lucky enough to be cooking where fava beans are available fresh, adjust the timing, as fresh beans cook more rapidly. Accompany Fava Bean Soup with bread and salad for a filling dinner.

2¼ cups dried fava beans

4 cups water

1 tablespoon delicate and mild olive oil

5 slices bacon, diced

1 onion, chopped

4 cups chicken stock or water

1 cup chopped parsley leaves, preferably flat-leaf parsley

Coarse sea salt and freshly ground black pepper, to taste

Small chunk of Parmesan cheese

Leafy green and grassy olive oil, for garnish

RINSE and pick over the fava beans.

SHELL the beans: Have a large bowl of ice water ready. Bring the 4 cups of water to a boil in a large pot. Add the beans and boil, uncovered, for about 10 minutes or until foam rises and the steam smells starchy. Drain the beans and plunge them into the cold water to stop the cooking. When the beans are cool enough to handle, drain them and peel them, using your thumbs to split the shell. Discard the shells.

IN a soup pot, slowly heat the delicate and mild olive oil until fragrant. Add the diced bacon and chopped onion, and cook over low heat until the onion is transparent, 3 to 5 minutes.

ADD the peeled fava beans and the chicken stock. Keeping the heat low, cover the pot and cook, simmering slowly, for 45 to 60 minutes, or until the beans are tender. Stir occasionally to make sure the beans are not sticking to the bottom.

ADD the parsley, salt, and pepper, and serve. Pass the cheese and a grater, along with a cruet or bottle of flavorful leafy green and grassy olive oil, to garnish the soup.

PASSING A CRUET OF OIL AT THE TABLE

Pass a cruet of green and grassy oil whenever you serve beans in any form, whether soup, puree, side vegetable, or spread. The herbal flavors and peppery bite of leafy green and grassy oils enhance dried legumes. Here's a good opportunity to use your most strongly flavored oil.

To illustrate the value Italians place on using just the right amount of good oil, there are specific traditions for pouring oil on soup. They go like this:

On an ordinary day, drizzle the oil in the shape of a "C."

On a Sunday, drizzle the oil in the shape of an "O,"

On a feast day, you are permitted to drizzle the oil more generously in a figure-8.

CHICKPEA SOUP WITH CAVOLO NERO

SERVES 6 TO 8
AS A MAIN COURSE

CAVOLO NERO IS ALSO called Tuscan cabbage, or lacinato kale, and it's becoming more and more available in this country. If you can't find it, substitute any kale or chard; the method and timing will be the same, although the taste will be slightly different. If you prefer a smooth soup, puree the chickpeas before adding the *cavolo nero*.

Don't worry about precise timing on soaking the chickpeas; what's important is that you do two long soaks in two changes of water before starting to cook them. You'll find that long soaking significantly reduces the cooking time. If you live in an area with hard water, adding ⅛ teaspoon baking soda to the cooking water will help the chickpeas cook to tenderness.

Serve some grilled or toasted country bread, rubbed with freshly cut garlic, alongside.

1 pound (2 cups) dried chickpeas

2 large Yukon Gold potatoes

¾ pound *cavolo nero*, kale, or chard

⅓ cup fruity and fragrant olive oil, plus more to drizzle over the soup

1 large onion, coarsely chopped

2 cloves garlic, peeled and finely chopped

4 anchovy fillets, salt-packed if possible (rinsed)

Generous pinch of red pepper flakes (optional)

Coarse sea salt and freshly ground black pepper

½ cup freshly grated Parmesan cheese, or more to taste

SOAK the chickpeas in water to cover by several inches all day or overnight (6 to 8 hours). When the water is largely absorbed, drain and rinse the chickpeas and cover them again with fresh water. Soak for another 4 to 6 hours. If your kitchen is very warm, find a cool place to soak the beans to avoid spoilage.

DRAIN and rinse the chickpeas again. Put them in a big heavy soup pot, such as an enameled cast-iron Dutch oven, and add water to cover by about 2 inches. Bring to a boil, skim off the starchy foam that forms, and then reduce the heat and simmer, covered, for 1½ hours.

PEEL the potatoes and cut them into a rough dice, and add them to the pot. Cook for another 30 minutes, or until both chickpeas and potatoes are tender but not mushy.

MEANWHILE, carefully wash the *cavolo nero*. Lay each leaf on a cutting board and fold it in half lengthwise so that the rib is exposed along one side. Using a sharp knife, cut off the rib. Do this with all the leaves, discarding the ribs. Pile 4 to 6 leaves on top of each other, and roll the stack into a cigar shape. Cutting across the "cigar," slice ¼-inch-wide ribbons. Repeat until all the leaves are cut into ribbons.

HEAT a large sauté or frying pan, and add the oil. Heat the oil until it shimmers and is fragrant. Add the chopped onion and garlic, and cook until limp, about 5 minutes. Then add the anchovies, mashing them into the onion mixture. Add the *cavolo nero*, the red pepper flakes if using, and a little salt and pepper. Toss, and cook covered, over low heat, for about 5 minutes.

WHEN the soup has cooked and the chickpeas are tender, decide if you want to puree the soup. If you do, this is the moment: Use an immersion blender if you have one; or puree the soup, in batches, in a blender or food processor, and return the puree to the pot.

CAREFULLY scrape all the *cavolo nero* mixture into the soup, and cook for 15 to 20 minutes, or until the kale is tender.

TASTE for salt and pepper, and add as needed. Serve the soup hot, sprinkled generously with freshly grated Parmesan cheese and a drizzle of good oil.

GREEN SPLIT PEA SOUP WITH CHICKEN-APPLE SAUSAGE

SERVES 4 TO 6

I FIND AIDELLS chicken-apple sausages have just the right amount of sweetness to complement green split peas, and they contribute to the lightness of this soup (see Resources). However, you could easily substitute any big (¾-inch-diameter) chicken- or pork-based sweet sausage for a similar flavor contrast. Surprisingly, this soup is good cold as well as warm, making it an all-season dish. In summer, garnish the cold soup with lightly blanched fresh peas and a small dollop of crème fraîche.

4 tablespoons leafy green and grassy olive oil, plus more to drizzle on the soup

2 large shallots *or* 1 small red onion, minced

1½ cups dried split peas, washed and drained

4 cups water

½ teaspoon fine sea salt

Freshly ground black pepper

4 to 5 links fully cooked chicken-apple sausage, cut diagonally into thin slices

Garnish

Plain yogurt or sour cream

Finely diced peeled apple

HEAT a Dutch oven or soup pot, add the olive oil, and then add the shallots. Cook over low heat until translucent and wilted, about 5 minutes.

ADD the drained split peas, and stir to coat them with the oil. Add the water, salt, pepper, and bring to a boil, skimming off any foam. Add sausages, and cook, partially covered, over medium-low heat for 30 to 40 minutes, or until the peas are soft and tender.

TOP each serving with a spoonful of yogurt or sour cream, some diced apple, and a drizzle of leafy green and grassy oil.

GAZPACHO

SERVES 4 TO 6

"RED" GAZPACHO HAS lots of variations—this one is mine. It's the perfect summer lunch: refreshing, cold, and full of good tastes. Although tradition calls for bread to thicken this soup, I prefer to scatter crisp croutons on top instead. The alcohol brings out the tomato's flavor, and Scandinavian aquavit amplifies it with a hint of caraway seed. If your liquor cabinet doesn't happen to hold any aquavit, you can use vodka.

1 clove garlic

6 ripe, juicy tomatoes, organic if possible

1 small sweet onion, Vidalia if possible

1 long European (hothouse) cucumber

1 green bell pepper

½ teaspoon coarse sea salt, or more to taste

Generous grinding of good black pepper

¼ cup sherry vinegar

⅓ cup fruity and fragrant olive oil

1 teaspoon aquavit or vodka

Garnish

2 tablespoons fruity and fragrant olive oil

3 to 4 slices good open-crumb country bread, such as ciabatta, crusts removed

PEEL and slice the garlic, and put it in the bowl of a food processor. Working over the processor bowl, core and cut the tomatoes into pieces with a paring knife, letting the juice drip into the bowl. Add the tomato pieces to the processor bowl.

PEEL the onion and cut it into wedges. Add them to the bowl. Peel and slice half the cucumber, (reserve the rest for the garnish), and add it to the bowl. Seed and coarsely slice the green pepper, and add it to the bowl as well. Add the salt, pepper, vinegar, oil, and aquavit.

PULSE the food processor to form a thick, toothy puree with bits of vegetables floating in it. Pour the gazpacho into a pitcher or jar, and refrigerate until very well chilled.

PREPARE the garnish: Heat the olive oil in a hot frying pan, and fry the bread slices on both sides until golden and crusty. Drain on paper towels and allow to cool; then slice into square croutons. Peel and finely dice the remaining half of the cucumber.

POUR the soup into chilled bowls, and top each serving with a sprinkling of croutons and cucumber.

ICED FRESH GINGER-PEA SOUP WITH TRUFFLE OIL

SERVES 4 TO 6
AS A FIRST COURSE

UNTIL VERY RECENTLY, I had lived my whole culinary life without buying truffle oil. When I finally did get some for a recipe I wanted to try, I was amazed at what a useful pantry item it turned out to be. I use truffle oil now with scrambled eggs, on pasta with olive oil, garlic, and cheese, and in this summer soup. While you can make this soup with frozen peas, it gains much of its sweetness and delicacy from those first early peas of summer. Try Mas Portell's White Truffle Olive Oil—it has a peppery finish that adds another dimension to any dish. This soup is beautiful served in white china teacups or in glass dessert goblets. Garnish it with a small spoonful of crème fraîche.

3 pounds fresh peas in their pods

1 tablespoon olive-y and peppery olive oil, plus more to drizzle on the soup if desired

2 shallots, finely chopped

1 teaspoon truffle oil

½ cup heavy cream

3 cups chicken stock

1½ teaspoons freshly grated ginger root

Coarse sea salt

Crème fraîche for garnish (optional)

SET a large bowl in the sink, and fill it with a tray's worth of ice cubes and cold water. Bring a large saucepan of salted water to a boil.

SHELL the peas, and cook them in the boiling water until all the peas float to the surface, about 1 minute. Take a pea out and taste it to see if it's sweet and only slightly crunchy. If so, drain the peas and add them to the ice water to stop the cooking.

HEAT a small frying pan, and then add the olive oil. When the oil is hot, reduce the heat to medium-low and cook the shallots until limp and translucent, about 3 minutes.

PUT the drained peas in a blender or a food processor, and add the cooked shallots, truffle oil, cream, chicken stock, and ginger. Process to a fine smooth puree, about 3 minutes.

SERVE cold, sprinkled with coarse sea salt, and garnished with crème fraîche and a drizzle of olive oil if desired.

ICED CELERY SOUP WITH FETA, TOASTED WALNUTS, AND APPLE

SERVES 4 TO 6
AS A FIRST COURSE

WHEN THE DOG DAYS of summer hit Vermont, it's hard to work up an appetite. Iced soups, I've found, are a great solution for both internal cooling and good nutrition. This soup is particularly tasty when made with farmer's market celery (which comes with plentiful leaves), but it's also good with the trimmed supermarket variety. If you want to skip the garnish, the soup is delicious plain.

1 whole head celery, leaves included, well washed and coarsely chopped (about 6 cups packed)

2 tablespoons delicate and mild olive oil

1 teaspoon coarse sea salt

1 cup apple juice (unfiltered organic, if possible)

2 cups buttermilk

½ teaspoon fennel seeds

1 scant teaspoon sugar

1 tablespoon Pastis, Pernod, aquavit, or vodka

Garnish

½ cup walnuts

½ cup (2 ounces) crumbled feta cheese

1 apple

Juice of 1 lemon

USING a vegetable steamer over boiling water, steam the celery pieces, leaves included, until soft, 20 to 30 minutes. Allow to cool.

COMBINE the steamed celery, olive oil, salt, apple juice, buttermilk, fennel seeds, sugar, and liquor in a blender. (You can add a couple of ice cubes if you are in a hurry.) Puree, and refrigerate to chill thoroughly.

PREPARE the garnish: Toast the walnuts in a cast-iron pan over medium heat, stirring, until they begin to color and smell fragrant, about 5 minutes. Immediately pour them onto a plate to cool. When the nuts are cool, chop them by hand or by brief pulsing in a food processor to create not too-small pieces.

PLACE the crumbled feta cheese in a small bowl.

PEEL the apple and cut it into quarters. Cut the core off each quarter, and chop each quarter into small dice. Put the apple pieces in another small bowl and toss with the lemon juice to prevent browning.

SERVE the chilled soup in small bowls, teacups, or glass goblets, garnishing each serving with toasted walnuts, crumbled feta, and diced apple.

COLD BEET SOUP

SERVES 4 TO 6

WHEN I WAS GROWING UP, cold borscht was a summer tradition, but most frequently we ate the store-bought variety. Now I make it myself, and it takes only a little more effort than going to the grocery store. Roasting the beets first adds robust flavor. I frequently put them in the oven early in the day, while it's still cool.

2 tablespoons delicate and mild olive oil

1 pound (about 8 small) beets, scrubbed but unpeeled, root and stem ends uncut

½ teaspoon coarse sea salt

5 cups chicken stock or water

½ cup fresh lemon juice (1 large lemon; see Note)

¼ cup sugar

1 tablespoon chopped fresh dill

Garnish

Sour cream

Chopped hard-boiled egg

Chopped fresh dill

Horseradish Cream
(recipe follows)

PREHEAT the oven to 475°F.

PUT the olive oil in a roasting pan, and roll the beets in the oil to coat them well. Sprinkle with the salt. Roast the beets for 30 minutes, or until they can be pierced with a fork and are wrinkled and earthy smelling. Allow the beets to cool until you can handle them.

WORKING over a sink or bowl, peel the beets. The skin will slip off easily, but the flesh will stain anything it touches as soon as you cut off the root and stem ends. Place the peeled beets in a bowl.

FIT a food processor with the fine grating disk. Using the feed tube, grate the beets.

PLACE the grated beets in a large jar or pitcher, and add the chicken stock, lemon juice, sugar, and dill. Stir or shake to blend; then chill until ready to serve.

SERVE very cold, accompanied by any of the garnishes.

Note: To get the most juice possible out of a lemon, roll the lemon on a work surface while pressing on it with your hand; then cut and squeeze it.

HORSERADISH CREAM

¼ cup sour cream

4 teaspoons prepared
horseradish

THIS is an excellent garnish for Cold Beet Soup or Tomato Toast.

BLEND the sour cream and horseradish in a small bowl. Refrigerate until ready to use.

Breads and pizza

OLIVE AND PEPPER KNOTS

MAKES 30 TO 40
LITTLE KNOTS

PERFECT FOR a cocktail party (they are *made* for a martini), these savory nibbles have just the right amount of flavor and crunch. This recipe can be doubled—this amount of dough is just enough to fill one baking sheet—and it is very easily and rapidly mixed by hand in a bowl.

1 heaping tablespoon pitted black olives, such as Kalamata

⅓ cup freshly grated Parmesan cheese

1 teaspoon freshly ground black pepper

½ cup olive-y and peppery olive oil

½ cup dry vermouth

¼ teaspoon coarse sea salt

1½ cups unbleached all-purpose flour

PREHEAT the oven to 350°F, and line a baking sheet with parchment paper.

CHOP the olives either with a knife or in a small food processor so that they are in tiny shreds. Put them in a mixing bowl and add the cheese, pepper, olive oil, vermouth, salt, and ¾ cup of the flour. Blend together, using a spatula or a wooden spoon. Gradually add more of the flour, mixing (you may not need the last ¼ cup). The dough is ready when it begins to clean the bowl and is moist and pliable but not terribly sticky.

PINCH off pieces of dough about the size of a big marble, and roll each piece between your hands to form a coil 3 to 4 inches long (don't worry if the ends are thinner than the middle) and about the same diameter as a pencil. Tie or twist each coil into a knot or ring. Place the knots on the baking sheet, leaving about ½ inch between them. Bake for 35 to 40 minutes, or until really golden and fragrant. Cool on wire racks, and store in tins if not serving immediately.

PIADINA

MAKES 8 FLATBREADS

AN ANCIENT FLATBREAD from Emilia-Romagna, these griddle cakes are easy to make and are fabulous for appetizers or a light dinner. Eat them hot off the griddle, wrapped around fresh tomatoes and smoked mozzarella drizzled with fragrant olive oil; around greens sautéed in olive oil with garlic; around crumbled goat cheese and arugula; or around ham and cheese. Think of them as Italian wrap bread or tortillas, and you'll get the idea.

2 cups unbleached all-purpose flour

1 teaspoon coarse sea salt

½ teaspoon baking powder

⅓ cup leafy green and grassy olive oil

⅔ cup warm water

LAYER all the ingredients except the water in the bowl of a food processor fitted with the steel blade. Process, adding the water gradually through the feed tube, until the mixture forms a soft ball of dough. Turn the dough out onto a lightly floured board or counter, knead it lightly, and let it rest, covered with a cloth, for 30 minutes.

MEANWHILE, prepare the ingredients for the filling of your choice (see headnote), and set it aside.

HEAT a griddle on the stove.

DIVIDE the dough into 8 pieces and form each piece into a ball. Using a lightly floured rolling pin, roll a ball out to form a circle 6 to 8 inches in diameter. Place it on the ungreased griddle. If your griddle is well heated, it will take about 15 seconds to puff and speckle on one side. Then turn, using tongs or a spatula, to speckle the other side as well. Remove the flatbread from the griddle and place it on a plate. Cover the plate with a cloth to keep the bread warm and pliable. Repeat until all the dough is cooked, piling the cooked flatbreads on the plate.

SERVE at once, accompanied by a filling and a cruet of olive oil. If you like, you can spread the filling over each griddle cake in the kitchen and roll it up; then slice on the diagonal and serve as an appetizer. Or of course you can simply eat filled Piadinas as wrap sandwiches.

SMOKED MOZZARELLA, TOMATO, AND BASIL FILLING

1 pound smoked mozzarella,
thinly sliced

2 large ripe tomatoes, thinly
sliced

12 to 18 leaves fresh basil

¼ cup leafy green and grassy
olive oil

Coarse sea salt and freshly
ground black pepper

O N each warm piadina, arrange rounds of cheese and tomato. Scatter the basil over, and drizzle with the olive oil. Season to taste with salt and pepper. Roll the piadina up, and place it seam side down on a cutting board. Press down on it slightly. Cut in half on the diagonal, and serve.

GOAT CHEESE AND ARUGULA FILLING

½ pound goat cheese, sliced

½ pound arugula, washed,
stemmed, and dried

¼ cup leafy green and grassy
olive oil

Coarse sea salt and freshly
ground black pepper

O N each warm piadina, arrange the slices of goat cheese and the arugula leaves. Drizzle with the olive oil, and season to taste with salt and pepper. Roll the piadina up into a fat roll, seam side down. Cut it in half or quarters, on the diagonal, and serve.

OVERNIGHT COUNTRY BREAD

MAKES 1 VERY LARGE
ROUND LOAF

THIS IS A PERFECT BREAD for olive oil—grill a couple of slices or leave them untoasted (rub a grilled piece with a cut garlic clove if you wish), salt with a great coarse sea salt, and pour a delicious olive oil on top. Along with a glass of wine, there's no better way to start an evening.

The best breads are made from dough that contains an aged starter and has a long, slow rising. This recipe is an easy version of such a bread, scaled and timed for our hectic lives. It's a perfect choice for a weekend, or whenever you have parts of a day free and 5 to 10 minutes of an evening beforehand to get started. Here's how it works: Make the starter the night before and let it rest, covered, overnight to develop the flavors (if your house is hot, do this in the refrigerator). The next day, make the dough, knead it very well, and let it rise for 3 hours if you are going to be at home or all day in the refrigerator if you're not. Then bring it to room temperature, punch it down, and knead it lightly. Allow the loaves a last slow 1½- to 2-hour rise before baking. This process creates a memorable bread with good flavor and keeping qualities.

Using a spray bottle to spray the loaves with a watery mist as they begin to bake greatly aids the development of a well-expanded dough and a good crust—you can find a mister at houseware and hardware stores.

Starter

½ teaspoon active dry yeast

1 cup warm water

1 cup unbleached all-purpose flour

To finish the dough

2 cups lukewarm water

½ teaspoon active dry yeast

5 to 6 cups unbleached all-purpose flour

1 tablespoon coarse sea salt

1 tablespoon delicate and mild olive oil

MAKE the starter: Dissolve the yeast in the warm water in a large mixing bowl, and let it stand for about 5 minutes, until bubbly. Then add the flour and mix to form a thick slurry. Cover, and leave in a coolish place (50° to 70°F) overnight.

THE next day, prepare the dough: Add the lukewarm water to the starter, and mix it vigorously to combine. Add the yeast, then 2 cups of the flour, mixing until incorporated. Add the salt, and then begin to add more of the flour, a little at a time, until the dough comes together. (This is a soft, wet dough, and although it will still work if you add more flour than is necessary, it won't have the best texture or taste.) Knead by machine or vigorously by hand, adding the minimum amount of flour to prevent the dough from sticking, until the dough is really smooth and elastic, about 15 minutes. Form the dough into a ball.

PLACE the olive oil in a large clean mixing bowl, and turn the dough in it so that it's coated with oil. Cover the bowl with plastic wrap to make an airtight seal, and let the dough rise for 3 hours or until doubled in size. (If you are refrigerating the dough overnight, this is the time to put it in the refrigerator.) When the dough has doubled (or after it has been removed from the refrigerator), punch it down and let it rest for 30 minutes.

KNEAD the dough again, vigorously, on a lightly floured surface for 5 to 10 minutes. Shape it into a ball, stretching the outside skin down to the center bottom to make a taut round. Place the round on an oiled cookie sheet, cover it with a cloth, and let it rise again for another 1½ to 2 hours, or until doubled.

PREHEAT the oven to 450°F. Have a water mister ready.

BRUSH the loaf with cold water, and slash the top crosswise, making two cuts with scissors, a clean craft knife, or a razor blade. Place the dough in the oven, and mist the dough and the walls of the oven as rapidly as possible so as not to lose too much heat. During the first 5 minutes of baking, open the oven slightly and spray a total of five times (once a minute), avoiding spraying the oven light and electric elements directly. After that, don't open the oven again until the bread is done.

BAKE for another 15 minutes. Then lower the heat to 400°F and bake for an additional 20 to 25 minutes, or until the loaf is golden brown, fragrant, and sounds hollow when thumped on the bottom. (Or use an instant-read thermometer—the loaf is done when it reads 200°F when poked into the middle.) Allow the bread to cool on a wire rack. Don't cut into the loaf until it is thoroughly cooled.

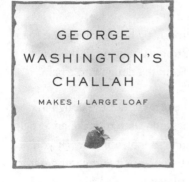

GEORGE WASHINGTON'S CHALLAH

MAKES 1 LARGE LOAF

OKAY, SO THE FATHER of our country wasn't Jewish and he probably never knew just how delicious this traditional Sabbath egg bread can be. But when we first added dried cherries to our version of challah, George Washington's exploits with a cherry tree were lodged so firmly in our imagination that there was no other possible name for this bread—it's been George Washington's Challah in our family ever since. (You can make *Pilgrim Challah* by substituting dried cranberries for the cherries.) This recipe yields one enormous presidential-size braided loaf, or two more conventionally sized loaves.

1 tablespoon (1 package) active dry yeast

2¼ cups warm water

4 tablespoons sugar

About 7½ cups unbleached all-purpose flour or high-gluten flour such as Sir Galahad from King Arthur Flour Co.

1 teaspoon coarse sea salt

1¼ cups dried cherries

⅓ cup plus 1 tablespoon delicate and mild olive oil

3 whole eggs

1 egg yolk

1 teaspoon water

STIR the yeast into the warm (not scalding) water in a large bowl to dissolve it. Add 1 tablespoon of the sugar, and let sit for 5 minutes, until bubbly.

ADD 3 cups of the flour to the yeast, mixing to combine (either by hand, in a very large stand mixer, or in a large food processor). Add the remaining 3 tablespoons sugar and the salt, along with the dried cherries, and combine.

ADD the ⅓ cup oil in a steady stream while mixing. Then add the eggs, one at a time. Mix in 2 more cups of the flour, adding more as needed to form a dough. Knead for 5 to 10 minutes, until the dough is smooth and elastic and cleans the sides of the bowl, sprinkling in more flour if needed. Form the dough into a ball. Put the remaining 1 tablespoon oil in a bowl, and turn the dough in it to coat it with oil. Cover the bowl tightly with plastic wrap and set aside in a warm draft-free place until the dough has doubled in bulk, about 1¼ hours.

OIL a baking sheet. Punch the dough down, knead it lightly on a lightly floured board, and divide it into 3 equal parts with a sharp knife or a dough scraper. Roll each part into an even snake of dough about the length of your baking sheet. Place the 3 strands on the sheet, pinch them together at the top, and braid the strands together, tucking the pinched ends under on both sides. Allow this shaped loaf to rise again in a warm place, covered with a clean cloth, for about 45 minutes.

WHILE the dough is rising, preheat the oven to 350°F.

BLEND the egg yolk with the water, and brush the loaf with this egg wash, taking care not to let it drip onto the baking sheet. Bake for 45 minutes, or until golden and hollow sounding when thumped on the bottom. Cool the loaf well on a wire rack before slicing it.

WHOLE WHEAT AND WALNUT BAGUETTES

MAKES 2 BAGUETTES
OR 1 WREATH

THIS RECIPE IS a compromise between expediency and tradition; I'd have to call it a very American take on French bread. It differs from tradition in two crucial ways: First, traditional baguettes are slow-risen with an aged dough starter, while this one rises fast using dry yeast. Second, unlike the traditional method of forming baguettes by pressing the dough into a rectangle, folding it in half the long way, sealing the seam, and folding and sealing again to form a long loaf, this bread is shaped by rolling it into a sausage shape. However, dispensing with tradition also has some benefits: You can turn this loaf into a bread wreath if you wish, which is a beautiful way to present it, especially with ripe cheese in the middle, drizzled with chestnut honey, as a dessert or cheese course. I also like to serve this loaf thinly sliced and spread with goat cheese, with a little shred of roasted red pepper on top and a tiny drizzle of great oil.

1¼ teaspoons active dry yeast

1½ cups lukewarm water

2 tablespoons fruity and fragrant olive oil

2 cups whole wheat flour

About 1½ cups unbleached all-purpose flour

1 teaspoon coarse sea salt

½ cup coarsely chopped toasted walnuts (see page 61)

STIR the yeast into the warm water in a large mixing bowl, the bowl of a large-capacity food processor, or the bowl of a large stand mixer. Let it sit for about 5 minutes, until bubbly. Add the oil.

IN another bowl, mix together the whole wheat flour and 1 cup of the all-purpose flour. Set it aside.

BY machine or by hand, gradually add about half the mixed flour to the yeast, and then add the salt. If the dough is too sticky to handle, gradually add more all-purpose flour, waiting until it is absorbed and feeling the dough with each addition, until the dough is only slightly sticky. Add the walnuts and knead until very smooth and elastic, about 15 minutes.

FORM the dough into a ball on a lightly floured board. Dust a cloth very lightly with flour, and cover the ball of dough with the floured cloth. Let rise in a warm, draft-free place for 1 hour.

ON a lightly floured surface, punch down the dough, and knead it well. If you are making baguettes, divide it into 2 parts. Stretch, pound lightly, and roll each portion out to form a 14-inch-long log, making them as even as possible. (For a wreath, form one long log.) Throwing the log down on the work surface as it is being formed will improve the texture of the finished bread—don't be afraid to be rough with this dough.

IF you are forming a wreath, set the log on a parchment-covered baking sheet, and curve it into a circle, pinching the ends together. Using scissors, cut diagonal "leaves" (slashes that extend to the middle of the log) alternately on the inner and outer curves of the circle. (These will expand as the bread rises.) If you are forming baguettes, simply place the 2 logs on a parchment-covered baking sheet.

COVER the wreath or the logs with the flour-dusted cloth, and let rise for 30 minutes in a warm draft-free place.

MEANWHILE, preheat the oven to 400°F. If you are using a baking stone, place it in the cold oven and preheat it with the oven.

USING scissors or a craft knife, cut four diagonal slashes in the top of each baguette. Very lightly brush the dough with cold water. Place the dough in the oven and rapidly spray the oven walls with water. Repeat this misting three more times in the first 5 minutes of baking, opening the door as little as possible with each spray. Take care not to spray the light bulb or electric elements directly. After those 5 minutes, do not open the oven again until the bread is baked.

BAKE for 35 to 45 minutes, or until golden and hollow sounding when thumped on the bottom. Cool thoroughly on a wire rack.

FOCACCIA WITH CARAMELIZED ONIONS

MAKES 1 LARGE FOCACCIA

USUALLY FOCACCIA is made in a pan, whereas pizza is cooked directly on a baking stone or hearth. I've reversed the technique in two recipes in this collection because in both cases the breads taste better when cooked in a less orthodox manner. If you don't have a baking stone, you can bake this bread on a cookie sheet. You can also make your own baking stone (see page 123).

Although these directions might look long, once you try this recipe you'll see how easy it is. Caramelized onions are a versatile condiment—you can use them to top pizza, on toast, as a side dish with roast meats (I always serve them at Thanksgiving), or mixed with green vegetables such as peas.

1 package active dry yeast

1½ cups warm water

5 tablespoons fresh rosemary needles, finely chopped

5 tablespoons leafy green and grassy olive oil

4½ cups unbleached all-purpose flour, or more as needed

2 teaspoons coarse sea salt

Caramelized Onion Topping (recipe follows)

DISSOLVE the yeast in the warm water in a large bowl, and set it aside for about 5 minutes, until bubbly. Add the rosemary and 3 tablespoons of the olive oil. Add 3 cups of the flour and the salt, and mix the dough together. You are aiming for a wet dough, so add more flour sparingly until you have made a soft dough that can be kneaded easily. Knead it for about 5 minutes on a lightly floured surface, and then form it into a ball. Pour 1 tablespoon of the olive oil into a mixing bowl, and turn the ball of dough in it to coat the dough well. Cover the bowl tightly with plastic wrap and leave it in a warm draft-free place until doubled in bulk, 1½ to 2 hours.

AFTER about 1 hour of the rising time, put a baking stone, or a cookie sheet lined with quarry tiles, on the lowest shelf of the oven. Remove any other racks in the oven, and preheat the oven to 450°F. (If you don't have a stone or tiles, just preheat the oven.) Prepare the onion topping.

WHEN the dough has doubled in size, punch it down in the bowl. Put a piece of parchment paper on a rimless cookie sheet or on the back of a sheet pan (this will serve as a peel). (If you are baking the focaccia in a baking sheet that is not lined with tile, put the parchment in the baking sheet.)

INVERT the dough from the bowl onto the parchment paper. Using your fingers, poke and stretch the dough into the shape and size, roughly, of your stone or pan. Let the dough rest for 5 to 10 minutes to relax the gluten, and then poke and dimple the dough from the center to the outer edges to thin it and further stretch it into the desired shape.

DRIZZLE the dough with the remaining 1 tablespoon olive oil, and spoon the onion topping over the whole surface. Open the oven, and carefully slide the parchment paper with the dough from the peel onto the hot baking stone or tile surface. (If you're baking the focaccia on a parchment-lined baking sheet, simply place it in the oven.) Remove the empty peel, shut the oven door, and bake until golden and puffed, about 25 minutes. Serve hot.

CARAMELIZED ONION TOPPING

MAKES 2 CUPS

3 tablespoons fruity and fragrant olive oil

1 pound large onions, sliced as thin as possible (4 cups sliced)

½ teaspoon sugar

½ teaspoon coarse sea salt

HEAT a heavy pan (do not use nonstick) and add the oil. When the oil is hot, add the thinly sliced onions, sugar, and salt, breaking the onions into rings with a wooden spoon. Allow to cook, undisturbed, over medium-low heat until the onions begin to color on their underside, and look limp and translucent. Give the onions a stir to expose the other sides to the heat, and continue cooking until they are golden brown with occasional flecks of darker brown caramelization. This will take about 30 minutes. Set the onions aside until ready to use. Caramelized onions can be stored in a covered jar for at least a week in the refrigerator.

MAKING A "BRICK HEARTH" FOR BREAD BAKING

To make a portable ceramic hearth for baking, take a baking sheet or a jelly roll pan to your local Home Depot. Choose unglazed quarry tiles (orange-red terra-cotta clay tiles)—the thicker the better. Buy enough tiles to fill your baking sheet from edge to edge. Use a tile cutter to cut the tiles as necessary to make a close fit. You now have a custom-made baking stone! Wash the tiles well when you get home, and keep them in the sheet.

Of course you can also purchase a baking stone from a kitchenware store.

PAN PIZZA DOUGH

MAKES 3 ROUND OR
2 RECTANGULAR PIZZAS

ALTHOUGH PIZZA traditionally is cooked directly on a pizza stone or clay hearth, this dough works best when dimpled into a pizza pan or a jelly-roll sheet; it tends to tear when pulled into a free-form pizza. On the other hand, it makes a gorgeous chewy crust. For even more flavor, you can make the dough the night before and let it slow-rise in the refrigerator overnight. Punch it down in the morning, return it to the refrigerator, and take it out a few hours before dinner. Let it rise again at room temperature before the final shaping.

If this is more pizza than you want to make at one time, you can freeze the dough in self-seal freezer bags for later use. Just bring it to room temperature in a covered oiled bowl, and let it have one rising and one punch-down before the final shaping.

This dough can be made in a stand mixer, in a large food processor, or by hand in a large mixing bowl.

1 tablespoon active dry yeast
(about 1 package)

½ teaspoon sugar

2 cups warm water (108°F)

4½ to 5 cups unbleached
all-purpose flour

1 tablespoon coarse sea salt

5 tablespoons leafy green and
grassy olive oil, plus additional
for drizzling over the pizzas

DISSOLVE the yeast and sugar in the warm water in a large bowl and set it aside for 5 minutes, until the yeast bubbles (if it doesn't, it means the yeast is too old). Add 4 cups of the flour, cup by cup, beating (or processing) after each addition. Add the salt and 4 tablespoons of the olive oil, and beat to incorporate. Check the dough. If it feels sticky and very wet, add more flour, ¼ cup at a time, feeling it after each addition. You want a fairly wet dough. When the dough feels loose and elastic, and starts to wrap around the beater of a stand mixer or the blade of a processor, cleaning the sides as it rotates, it's ready for the next step.

KNEAD the dough by hand on a lightly floured board for 10 minutes or for 5 minutes by machine, until it feels very smooth and elastic. Remove the dough and form it into a large ball. Place 1 tablespoon of the oil in a large mixing bowl, and turn the dough in the bowl to coat both dough and bowl with oil. Cover with a kitchen towel or plastic wrap, and leave in a warm place until doubled in bulk, about 1½ to 2 hours.

PUNCH the dough down and hand-knead it lightly. (If you are freezing a portion of the dough, freeze it now. If you are chilling the dough overnight, this is the point at which to refrigerate it.) Return it to the bowl, cover, and let it rise again, about 45 minutes.

PUNCH the dough down again and divide it into 2 or 3 parts, depending on the pans you are planning to use: It will fill three 15-inch round pizza pans or two 12 x 15-inch jelly-roll pans.

PREHEAT the oven to 475°F. Oil the pizza pans.

SHAPE each piece of dough by using a rolling pin on a floured board, or by gently turning and stretching the dough between your hands. When the dough is approximately the right size, place it in the prepared pan and let it rest for 10 minutes. (Don't worry if it is too small; this resting period will allow the gluten to relax and the dough will stretch further.)

DIMPLE the dough with your fingers, starting from the center and working out toward the edges to stretch it further. Leave a thicker rim of dough around the edges. When the dough is the size you want, sprinkle the whole surface with about 1 tablespoon olive oil before adding the toppings of your choice.

REDUCE the oven heat to 425°F and bake the pizza for 15 to 20 minutes, or until cooked through and brown at the edges.

PIZZA TOPPING IDEAS

SAVORY PIZZAS—any combination of the following, drizzling the dough first with a leafy green and grassy oil:

- Sliced roasted red or raw green peppers

- Fresh tomato slices

- Slivered or mashed garlic cloves

- Thin slices of ice-water-soaked red onion, drained well

- Crumbled cooked sausage

- Salami, thinly sliced and/or chopped

- Pitted black olives, chopped

- Cheeses like chèvre, ricotta, feta, Parmesan curls, or mozzarella slices

- Arugula, scattered over the pizza as it emerges from the oven—it will cook in the residual heat

BLACK OLIVE, MOZZARELLA, CHÈVRE, AND ARUGULA PIZZA

MAKES 2 PIZZAS

WE MAKE PIZZA OFTEN, and this is one of our favorites. You can use ricotta cheese instead of chèvre, and watercress can be substituted for the arugula, should you prefer it. You could also add chopped tomato or slices of roasted red pepper for color and added flavor.

Pizza dough for 2 large pizzas (page 124), at room temperature

Fruity and fragrant olive oil, to drizzle on the pizzas

1 whole head garlic, cloves peeled and coarsely chopped

30 pitted black olives, preferably oil-and-herb-cured, split or chopped

1 pound shredded or sliced good-quality mozzarella cheese

½ pound goat cheese (chèvre)

½ pound arugula, washed and dried, stems removed

½ pound fresh basil, washed and dried, stems removed

PREHEAT the oven to 475°F. If you are using a baking stone, put it in the cold oven and preheat it with the oven. If you don't have a pizza stone, you can line a baking sheet with quarry tiles (see page 123).

ROLL, stretch, and shape the pizza dough. If using lightly oiled pans, stretch it to nearly fit the pan size. If using a peel and a baking stone, shape the pizzas on a floured board to fit the peel. Let the dough rest for 15 minutes before the final stretching. When it's finally shaped, place the dough on floured parchment paper or directly on a well-floured pizza peel if you are using a stone. If using pans, the dough will now be ready.

SPRINKLE the dough (in this order) with drizzles of olive oil, chopped garlic, olives, and mozzarella. Crumble the goat cheese over all.

LOWER the oven heat to 425°F. If using pans, place them in the oven. If using a stone, slide the pizza from the peel or paper to the hot stone. Close the oven door as fast as you can, and bake for 15 to 20 minutes, or until the crust is golden and the toppings cooked. Remove from the oven, scatter the arugula on top, and garnish with the basil leaves. Serve at once.

PASTA

WHOLE WHEAT GOBBETTI WITH RED PEPPER, POULTRY SAUSAGE WITH SUN-DRIED TOMATOES, AND KALE

SERVES 4 TO 6

SOMETIMES I GET A CRAVING for whole wheat and other hearty flavors, and this pasta dish always satisfies. I buy whole wheat gobbetti, made by the organic pasta company Bionaturae, at my local health-food store. Gobbetti are large curved tubes that are ridged and twisted, and they are perfectly designed for holding bits of sauce. For sausage, I use Bruce Aidells' sun-dried tomato sausage, which is sold fully cooked and is made with smoked turkey and chicken. Use a big bunch of kale here to complement the robust flavors, and add a generous grating of flavorful Parmesan to finish the dish.

If you can't find Aidells, there are other very good poultry sausages available—look for ones that have a lot of flavor, and cook them through if they are not sold pre-cooked. It may be harder to find other whole wheat pastas in a tubular shape; if you can't, try this with a good white-flour pasta. You'll need a pretty big frying pan, a sauté pan with a good cover, or a large Dutch oven to cook the sauce in because you mix the pasta with the sauce at the end.

1 red bell pepper

3 links Aidells Sun-Dried Tomato Poultry Sausage (see Resources)

4 tablespoons leafy green and grassy olive oil

1 clove garlic, finely chopped

1 small red onion, diced

1 large bunch kale (¾ to 1 pound), washed, ribs removed, leaves coarsely chopped

1 pound whole wheat gobbetti

BRING at least 6 quarts salted water to a boil.

WASH the red pepper, remove the inner ribs and seeds, and cut it into ½-inch dice. Set it aside.

HEAT a large frying pan. Cut the sausages in half lengthwise and place them, cut side down, on the hot pan. Lower the heat to medium and cook until the sausages are browned on both sides. Remove from the pan and set aside to cool. When they are cool, cut the cooked sausages into ¼-inch-thick slices.

**1 potato (I like Yukon Gold),
peeled and thinly sliced**

Freshly grated Parmesan cheese

ADD 1 tablespoon of the olive oil to the pan. Then add the chopped garlic and red onion, and cook for 2 to 3 minutes over low heat. Add the greens, give them a good stir to coat with the flavorful oil, and place the cover on the pan. Cook until the greens are wilted, about 3 minutes. Uncover the pan and add the bell pepper, and continue to cook, uncovered, stirring occasionally, for about 5 minutes over low heat (the pepper will still have some crunch). Add the sausage slices and heat gently.

ADD the pasta and the potato slices to the boiling water, and cook until the pasta is al dente (the potatoes will be cooked through in the same time if thinly sliced). Reserving ½ cup of the pasta water, drain the pasta. Add the drained pasta and potato to the sauce, along with the remaining 3 tablespoons olive oil. Add the reserved pasta water if the sauce seems dry. Mix, turn out onto a serving platter, and dust generously with freshly grated Parmesan. Serve at once.

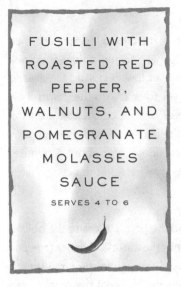

FUSILLI WITH ROASTED RED PEPPER, WALNUTS, AND POMEGRANATE MOLASSES SAUCE

SERVES 4 TO 6

THE COMBINATION of ingredients in this sauce is found in many parts of the eastern Mediterranean; in Turkey it's called Muhammara. I thought of using them for a pasta sauce after seeing Sara Jenkins, chef at New York's Il Buco restaurant, use these elements for crostini. This sauce gets better as it sits, so it's a good idea (although not essential) to try to make it a day ahead to let the flavors merge, and then bring it to room temperature before you cook the pasta. Pomegranate molasses is inexpensive and is available from specialty food stores and Middle Eastern shops as well as from Global Food Market.

If you want to follow Il Buco's lead, this sauce, minus the added pasta water, is just wonderful as a spread on crisp grilled bread. If you want to serve it that way as an appetizer, be sure to drizzle some olive oil on the bread after spooning on the spread.

1 clove garlic, peeled

1 red bell pepper, roasted and coarsely chopped (page 68)

½ cup toasted walnuts (page 61)

½ cup olive-y and peppery olive oil, plus more for drizzling

1 teaspoon pomegranate molasses

Grated zest of ½ lemon

Coarse sea salt and freshly ground black pepper, to taste

1 pound fusilli

BY hand in a mortar and pestle, or in a food processor, chop the garlic to a very fine paste. Add the red pepper and walnuts, and chop to a slightly chunky puree. Slowly add the olive oil, stirring or processing as you add it, and then add the pomegranate molasses. Stir in the lemon zest, salt, and pepper. Taste and correct the seasonings. If possible, place in a closed container and refrigerate for a day or so; otherwise use at once.

BRING at least 6 quarts salted water to a boil in a large pot. Add the pasta, and cook until al dente, 10 to 12 minutes.

MEANWHILE, put the sauce in a large sauté pan or Dutch oven, and heat it very gently over the lowest possible heat—it should be just warm, not hot. Scoop out ½ cup of the pasta water and add it to the sauce, stirring. Drain the pasta, add it to the slightly warm sauce, and toss. Serve at once, passing more olive oil to drizzle over the pasta at the table.

OLIVE OIL–BATHED SPRING VEGETABLES *page 177*

FRESH TOMATO TART *page 79*

facing page
GREEN SPLIT PEA SOUP WITH CHICKEN-APPLE SAUSAGE *page 106*

ORANGE, ONION, AND OLIVE SALAD *page 86*

facing page
CHICKEN BRAISED WITH SAFFRON, CINNAMON, AND
LAVENDER, TOPPED WITH ALMONDS *page 166*

RADIATORE WITH PARSLEY SAUCE AND SWEET CORN *page 146*

facing page
YOGURT-MARINATED GRILLED SWORDFISH STEAKS *page 154*

APPLE-CHERRY CARDAMOM STRUDEL *page 202*

There are lots of myths about how to cook dried pasta. Let me explode a few of them. First of all, *don't* add oil to the pasta water—it only makes it harder for the sauce to cling to the pasta. *Do* add plenty of salt—it helps to flavor the pasta. *Do* use plenty of water—6 to 8 quarts of boiling salted water for each pound of dried pasta. *Don't* rinse pasta after cooking—it's completely unnecessary. *Don't* cook pasta ahead—call everyone to the table while it's still cooking, and get it from pot to platter to table as fast as you can.

Consider adding cooked pasta to the sauce while the sauce is still in the pan; this allows the pasta to cook a little in the hot sauce and absorb it. I always reserve a little pasta water (see page 135) to thin the sauce, if necessary, and I try to make sure that the pasta does not swim in too much sauce.

Think too about the shape of pasta you choose for a particular sauce. You need a rounded form with crevices for some kinds of sauces, such as those with small chunks of meat or vegetables or cheese. Some thinner sauces also demand a pasta with some complexity of shape, so that the sauce can pool and create intense pockets of flavor. I've made suggestions with each pasta recipe, and I encourage you to try other shapes to discover which ones you like best with your sauces. To see how an Italian cook classifies pasta shapes and the sauces they require, see page 141.

To cook dried pasta: Put the pasta in a pot of boiling salted water, give it a stir, and cover the pot to return it rapidly to the boil. When it boils, remove the cover and cook until al dente (slightly resistant to the touch or bite). Drain in a colander in the sink, or dip out scoops of pasta with a perforated pasta scoop and shake the pasta to remove some of the water that clings to it. Place the cooked pasta in its sauce in the saucepan or on a platter, toss, and serve, accompanied by a cruet of olive oil for drizzling and a wedge of Parmesan cheese to grate. Have coarse sea salt and a pepper grinder at the table for those who want to season their pasta more.

PENNE WITH SWEET ITALIAN SAUSAGE AND SPINACH

SERVES 4 TO 6

FOR A RAPID ONE-DISH weeknight meal, Pasta with Sweet Italian Sausage and Spinach is a family favorite—provided I serve the sausage on the side for the sake of the vegetarians. I prefer a toothy pasta here, like penne or orecchiette. Adding the potato to the pasta water is a useful trick to make dried pasta taste fresher, but it's by no means essential. I've used spinach in this recipe, but you can also use chard or kale—just cut off and discard the whole length of thick stem, chopping the leaves into slivers. Boil the leaves of tougher greens like chard or kale longer by adding them along with the pasta, since they require more time to cook to tenderness.

Try adding grilled bread crumbs to elevate this dish sensationally: Pan-fry crustless slices of good country bread along with a chopped clove of garlic in a puddle of flavorful leafy green and grassy olive oil until toasted and golden brown. Let cool, and then grate on a hand grater, or cut into chunks and process in a food processor, until you have coarse crisp crumbs. Sprinkle over the top of the pasta.

½ to ¾ pound sweet Italian pork sausages

1 cup white wine or water

1 pound penne or orecchiette

1 potato, such as Yukon Gold, peeled and thinly sliced (optional)

1 pound fresh spinach, stemmed, washed, and coarsely chopped

About 3 tablespoons leafy green and grassy olive oil

Coarse sea salt and freshly ground black pepper, to taste

BRING at least 8 quarts salted water to a boil in a large pot. While the water is heating, heat a heavy frying pan over medium-high heat, and when it is hot, add the sausages. Prick them all over with a fork, and cook them, turning, until browned, about 2 minutes per side. Add the wine, cover, and cook over medium-low heat until cooked through, about 20 minutes more. Let cool, and then cut into thin slices. Set aside until ready to use.

ADD the pasta, and the potato slices if using, to the boiling water and cook, stirring occasionally, for 5 minutes. Then add the chopped spinach and

Large pinch of red pepper flakes (optional)

Wedge of Parmesan cheese for grating

cook until al dente, another 5 to 6 minutes. Drain well in a colander, and place on a serving platter. Immediately pour the olive oil over the pasta and greens, add the sliced sausage, and mix all together. Sprinkle with salt and pepper, and red pepper flakes if desired. Grate Parmesan generously over the top, and mix again. Serve immediately, passing additional olive oil and cheese at the table.

RAW POTATOES AND DRIED PASTA

Dropping a sliced raw peeled potato into pasta water as it comes to a boil provides added starch to dried pasta and makes it taste better. You'll find that if you thinly slice the potato, it will finish cooking at the same time as the pasta. The potato makes a delicious addition to most sauces (but it's not recommended with cream sauces).

CELLENTANI PASTA WITH OVEN-DRIED TOMATOES AND GORGONZOLA

SERVES 4 TO 6

CELLENTANI ARE THICK, toothy pasta spirals; you can also use any thick pasta shape like rigatoni or fusilli. If you don't have homemade oven-dried tomatoes (see page 62), you can use commercial sun-dried tomatoes instead, although they may require more liquid to soften them—add a little water. You can also use sun-dried tomatoes packed in oil, but drain them before using. The vodka in this recipe is essential—it brings out the flavor of the tomatoes even though the alcohol is completely cooked off. Taste your Gorgonzola to see how strong it is, and use your own judgment about how much you want to use to flavor the pasta sauce (sweet, or *dolce,* Gorgonzola doesn't work here).

2 tablespoons olive-y and peppery olive oil, plus more to drizzle over the pasta

2 cloves garlic, peeled and chopped

1 large sweet onion, such as Walla Walla or Vidalia, *or* 1 small yellow onion, chopped

1 cup oven-dried tomatoes, coarsely chopped

½ cup vodka

1 pound cellentani pasta

About ¾ cup chopped flat-leaf parsley

½ cup coarsely chopped flavorful black olives

4 to 6 ounces Gorgonzola cheese, cut or crumbled

Coarse sea salt and freshly ground black pepper, to taste

1 tablespoon capers, drained (rinsed if salt-packed)

HEAT a very large sauté pan or a large Dutch oven. When the pan is hot, add the olive oil and reduce the heat to medium. When the oil is warm and fragrant, add the garlic and cook over low heat for a minute or two. Add the onion and cook until limp and translucent.

ADD the tomatoes and cook them slowly, dribbling in the vodka as needed to keep them moist. Cook over low heat for 10 to 15 minutes, until soft and fragrant.

MEANWHILE, bring 6 to 8 quarts salted water to a boil in a large pot. Add the pasta and cook until al dente, 10 to 12 minutes.

WHILE the pasta is cooking, add the parsley, olives, and crumbled cheese, along with any remaining vodka, to the tomatoes. Cook, covered, over the lowest possible heat. If the sauce gets too dry, add a ladle of pasta water. Add salt and pepper to taste.

RESERVING 1 cup of the pasta water, drain the pasta and toss it with the sauce. Add the capers, and the reserved pasta water if the sauce seems too thick.

SERVE immediately, passing more olive oil at the table to drizzle over the pasta.

ADDING PASTA WATER TO SAUCES

The traditional technique of reserving some of the starchy pasta water to thin or stretch a sauce is less well known than it should be. It's especially useful when a pasta sauce is very rich; I always use pasta water when making pesto pasta for just this reason. Don't limit yourself to Mediterranean dishes—pasta water added to a Thai peanut sauce or Chinese cold sesame noodles makes these dishes more delicious and helps the sauce stick to the pasta.

PESTO WITH
WALNUTS
SERVES 4 TO 6

WHILE YOU CAN MAKE a pesto sauce out of many different greens—arugula, parsley, and cilantro come to mind—basil pesto is the most well-loved around here. Although it's traditionally made with pine nuts *(Pesto Genovese)*, I like the heartier taste of walnuts with this dish. I usually make it in a food processor, but recently I've been using a mortar and pestle, and I can't get over the difference it makes: The flavor is more pungent. My mortar and pestle came from a Thai grocery, and although it's made of stone and very heavy, it was remarkably inexpensive. In terms of pasta forms, I like to be traditional and use linguini with pesto.

About 4 cups fresh basil leaves

2 or 3 large cloves garlic, peeled

½ cup walnuts, toasted

1 teaspoon coarse sea salt

Freshly ground black pepper
to taste

½ cup fruity and fragrant
olive oil

½ cup freshly grated Parmesan
cheese

1 pound linguini

Wedge of Parmesan cheese to
grate at the table

WASH and dry the basil, and put it in the bowl of a food processor or in a mortar. Add the garlic, walnuts, salt, and pepper, and process or pound to a pulp. Gradually add the olive oil, processing as it is added. Add the grated cheese. (If using a food processor, diced pieces of Parmesan can be used instead of grated cheese, as the steel knife will grind them into small bits.)

BRING 6 to 8 quarts salted water to a boil in a large pot. Add the linguini and cook until al dente, 8 to 10 minutes. Reserving ½ cup of the pasta water, drain the pasta and put it in a large bowl or platter.

GRADUALLY add the reserved pasta water to the sauce until it reaches the consistency you like, and then immediately toss the pasta with the pesto and serve. Pass the wedge of cheese and a grater at the table for those who like more cheese.

RADIATORE WITH NEAPOLITAN PESTO

SERVES 4 TO 6

MAUREEN FANT, in a travel piece in *The New York Times,* described a dish she'd eaten in Naples. It sounded so wonderful to me, I just had to figure it out and cook it. This is the result—a sauce made of basil-rich Pesto Genovese mixed with tomatoes, black olives, toasted pine nuts, and capers. Once you try it, you may agree with one previously loyal pesto fiend who said, "This is even better than plain pesto."

½ cup pine nuts

About 4 cups loosely packed fresh basil leaves

3 cloves garlic, peeled

½ cup freshly grated Parmesan cheese

4 anchovy fillets, drained (cleaned and rinsed if salt-packed)

½ cup fruity and fragrant olive oil

½ teaspoon vodka (optional)

½ teaspoon coarse sea salt

Generous grinding of black pepper

½ cup olive oil–cured black olives, pitted

1 very large tomato

1 tablespoon capers, preferably unrinsed salt-packed

1 pound radiatore or other spiral pasta

Wedge of Parmesan cheese to pass at the table

IN a cast-iron frying pan, toast the pine nuts, stirring until the nuts are golden and aromatic, about 5 minutes. Transfer the nuts to a plate to stop them from cooking further.

WASH and dry the basil leaves. Place them in the bowl of a food processor, and add the garlic cloves, grated cheese, anchovies, olive oil, and the vodka if using. Process to a smooth paste, stopping the processor and scraping down the sides as necessary. Taste, and then add the salt and pepper. Pour the pesto onto a serving platter.

WITHOUT washing the food processor bowl, add the pitted olives and pulse to coarsely chop them. Add to the pesto on the platter. Working over the platter, cut the tomato into small dice and add it to the pesto. Add the capers as well.

MEANWHILE, bring 6 to 8 quarts salted water to a boil in a large pot. Add the radiatore and cook until al dente, 10 to 12 minutes.

RESERVING ⅛ cup pasta water, drain the pasta. Stir the reserved pasta water into the sauce on the platter. Put the cooked pasta on top, and toss. Scatter the toasted pine nuts over the pasta, and serve immediately, passing a wedge of Parmesan with a grater at the table.

SPAGHETTI WITH BOTTARGA DI TONNO

SERVES 4 TO 6

BOTTARGA DI TONNO is dried tuna roe, an intense salty, fishy ingredient that pairs just wonderfully with pasta. It's one of those very ancient foods that's still made exactly as it always was—sun-dried and salted. Some of the best bottarga comes from Sicily, and it's available from Esperya (a jar makes at least four meals). Bottarga is also available pressed into flat cakes that can be finely grated, but I find it most convenient when it's already in granulated form, packed in a glass jar.

Unfortunately, there is no real substitute for bottarga. However, there is an option for a variation. In this case, you don't have to start ahead; you can make the sauce as the pasta cooks. To make *Spaghetti with Parsley and Olive Oil*, cook the pasta and make the sauce of olive oil and finely chopped parsley, adding ½ to 1 cup freshly grated Parmesan cheese to increase both flavor and protein levels, and adding salt as well.

3 tablespoons dried bottarga grains or finely grated pressed bottarga

½ cup leafy green and grassy olive oil

1 cup finely chopped flat-leaf parsley leaves

1 pound spaghetti

Freshly ground black pepper

EARLY in the day you plan to serve the dish, place the bottarga in a bowl, and add the olive oil and the chopped parsley. Allow to marinate, covered with plastic wrap, at room temperature for at least 6 hours.

BRING 6 to 8 quarts salted water to a boil in a large pot. Add the spaghetti and cook until al dente, 8 to 10 minutes. Drain the pasta, and toss it in a bowl with the bottarga mixture. Season with black pepper and serve at once.

FUSILLI WITH RED ONION, PARSLEY, TUNA, CAPERS, AND MOZZARELLA

SERVES 4 TO 6

1 red onion

One 6-ounce can high-quality tuna, preferably imported and packed in olive oil

1 pound mozzarella, diced

2 ripe tomatoes, chopped

Garlic slivers slow-cooked in olive oil (optional)

One 16- or 19-ounce can chickpeas (garbanzo beans), drained and rinsed (optional)

1 pound fusilli

1 cup flat-leaf parsley leaves, washed and dried

1 heaping tablespoon capers, preferably unrinsed salt-packed

2 anchovy fillets, drained (cleaned and rinsed if salt-packed)

½ cup fruity and fragrant olive oil

½ to ¾ cup wrinkled black olives, preferably packed in olive oil, pitted and coarsely chopped

Wedge of Parmesan cheese to pass at the table

SALAD INGREDIENTS and pasta combine to make a robust dish that's good hot or cold.

BRING 6 to 8 quarts salted water to a boil in a large pot.

WHILE the water is heating, peel and thinly slice the onion. Place the onion slices in a bowl of ice water, and let soak while you proceed with the recipe.

OPEN the can of tuna, drain it, and place the contents in the center of a big serving platter. Break apart the tuna. Put the mozzarella pieces and the chopped tomatoes on the platter, as well as the cooked garlic and drained chickpeas if using.

ADD the fusilli to the boiling water, and cook until al dente, 10 to 12 minutes.

WHILE the pasta is cooking, chop the parsley to a fine texture in a food processor. Add the capers, anchovies, olive oil, olives, and drained onion, and process to a slightly chunky consistency. Leave this sauce mixture in the processor.

RESERVING 1 cup of the pasta water, drain the pasta and put it on the platter with the tuna, mozzarella pieces, and tomatoes.

CHECK the sauce—is it too thick or is its flavor too intense? If so, add some of the reserved pasta water (½ cup to start) to dilute it. Process, then pour the sauce over the pasta, toss well, and serve.

PASS the wedge of Parmesan and a grater at the table, along with a pepper grinder.

CHIOCCIOLI WITH SWORDFISH IN TOMATO SAUCE

SERVES 4 TO 6

CHIOCCIOLI ARE short wide curved tubes, made by the organic pasta company Bionaturae. They are not essential; you can easily substitute any curved sauce-holding pasta shape such as large shells, elbows, or orecchiette (little ears). The combination of swordfish, eggplant, and tomato is a traditional Sicilian triumvirate; I've added olives and capers to further increase the brininess. If this were a traditional recipe, the eggplant would be deep-fried to a crisp. I sauté it in much less oil, but it is important to get a good brown crust on the eggplant, so use a pan that is *not* nonstick and that browns food well, such as a black cast-iron frying pan.

2 small Japanese eggplants *or* 1 large eggplant

½ cup plus 2 tablespoons leafy green and grassy olive oil

2 cloves garlic, peeled and finely chopped

½ to ¾ pound fresh swordfish (about half a steak), skin removed, cut into ½-inch dice

1 teaspoon white balsamic vinegar or other white wine vinegar

One 14-ounce can diced tomatoes

1 teaspoon dried oregano *or* 2 teaspoons fresh oregano

1 pound chioccioli, elbows, or orecchiette pasta

½ cup freshly grated Parmesan cheese, plus more for serving if desired

¼ cup finely chopped fresh flat-leaf parsley

CUT the eggplant into ½-inch dice. Preheat a heavy sauté pan over medium-high heat, and when the pan is hot, add the ½ cup olive oil—it should be at a depth of about ¼ inch. Put a shred of eggplant in the oil, and if it immediately sizzles, the oil is hot enough. Add the eggplant to the pan in one layer, immediately lower the heat to medium-low, and cook, without disturbing, until brown on one side. Then gently turn the eggplant and brown it on all sides. This will take about 45 minutes in all. When the eggplant is cooked, use a slotted spoon to remove it, leaving the oil in the pan. Reserve the eggplant and discard any oil that remains.

ADD the remaining 2 tablespoons olive oil to the empty pan, scraping up any browned bits from the eggplant, and gently cook the garlic over low heat until it is tender, 1 to 2 minutes. Add the swordfish cubes and cook them until they are just starting to turn white and opaque, about 5 minutes. Add the vinegar, then the tomatoes and oregano. Cook for 1 minute, and then return the eggplant to the pan.

¼ cup pitted black olives, finely chopped

1 tablespoon capers, drained (rinsed if salt-packed)

Coarse sea salt and freshly ground black pepper, to taste

Simmer uncovered over very low heat for about 15 minutes or until slightly reduced in volume.

MEANWHILE, bring 8 to 10 quarts salted water to a boil in a large pot, and add the pasta. Cook until al dente, 10 to 12 minutes. Drain the pasta and place it on a serving platter. Pour the swordfish sauce over the pasta and toss. Dust it with the cheese, parsley, olives, and capers, along with salt and pepper to taste. Toss again. Serve at once, passing more cheese at the table if desired.

FITTING THE PASTA SHAPE TO THE SAUCE

Beatrice Ughi of Esperya has explained in her newsletter how Italians decide which pasta to use with different kinds of sauces. Here is her formulation:

Long strand pasta—such as spaghetti, spaghettini, capellini, and linguini—is best with smooth sauces.

Wide long noodles, such as fettuccine, support slightly chunkier sauces.

In general, short tubular or molded pasta shapes do an excellent job of trap-ping chunkier sauces: Small to medium chunks make more sense with fusilli, pennette, and gnocchette, while large chunks work best with rigatoni or other large tubes.

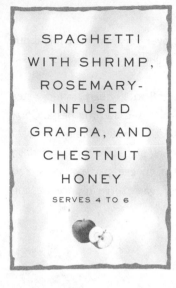

SPAGHETTI WITH SHRIMP, ROSEMARY-INFUSED GRAPPA, AND CHESTNUT HONEY

SERVES 4 TO 6

INFUSING ALCOHOL with herbs is very easy and produces a wonderful effect. In fact, this rosemary-infused grappa is so delicious that you might want to consider making a larger amount and serving it as a *digestivo* in small glasses. If grappa is hard to come by where you live, you could substitute a flavorless vodka. Similarly, if you don't have chestnut honey, use any strong dark honey instead.

½ cup grappa or vodka

2 lush sprigs fresh rosemary, washed and dried

8 tablespoons fruity and fragrant olive oil

6 cloves garlic, peeled, crushed, and finely chopped

2 tablespoons finely minced shallots

1 pound medium shrimp, thawed if frozen, peeled and deveined, cut in half crosswise

Coarse sea salt and freshly ground black pepper, to taste

1 teaspoon chestnut honey or other dark strong honey

1 pound spaghetti

¼ cup heavy cream

¾ cup chopped fresh basil leaves

USING a small saucepan, heat the grappa to hot but not boiling, and add the whole rosemary sprigs. Remove the pan from the heat, cover, and let infuse for 15 minutes, pressing on the rosemary with a spoon to make sure it is as submerged as possible. Remove the rosemary. Mince the leaves from one sprig and then set aside (you should have 1 tablespoon). Discard the other sprig.

BRING 6 to 8 quarts salted water to a boil in a large pot.

WHILE the water is heating, heat a large sauté pan or frying pan, and add 6 tablespoons of the oil. Sauté the garlic and shallots over medium-low heat until the shallots are limp and translucent (but not browning), 3 to 4 minutes. Increase the heat to medium-high and add the shrimp, stirring and cooking until they are pink on all sides, 2 to 3 minutes. Add the infused grappa, and a little salt and pepper to taste. Boil for 1 minute to evaporate the alcohol. Remove from the heat and stir in the honey.

COOK the pasta in the boiling water until al dente, 8 to 10 minutes. Reserving ¼ cup of the pasta water, drain the pasta. Put the pasta in the sauté pan and toss it with the sauce over low heat for a minute or two. Add the cream, basil, reserved chopped rosemary, and remaining 2 tablespoons olive oil. Toss again, put on a platter, and serve at once.

CAREFUL!

Watch the grappa closely when you're heating it—you don't want it to boil. Keep the pot lid handy, and if the alcohol combusts, quickly clamp the lid on the pot to smother the flames.

COOKING PASTA IN ITS SAUCE

When you make a pasta sauce in a large shallow sauté pan, you can take the drained pasta and add it to the pan over low heat. This allows the pasta to absorb some of the sauce and to finish cooking in the sauce. The flavor difference is noticeable. If you do this, remember to drain the pasta before it is fully cooked, as it will continue to cook a little in the sauce—aim for the firm side of al dente. If you scoop the pasta from the cooking water rather than draining it in a colander, you'll get the benefit of the water that clings to the pasta in your sauce, and you will have more hot pasta water right at hand should you decide you need more.

SUMMER PASTA WITH RAW TOMATO SAUCE

SERVES 4 TO 6

SALSA CRUDA, OR RAW SAUCE, is much thinner than a cooked tomato sauce, with an addictive and intense flavor that actually improves after resting for an hour. If you can, make the sauce when you get home and let it age, so that there's a time gap between blending and serving. Serve this sauce with fusilli, bow ties (farfalle), or orecchiette pasta (all of which catch the sauce in the curves of the pasta), and put it in shallow bowls so that you can gather up all the goodness with a spoon. A crusty loaf of bread is also a good addition, and with a green salad makes a satisfying meal. This recipe can be doubled if you are feeding a crowd. Leftover sauce can be refrigerated and used the next day with little loss of flavor; it's great on cottage cheese!

Raw tomato sauce

2 cloves garlic, peeled, cut in half, green sprout removed

2 pints ripe cherry tomatoes, washed and drained

2 whole anchovy fillets, preferably packed in olive oil, drained

5 flavorful green or black olives, pitted

1 generous tablespoon salt-packed capers, lightly rinsed

½ cup arugula leaves, washed and dried

Freshly ground black pepper

¼ cup leafy green and grassy olive oil

1 tablespoon vodka or aquavit

For the pasta

1 pound fusilli, bow ties, or orecchiette

For serving

Wedge of Parmesan cheese

PREPARE the tomato sauce: In a food processor, pulse the garlic to form a fine puree. Then add all of the remaining sauce ingredients and pulse until they are reduced to small chunks. Be careful not to overprocess the sauce into a liquid.

IF possible, let the sauce sit at room temperature for an hour or so to merge. Taste, and see if you need to add any salt.

BRING 6 to 8 quarts salted water to a boil in a large pot. Add the pasta and cook until al dente, 10 to 12 minutes. Drain the pasta, pour it into a serving bowl, and pour the sauce over the top.

SERVE immediately. Pass a wedge of Parmesan cheese and a grater at the table.

Shirley Corriher, the great food scientist, once told me that real food flavors are made up of a great many elements, not all of which can emerge on their own. Shirley then went on to give me the most helpful tip of my cooking life: There are five "magic" ingredients that release otherwise hidden flavor elements in food—sugar, salt, alcohol, fat, and water. A small amount of any of these substances will effect this release, and each one of them releases different flavor elements than the others. It's always useful to check your recipes for the presence of each of the five magic ingredients. If one is missing, try adding it to see if the overall flavor improves.

For example, in baking, the alcohol in vanilla extract is an important element—try a non-alcohol extract to taste the difference. The presence of salt in cakes and cookies serves to amplify the sweetness. Similarly, in savory dishes, adding a tiny bit of sugar and alcohol to a tomato-based sauce or dish increases the tomato's flavor by bringing out taste notes that would otherwise be hidden.

Most important, fat carries flavor. Cookbook author Lorna Sass recently told me a story about making a white bean and basil puree. She had made the puree with a spoonful of olive oil and lots of basil, but the basil flavor wasn't coming through. She added more basil, but there was still no robust taste. Finally she added another spoonful of olive oil, and suddenly the basil came alive.

RADIATORE WITH PARSLEY SAUCE AND SWEET CORN

SERVES 4 TO 6

ALTHOUGH THIS IS BEST when made with summer's fresh sweet corn cut off the cob, it's also good with frozen corn. It's an almost-instant kid- and crowd-pleasing main course. You could add pieces of crisp bacon to the mix, for added crunch and flavor.

4 to 5 ears fresh corn, shucked, *or* 2 cups frozen corn kernels

1 pound radiatore or other spiral pasta

2 cups flat-leaf parsley leaves

2 cloves garlic, peeled

1 anchovy fillet, drained (cleaned and rinsed if salt-packed)

1 heaping teaspoon salt-packed capers, unrinsed

1 small red onion, cut into wedges

⅓ cup fruity and fragrant olive oil

½ cup heavy cream

Coarse sea salt and freshly ground black pepper, to taste

2 ripe tomatoes, finely diced

1 pound mozzarella, diced

IF you are using fresh corn on the cob, steam or boil the corn until done. Cool it briefly in cold water; then drain, and slice the kernels off the cob. If using frozen corn, steam it briefly to defrost it, cool briefly in cold water, and drain. Set the cooled cooked corn aside.

BRING 6 to 8 quarts salted water to a boil in a large pot. Add the pasta and cook until al dente, 10 to 12 minutes.

WHILE the pasta is cooking, make the sauce: Combine the parsley, garlic, anchovy, capers, and onion in the bowl of a food processor. Process the mixture to form a smooth puree, adding the olive oil, then the cream, in a stream through the feed tube. Taste the sauce, and add salt and pepper to taste.

RESERVING about ½ cup of the pasta water, drain the pasta and put it in a large shallow bowl or platter. Pour the sauce over it and toss, adding some of the reserved pasta water if the sauce needs thinning. Add the corn kernels, diced tomatoes, and cubes of mozzarella, toss again, and serve.

NOT MY NANNA'S NOODLE KUGEL

SERVES 4 TO 6

FRANKLY, I COULDN'T FIGURE OUT where to put this recipe, because although it's essentially a sweet dish, the truth is that in our house this is a favorite dinner. When my daughter Abby comes home for a weekend from college exhausted, or when my younger daughter, Lizzie, has had a long day, this is the meal I serve to make them feel better. I like to think that if my Nanna were still here and cooking, this would be her new favorite version.

Lizzie (who loves the texture and sweetness of canned fruit) thinks Noodle Kugel is even better when tossed just before cooking with drained canned pineapple chunks, or sliced canned pears, apricots, or peaches.

3 tablespoons delicate and mild olive oil

One 12-ounce package egg noodles

5 eggs

1 pound sour cream

1 pound cottage cheese

1½ cups sugar

1 teaspoon ground cinnamon

1 teaspoon vanilla extract

½ cup dried cranberries, raisins, or drained canned fruit

PREHEAT the oven to 350°F. Using 1 tablespoon of the oil, grease a 9 x 12-inch lasagna pan or gratin dish.

BRING at least 6 quarts salted water to a boil in a large pot. Add the noodles and cook until just done, 6 to 8 minutes. Drain.

WHILE the noodles are cooking, combine the eggs, sour cream, cottage cheese, sugar, cinnamon, vanilla, cranberries or raisins, and remaining 2 tablespoons olive oil in a large mixing bowl. Add the noodles as soon as they're drained, and mix them in. If you are adding canned fruit, add it now.

POUR this mixture into the greased pan, and bake for 1 hour. Serve hot, cut into squares.

FISH, MEAT, AND POULTRY

OVEN-ROASTED WHOLE RED SNAPPER

SERVES 4 TO 6

THIS METHOD OF COOKING FISH in the oven is virtually foolproof. You'll want to cook this whole fish in a pan that is heavy, shallow, and big enough to hold the fish (although you can certainly cut off the head and tail). A large cast-iron skillet is a good choice, as is an oval fish frying pan, or a large cast-iron or ceramic gratin dish. I like to serve this with Orange, Onion, and Olive Salad (page 86).

How do you tell when fish is done? When the flesh is translucent, it's raw. When the flesh is opaque but moist, it's done. When it's opaque and flaky, it's overdone.

One 3-pound whole red snapper, cleaned and scaled

2 tablespoons fruity and fragrant olive oil

Coarse sea salt and freshly ground black pepper, to taste

Garnish

1 lemon, cut into wedges

Fruity and fragrant olive oil to pass at the table

PREHEAT the oven to 425°F for at least 10 minutes, preheating an ovenproof pan at the same time.

CUT off the head and tail if necessary to make the fish fit in the pan. Run the back of a knife over the surface of the fish to remove any scales that may be left. Rinse the fish under cold running water and pat it dry with paper towels.

RUB both sides of the fish with the olive oil, and scatter salt and pepper over the fish. Remove the hot pan from the oven, place the fish in it, and return it to the oven.

ROAST for 20 to 30 minutes, or until the flesh is opaque but still moist. Serve with lemon wedges, and pass additional olive oil at the table.

BONING A WHOLE FISH

When fish is cooked, the flesh separates easily from the bone. Using a spatula and a knife, remove the top half of the fish in large pieces (or in one piece,

if possible), exposing the bone. Arrange these pieces on a serving platter. Grasp the large spine bone and pull and remove it in one fluid motion—most of

the smaller bones will come out with this piece. Remove any other visible bones, and place the rest of the fish on the platter.

FLASH-ROASTED SALMON WITH SABA

SERVES 2 TO 4

FLASH-ROASTING SALMON in a very hot oven is the simplest way I know to cook a flavorful fillet. If I'm starting with soup or a salad, I assume that a pound of thick boneless salmon fillet will feed four when served with a starch and a green vegetable. If there is no first course, then I allow ½ pound per person.

You may not be familiar with saba. It's used much like aged balsamic vinegar, although it is made from cooked-down (rather than aged) grape must. Available at specialty food shops and from purveyors such as Corti Brothers, saba costs much less than real aged *balsamico* (and has a very different quality). It's a nice item to have in your pantry.

I like saba's fruity flavor in contrast with the fattiness of the salmon; it acts much like lemon with chicken or orange with duck. If you don't have any saba, try making the Fig "Balsamico" Agrodolce on page 64 and use that instead. Or just drizzle fresh lemon juice and a great fruity and fragrant olive oil over the roasted salmon.

1 tablespoon fruity and fragrant olive oil

1 to 2 pounds salmon fillet

Coarse sea salt and freshly ground black pepper, to taste

¼ cup saba

PREHEAT the oven to 500°F. Put a cast-iron or other ovenproof metal frying pan in the oven to preheat at the same time, about 10 minutes.

WHEN the pan is hot, pour a very little of the olive oil into the pan (it should immediately thin), tipping the pan to coat the bottom with a thin film of oil.

CAREFULLY place the salmon fillet in the pan, skin side down (cut it into serving-size pieces if necessary to make the fish fit in the pan). The oil should sizzle when you add the fish. If it doesn't, it's not hot enough. Carefully, using your hands or a pastry brush, smooth the rest of the oil over the top of the fish.

ROAST the fish in the oven for 12 to 15 minutes, depending on the thickness of the fillet. The fish is done when the flesh is opaque and when it flakes very slightly when prodded with a fork. Remove it immediately from the pan and place it on a serving platter or plates. Season with salt and pepper to taste. Sprinkle with the saba, or pass it at the table. Serve at once.

I started flash-roasting fish after reading Theresa Laursen's cookbook, *From Bangkok to Bali.* Her recipe for Asian-flavored flash-roasted salmon got me started, and now I often use her technique. I used to use a large cast-iron frying pan, and any good heavy metal pan—whether iron, aluminum, or steel—will work as long as the pan has a metal (not plastic or nylon) handle that can take intense heat and preheating. I now use an oval frying pan made by Calphalon (they call it a fajita pan). This pan is lighter on the wrist, and because the oval surface is perpendicular to the handle, it can hold a whole fish and still fit in a standard 27-inch oven. The dark hard-anodized aluminum conducts heat extremely well, needs little preheating time to come to temperature, and gives the fish a great crust. Note that any pan with a non-stick finish is a poor choice for this method because nonstick coatings are not made for high heat.

TURBOT WITH FENNEL, POTATOES, OLIVES, AND LEMON

SERVES 4

APPARENTLY MOST OF THE FLATFISH sold as turbot in the United States is not the same variety as the prized turbot one finds in the Mediterranean, but they still taste very good. If you should find turbot fillets at your fish store, don't hesitate to buy them, because this dish is well worth cooking.

1 whole fennel bulb, thinly sliced

6 Yukon Gold potatoes, peeled and thinly sliced

½ cup pitted and halved black Spanish olives

1 ripe tomato, coarsely diced

1 large shallot, finely chopped

Grated zest and juice of 1 lemon

4 turbot fillets (about 3½ pounds)

¼ cup leafy green and grassy olive oil

Coarse sea salt and freshly ground black pepper, to taste

1 lemon, cut into quarters

PREHEAT the oven to 475°F.

OIL a large baking dish or shallow casserole, and layer the ingredients in it in the order given, ending with the fish drizzled with the olive oil, salt, and pepper. Make sure to drizzle oil over any exposed vegetables as well.

USING a generous amount of aluminum foil, completely wrap the baking dish so that it's airtight (I use two or three layers, wrapping from top to bottom and then from bottom to top). The goal here is to steam-roast the fish with all the aromatics, and not to allow any of the juices to escape.

ROAST for 45 minutes. Then uncover the pan and cook for an additional 10 minutes to reduce and intensify the flavors of the liquid. Put the fish, potatoes, tomatoes, fennel, and olives on a serving platter. If any juices remain, pour them into a small saucepan and further reduce them over high heat if necessary. Pour the juices over the fish, and serve, along with the lemon wedges.

FLASH-ROASTED TURBOT FILLET

You can also flash-roast turbot fillet by preheating a cast-iron pan, rubbing the fillet with olive oil on both sides, and roasting it for 15 minutes at 450°F. Flash-roasting the fish produces a very different flavor from steam-roasting it with aromatics—the fish is more delicate and buttery, with an almost custard-like texture.

STEAM-ROASTING WHOLE RED SNAPPER WITH LICORICE FLAVORS

Wash and thinly slice a whole head of fennel (fronds and all), along with a whole head of celery (including the leaves), and place a cleaned and scaled red snapper on this bed of green vegetables in a shallow glass or porcelain baking dish. Add a good splash of French licorice-flavored liqueur, such as Pastis or Pernod, and cover the pan very tightly with aluminum foil (see page 152 for wrapping directions). The fish will be cooked in about 45 minutes, and perfumed with complex licorice flavors. After you've removed the cooked fish and the cooked vegetables, you can reduce the juices left in the pan, add a spoonful of cream off the heat, and pour this sauce over the fish.

YOGURT-MARINATED GRILLED SWORDFISH STEAKS

SERVES 6

WHILE THESE ARE most delicious when cooked on an outdoor grill, you could also use a broiler or a stovetop grill pan. I like to serve the swordfish on a bed of rice or couscous, and I often grill some vegetables on the side as the fish cooks. It's also very good on a bed of mixed salad greens tossed with Dione Lucas's French Dressing (page 83). Turkish chili paste is a potent and fiery blend that comes in a glass jar and can be found in Near Eastern groceries. You can substitute any hot pepper such as hot paprika, or chili paste or powder.

Three 1-pound swordfish steaks

Marinade

¼ cup whole-milk yogurt

¼ cup leafy green and grassy olive oil

1½ teaspoons Turkish chili paste or hot paprika

Juice of 1 lemon

2 teaspoons chopped fresh mint leaves *or* 1 teaspoon dried mint

¼ cup finely chopped mild onion

Garnish

Lemon wedges

Leafy green and grassy olive oil to pass at the table

CUT each swordfish steak in half down the center to make six ½-pound serving portions. Combine all the ingredients for the marinade in a large shallow nonreactive dish, such as a glass baking dish. Add the fish and spread the marinade over it. Cover with a lid or plastic wrap and refrigerate for 1 hour. (If you marinate fish for a longer period, it "cooks" in the marinade and becomes unpalatably mushy.)

REMOVE the fish from the refrigerator and allow it to come to room temperature. Drain off any excess marinade.

HEAT an outdoor grill or a stovetop grill pan to high heat. Oil the cooking surface very lightly, and grill the fish (covered if on an outdoor kettle grill) for 5 to 7 minutes per side. The fish is done when it is slightly charred, opaque, and just beginning to flake.

SERVE with lemon wedges, and pass the olive oil to drizzle on top.

PAN-FRIED TROUT WITH POLENTA CRUST AND ALMONDS

SERVES 4

CLASSIC TROUT AMANDINE is prepared like this, except that it relies on butter for flavor. I find that olive oil imparts a terrific flavor variation. To make *Chicken or Turkey Tenders with Polenta Crust and Almonds,* the procedure is nearly the same: First dredge the cutlets (scallops of breast meat) in a beaten egg, and then in the polenta. Lay them flat in the pan just like the trout, and do check to make sure they are cooked through before serving—there should be no trace of pink with poultry.

I like to serve this with plain rice and a flavorful green salad made with lots of different greens and a garlic-rich dressing.

1 cup instant polenta

2 whole trout, split and boned, rinsed and patted dry

2 tablespoons olive-y and peppery olive oil

1 lemon, cut into 4 wedges

⅔ cup slivered blanched almonds

POUR the polenta onto a piece of parchment paper, waxed paper, or a plate, and dredge each piece of trout in the polenta, coating both sides. Shake off the excess.

HEAT a cast-iron frying pan, and when it is hot, add 1 tablespoon of the olive oil. When the oil is hot, add the fish. Brown the fish on both sides, about 4 minutes per side. Put one piece on each plate, along with a wedge of lemon.

POUR off any fat in the pan. Immediately heat the remaining 1 tablespoon olive oil in the same pan, and brown the almonds over medium-high heat, stirring constantly as they start to brown. As soon as they are golden and aromatic, pour the almonds and oil over the fish, and serve.

YELLOWFIN TUNA POACHED IN OLIVE OIL

SERVES 2 TO 3

I HAD ORDERED OLIVE OIL–poached fish in restaurants, but I had never tried to make it at home until I started working on this book. It was hard to use such a quantity of good oil in one fell swoop, but the results convinced me that poaching fresh tuna in olive oil is well worth it. The fish comes out not at all greasy, but outstandingly moist and delicate in texture, with a pure flavor unmatched by any other cooking method. The amount of olive oil you use will be determined by the size of the fish and the size of your pan. Each time I do this, I look for the deepest pan that will closely accommodate the fish I've bought. You want depth so that the oil won't overflow, and you want as little space around the fish as possible so as to conserve the amount of oil you'll need; the aim is to have enough oil to half-submerge the fish. I've found a Windsor saucepan, which has flaring sides, or other small saucepan is ideal, as is a small enameled cast-iron Dutch oven or a small braising pan. Sauté pans are deep enough, but tend to be larger in diameter than necessary, which means you have to use a lot more oil to get some depth. The key here is to cook the fish over *low* heat—not to deep-fry it.

¾ pound yellowfin tuna loin steak (about 1 inch thick)

1 to 1½ cups fruity and fragrant olive oil

Lemon Mayonnaise (page 66) or lemon wedges and fruity and fragrant olive oil to drizzle

Coarse sea salt and freshly ground black pepper, to taste

RINSE the fish and pat it dry. Cut off any skin that may be attached. Cut off a tiny shred of fish to use to test the oil's heat, or have ready some bread cut into tiny bits.

GENTLY heat a deep wide saucepan or sauté pan that is just larger than the fish; then add the oil. After 2 to 3 minutes, test the oil by dropping a shred of fish or a crumb of bread into it. If the oil immediately bubbles around the food and sizzles softly, the oil is ready.

IMMEDIATELY lower the fish into the oil (it should reach halfway up the sides of the fish). Poach the fish in the oil over low heat for about 4 minutes. The sound of the sizzle should be like a whisper. Using tongs, turn the fish and poach the other side for 2 minutes. At this point, the tuna will have a small rare streak down the center, which is ideal in my view. But if you prefer more well-done tuna, you can cook it slightly longer, taking great care not to overcook and dry out the fish.

USING the tongs, remove the fish and lay it on a piece of paper towel to drain. Pat the top side with another piece of paper towel. Lay the fish on a cutting board and divide it into 2 or 3 pieces, depending on how many people you are serving. Place the fish on individual plates and serve topped with Lemon Mayonnaise, or with wedges of fresh lemon and more olive oil to drizzle on the fish at the table. Season with salt and pepper.

SEARED SCALLOPS ON CHICKPEA CREPES

SERVES 4

THIS ABSOLUTELY luscious combination of flavors makes it well worth the trouble to seek out Italian chickpea flour from an Italian specialty store or to mail-order it from Corti Brothers. Sea scallops are the big scallops, with a rich meaty texture and flavor. I make the crepes first and keep them warm in a low oven while I fast-cook the scallops to layer on top. With an appetizer to start and a green salad course to follow, this is a luxurious and festive company meal. Note that you need to mix the crepe batter an hour before cooking the crepes (it's enough batter for 6 large crepes, which leaves room for error).

For the chickpea crepes

1 cup Italian chickpea flour

1¾ cups water

Coarse sea salt and freshly ground black pepper, to taste

6 tablespoons leafy green and grassy olive oil

For the scallops

1 pound sea scallops

½ teaspoon coarse sea salt

¼ teaspoon freshly ground black pepper

3 tablespoons leafy green and grassy olive oil, plus more for serving at the table

2 cloves garlic, peeled and finely chopped

4 teaspoons chopped fresh thyme leaves

Grated zest of 1 lemon and some of its juice

PREPARE the crepes: In a mixing bowl, beat together the chickpea flour, water, salt and pepper, and olive oil. Let the batter sit for 1 hour at room temperature.

PREHEAT a well-seasoned crepe pan or other frying pan, and add a thin layer of olive oil to coat the hot pan. Ladle on enough of the crepe batter to make 1 big thin crepe, tilting and swirling the pan to coat it with a thin layer of batter. When the surface is pocked with tiny holes and the underside is brown and crisp, about 2 minutes, use a wide spatula to detach and flip the crepe to cook the other side. When the crepe is cooked, place it on a dinner plate, and put the plate in a warm oven set at the lowest temperature possible. Repeat for the rest of the batter, reserving or discarding the extra crepes.

PREPARE the scallops: Season the scallops on all sides with the salt and pepper. Heat the oil in a preheated pan over medium-low heat, and cook the garlic until limp, about 3 minutes. Remove the garlic with a slotted spoon and place it in a small bowl. Add the thyme leaves and toss with the garlic.

ADD the scallops to the frying pan and raise the heat to medium-high. Cook until golden brown and caramelized, about 1 minute per side. Remove the pan from the heat, return the garlic/thyme mixture to the pan, and add the lemon zest and a spoonful or two of lemon juice.

SPOON a quarter of the scallops and their juices onto a giant crepe on each dinner plate. Serve at once, passing olive oil to drizzle at the table.

Carpineto®

Olio
ExtraVergine
di Oliva
EXTRA VIRGIN
OLIVE OIL

FIRST COLD PRESSED

PRODUCED AND BOTTLED BY
Carpineto s.n.c.
VIA DUDDA 17/B
GREVE IN CHIANTI
ITALY

PRODUCT OF ITALY

NET CONT 500ML (16.9 FL OZ)

LEMON THYME ROAST CHICKEN WITH CARAMELIZED ROASTED VEGETABLES

SERVES 4

EVERY COOK I KNOW loves his or her own roast chicken. While I don't know if this one is the best in the world, it's certainly one we're very fond of. You can buy fresh lemon thyme in most super-market produce sections, but if you can't find it, use any fresh thyme—or for a completely different flavor, fresh sage leaves. I find that hormone-free air-chilled chickens (this 3-pound size is often labeled "fryer") taste far better than the conventional kind; in my area they can be found in the big chain supermarkets as well as in the alternative coops. You can also use this recipe for larger roasting chickens, cooking a bigger bird for 45 minutes at 450°F, and then for about another 45 minutes at 375°F, or until the leg moves easily, there is no trace of pink at the bone, and the chicken is cooked through. For a bigger bird, cut the vegetables in large wedges (since they'll cook longer), and double the amount of vegetables to fill a larger pan.

This chicken tastes best when roasted in either a cast-iron frying pan or a shallow enameled cast-iron roasting pan such as those made by Le Creuset. However, although I think the way cast iron holds heat contributes to the caramelization of the vegetables, I've also cooked this successfully in large ceramic and glass gratin dishes.

---

1 3-pound chicken, hormone-free if possible

8 to 12 large sprigs lemon thyme or plain thyme *or* 8 to 10 fresh sage leaves

1 lemon, cut in half

1 large onion, peeled and cut into 8 wedges

2 tablespoons leafy green and grassy olive oil, plus more to pass at the table

1 garnet yam, washed, peeled, and cut into ½-inch-thick slices

PREHEAT the oven to 450°F, and set the rack slightly above the middle of the oven.

WASH and dry the chicken, removing the innards and cutting off any big lumps of fat. Setting the chicken on a cutting board, use both hands to loosen the skin from the breast, working from the neck downward, gently pushing your fingers between skin and meat to make a pocket. Stuff this pocket on each side with 2 or 3 sprigs of lemon thyme, or with most of the fresh sage leaves. Stuff the interior of the bird with both lemon halves, as

2 to 4 Yukon Gold potatoes, washed, peeled, and cut into ½-inch-thick slices

2 to 3 fat carrots, washed, peeled, and cut into ½-inch-thick rounds

4 to 5 cloves garlic, unpeeled

Coarse sea salt and freshly ground black pepper, to taste

1 teaspoon Fig "Balsamico" Agrodolce (page 64) or balsamic vinegar

many more sprigs of lemon thyme as you can fit inside (or with 4 fresh sage leaves), and 1 or 2 of the onion wedges.

LIGHTLY grease the pan with some of the olive oil. Arrange the remaining onion wedges and any remaining herb sprigs on the bottom of the pan to make a bed for the chicken. Set the bird on the bed, and surround it with the slices of yam, potato, and carrot and the unpeeled garlic cloves. Pour some of the remaining olive oil over the chicken, using your hands to spread it over all the skin. Drizzle any olive oil that's left over the vegetables.

SPRINKLE salt and pepper over all, and roast for 30 minutes, basting every 15 minutes or so, using a spoon to collect and drizzle the juices over both chicken and vegetables. Turn the vegetables once during the cooking process. Then lower the heat to 375°F and roast for another 20 to 30 minutes, continuing to baste regularly, until the chicken is not pink anywhere near the thigh bone (check with the tip of a sharp knife).

SPRINKLE the Fig "Balsamico" over the top of the bird, and roast for an additional 5 minutes to glaze it. Pour the pan liquids into a defatting pitcher, and reserve the fat-free pan juices to use as a sauce. Let the chicken rest for 10 minutes before carving.

SERVE the chicken with the roast vegetables, squeezing the garlic out from their papery skins and putting a portion of this garlic paste on each plate. Pass the pan juices, along with a cruet of oil, to drizzle over the chicken.

HONEY-GLAZED ROLLED TURKEY BREAST WITH HERBS AND POTATOES

SERVES 4 TO 8

THIS IS ONE OF THOSE DISHES that taste wonderful hot or cold, so it's a good choice for a buffet. Don't be put off by the necessity of boning the turkey—it's not hard to do, and you needn't worry too much about perfection because as the meat gets rolled around the herb paste, any errors are concealed. When you slice the meat, it reveals pretty spirals of herbs in each piece. This turkey meat is moist and flavorful, with a sweetness from the honey that also permeates the potatoes. The honey coats the skin and makes it cook to a caramelized crispness; it also seems to seal in flavor.

Recently I found something labeled "Roaster Chicken Breast" in my grocery store—it was skin-on and huge (much bigger than the conventional chicken breast since it was from a roasting chicken). I tried boning it, rolling it around the herb paste, and trussing it as if it were turkey. It was delicious, and the only change from the recipe as written here is that it takes only about 30 minutes of roasting before the very large rolled chicken breast is cooked through.

1 fresh whole or half turkey breast, boned or bone-in (a whole bone-in breast weights 6½ to 8½ pounds), skin attached

¼ cup fresh rosemary needles

¼ cup fresh tarragon leaves

¼ cup fresh oregano or thyme leaves

⅓ cup fruity and fragrant olive oil, plus more to drizzle before roasting

6 to 8 Yukon Gold potatoes, washed and cut in half

Coarse sea salt and freshly ground black pepper, to taste

PREHEAT the oven to 450°F.

IF the turkey breast is bone-in, rinse and cut off the wings and remove the pop-up thermometer, if there is one. Bone the turkey breast, using a sharp boning knife and trying to keep the meat in one large piece per side. Leave the skin on the meat. If you should end up with two turkey breast halves, don't worry—you can stuff and roll each one separately and cook them side by side. (Save the carcass with meat clinging to it to make turkey stock.)

COMBINE the rosemary, tarragon, oregano, and olive oil in a food processor and process to make a fairly thick paste. Spread out the turkey, skin side

1 to 2 heaping tablespoons dark flavorful honey, such as chestnut, pine, or clover

down, and spread most of the herb mixture over the meat. Turn the meat over and push the rest of the herb paste under the skin. Lightly oil a baking dish or roasting pan. Roll up the turkey, keeping the skin on the outside. If, and this is unlikely, it seems that your roll may fall apart, tie it with kitchen string or thread toothpicks like staples along the seam. Place the turkey roll, seam side down, in the center of the pan. Arrange the potato halves around the turkey, and drizzle everything with olive oil and salt and pepper. Pour about 1 inch of water into the pan.

BAKE, basting every 15 minutes or so, until done, 45 to 60 minutes. When the turkey is cooked, drizzle the honey over the turkey and potatoes, and bake an additional 5 minutes.

REMOVE the pan from the oven and let the meat rest for 10 minutes before slicing and serving it.

SHARPENING KNIVES

A sharp knife is safer than a dull one, because you'll use it with more care and less effort. Knives need sharpening, or more properly realigning, after almost every hard use. While there are any number of different tools for this purpose, from electric sharpeners to stones and steels, I like my manual pull-through knife sharpener the best. It's small, so it doesn't take up lots of drawer space, and it's impossible to use incorrectly because the slots are angled so precisely. I've used a number of different brands, and they've all worked well. At less than $25, a manual knife sharpener is a good investment.

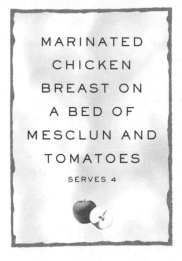

MARINATED CHICKEN BREAST ON A BED OF MESCLUN AND TOMATOES

SERVES 4

VIANA LA PLACE and Evan Kleiman's book *Cucina Rustica* taught me that marinating boneless skinless chicken breasts in olive oil and herbs produces lots of flavor and keeps the meat moist. I usually marinate the chicken while I prepare a side vegetable or enjoy a glass of wine, and I still have time to get dinner on the table within half an hour. When I'm more organized, I start the chicken marinating the night before. Either way, it's always delicious.

You have a choice about pounding the chicken fillets into paillards: If you do, the chicken will cook even faster, and it will fill up most of the plate. If you don't pound the meat, you'll need to be more careful about checking that it is not pink in the center; on the other hand, it will be moister.

You can change the flavor of the marinade by using fresh oregano and fresh thyme; you can also serve the chicken on a bed of rice or polenta.

2 whole boneless, skinless chicken breasts

For the marinade

Grated zest and juice of 1 lemon

½ cup fruity and fragrant olive oil

Coarse sea salt and freshly ground black pepper, to taste

5 to 7 fresh basil leaves

1 teaspoon fresh tarragon leaves *or* 1 tablespoon dried tarragon

1 teaspoon fresh sage leaves *or* 1 tablespoon dried sage

DIVIDE each whole chicken breast into two parts. Using a sharp knife and working horizontally, cut into the thicker part of the meat to make it even in thickness with the rest of the meat. By not cutting all the way through, you will have formed a scallop, which you can open out to lie flat. Do this with all 4 pieces.

TO create a paillard (see headnote), put each piece of meat between two sheets of waxed paper, and using a flat meat pounder or the bottom of a wine bottle, pound from the center outward to create a flat piece that's about ¼ inch thick.

For serving

4 cups mesclun or other mixed baby salad greens, washed and dried

4 ripe tomatoes, coarsely chopped

3 tablespoons fruity and fragrant olive oil

1 tablespoon balsamic vinegar

MIX the lemon zest and juice with all the rest of the marinade ingredients in a large shallow bowl, such as a soup bowl. Dip each piece of flattened chicken in the marinade to coat it thoroughly. After the pieces have been coated on both sides, layer them in the marinade bowl and let sit for about 15 minutes at room temperature, or covered and refrigerated overnight.

PREPARE a bed of mesclun on a serving platter or on individual dinner plates.

PREHEAT a heavy frying pan or grill pan on the stove. When the edges of the pan are hot to the touch, add 1 tablespoon of the marinade and let it cook for about 1 minute, or until fragrant and thin. Now lay the marinated chicken in the pan, discarding all the rest of the marinade. Cook the chicken on both sides until golden and flecked with dark spots (if the pieces were pounded, they'll cook very, very quickly and you'll need to do them in batches). Cut into a piece of chicken to make sure it is cooked through. Immediately place the warm chicken on the bed of greens. Scatter the tomato cubes on top of the meat, and drizzle the olive oil and balsamic vinegar over all. Serve at once.

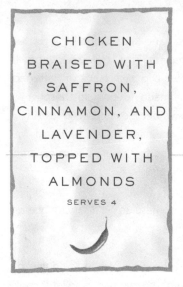

CHICKEN BRAISED WITH SAFFRON, CINNAMON, AND LAVENDER, TOPPED WITH ALMONDS

SERVES 4

BASED ON A LIST OF ingredients in an anonymous 13th-century Andalusian cookbook, this recipe reflects the way aromatic spices were used in Islamic Spain. I think they create an exotic yet homey dinner in cold or wet weather. You can buy dried lavender buds in stores that sell bulk teas and spices, or by mail (see the Resources section); make sure they are pesticide-free and fit for human consumption. The flavor of this dish improves over time, so it's a good candidate for making ahead and reheating, or for leftovers for later in the week. Serve it over rice, couscous, Olive Oil and Rosemary Mashed Potatoes (page 188), or Polenta (page 186).

2 tablespoons olive-y and peppery olive oil

4 whole chicken legs, thigh and drumstick separated *or* 1 whole chicken, cut up

2 small onions, chopped

1 teaspoon ground cinnamon

1 teaspoon ground coriander

Coarse sea salt and freshly ground black pepper, to taste

½ cup dry sherry or Marsala

½ teaspoon saffron threads dissolved in 1 tablespoon very hot water

½ cup water

2 tablespoons Fig "Balsamico" Agrodolce (page 64) or balsamic vinegar

½ cup vodka

HEAT a large heavy Dutch oven or braising pot over medium heat until the pot's edges are warm to the touch; then add the olive oil. When the oil is hot and shimmery and is beginning to thin and flow, add the pieces of chicken, skin side down, until the floor of the pot is filled. Don't overcrowd the pot. You will need to brown the chicken in at least two batches unless your pan is very large. As pieces brown, turn them and brown the other side. Remove the browned pieces and hold them on a platter. When all of the chicken is browned, drain off all but a very thin film of fat and oil.

ADD the onions to the pot and cook over low heat until limp and translucent, 5 to 10 minutes. Then add the spices and cook for another minute or two. Mix in the sherry, saffron water, and Fig "Balsamico," and return the chicken to the pot. Cover tightly and let cook slowly, over the lowest possible heat, turning once, for 45 minutes or until just cooked through.

1 heaping tablespoon dried
lavender buds

1 tablespoon honey

1 cup chopped toasted almonds
(see page 61)

CAREFUL!

Watch the vodka closely when
you're heating it—you don't
want it to boil. Keep the pot lid
handy, and if the alcohol combusts, quickly clamp the lid on
the pot to smother the flames.

REMOVE the chicken pieces, and pour the excess
fat into a defatting pitcher or scoop it off with a
spoon. (If you are serving the chicken later in the
day or the next day, you can chill the liquid and
then remove the hardened fat with a spoon.)
There will be about 1¼ cups liquid.

ABOUT 20 minutes before serving time, heat the
vodka to just below boiling in a small pan. Take it
off the heat and add the lavender buds. Allow to
steep for 15 minutes. Then strain out and discard
the flowers, and add the vodka to the defatted pan
juices. Heat the juices to cook off the alcohol, 3 to
4 minutes.

RETURN the chicken and its sauce to the pot and
heat gently until warmed through. Pour the honey
over the top, add the toasted almonds, and serve.

SPANISH RICE WITH MIXED SAUSAGES

SERVES 4 TO 6

I LOVE CHINESE-STYLE sausages! Labeled Kam Yen Jan, Chinese-Style Sausages, Lap Xuong Thuong Hang, or Lop Cheung, they're made in the U.S. and are sold in 1-pound packages. They're widely available—I've found them in every Chinese grocery store I've ever been in, even in small towns in New England. They are kept in the refrigerator or freezer section, and I usually buy a couple of packages and keep a supply in my home freezer. They are sweet and savory at the same time, and are unique in my experience because they are cooked by steaming rather than frying. If you don't have Chinese sausages, you can also make this dish with a wide variety of other sausage types—each will contribute its own unique flavor. I've tried it with Bruce Aidells' chicken and apple sausages, with his chorizo (you can find these at Costco, among other places), and with kielbasa. The dish is very good with a combination of different sausages, especially when half are Chinese-style and the rest are another kind. Just remember to cook whatever sausages you use thoroughly before adding them to the rice, unless they are precooked.

Bomba is definitely the best rice for this dish; use Arborio only if you don't have Bomba. You can order Bomba rice from La Tienda or The Spanish Table (see the Resources section).

You can vary the taste of this dish by using the optional ingredients—they add a depth of flavor.

1 to 1½ pounds Chinese and other sausages

2 tablespoons fruity and fragrant olive oil

1 onion (Vidalia or other sweet onion, if possible), coarsely chopped

2 cloves garlic, peeled, mashed, and chopped

¾ cup finely chopped flat-leaf parsley leaves

THOROUGHLY cook the sausages: Chinese-style sausages are best cooked in a steamer over boiling water for 15 minutes. Most chicken sausage is precooked and needs no additional cooking; the same is true of kielbasa. Slice all the sausages thinly on the diagonal with a sharp knife. Set aside.

IN an earthenware *cazuela* (see page 169), a sauté pan, a large shallow skillet, or a braising pot, gently heat the olive oil over medium heat until it shimmers. Add the onion and garlic, and slowly cook

½ teaspoon ground cinnamon

1 ripe tomato, chopped
(optional)

4 leaves fresh sage, finely
chopped (optional)

Generous pinch saffron threads
(optional)

3 cups chicken stock or water

½ teaspoon coarse sea salt

1 cup Bomba or Arborio rice

them down until they are limp but not brown, 3 to
5 minutes. Add the parsley and cinnamon, and the
tomato, sage, and saffron if using, and stir. Add the
stock and heat until nearly boiling. Add the salt and
the rice, and stir to combine.

DISTRIBUTE the sausage slices over the surface
of the dish. Reduce the heat to a simmer and cook,
uncovered, without stirring, for 30 to 40 minutes
or until the rice is cooked through. The timing will
vary depending on the pot that is used—this timing
is for a *cazuela*.

SERVE immediately.

CAZUELAS

A *cazuela* is a shallow earthenware cooking pot, and food cooked in it seems to have a different texture than food cooked in metal pans. I particularly like to cook rice dishes in *cazuelas*—it's what they were made for. You can buy a *cazuela* remarkably inexpensively from La Tienda or The Spanish Table. Most people advise using a flame-tamer under a stovetop clay pot; it is certainly essential with an electric cooktop. I find, however, that I can use a *cazuela* directly on a gas flame, as long as I heat it up slowly from room temperature and never take it directly from refrigerator to range.

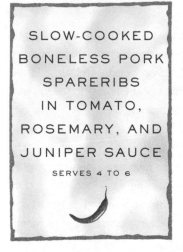

SLOW-COOKED
BONELESS PORK
SPARERIBS
IN TOMATO,
ROSEMARY, AND
JUNIPER SAUCE

SERVES 4 TO 6

THIS BRAISE OF HEARTY FLAVORS makes a great combination with soft polenta (page 186) or rosemary mashed potatoes (page 188). I owe the idea of combining pork with juniper berries to Marcella Hazan. Juniper berries can be surprisingly hard to find; I buy mine in a food coop that sells spices in bulk, but they are also available from specialty stores such as A Cook's Wares and from spice merchants such as Penzey's. Muir Glen makes organic fire-roasted crushed tomatoes. Their distinctive taste is worth seeking out, but any good-quality canned crushed tomatoes will serve. This is a dish that tastes best when cooked in an enameled cast-iron Dutch oven, such as those made by Le Creuset.

I always try to cook this dish in advance because the flavor improves with age and because removing the fat is easier after chilling. Then all I have to do to finish dinner on a busy night is make the starch and a salad. This dish also freezes well.

2 tablespoons olive-y and peppery olive oil

½ cup finely chopped mild onion

1½ pounds boneless "country-style" pork spareribs, cut into 1½- to 2-inch cubes

½ cup dry vermouth or gin

2 tablespoons red wine vinegar

One 28-ounce can fire-roasted crushed tomatoes or other crushed tomatoes

30 juniper berries

3 anchovies

3 tablespoons fresh rosemary needles

HEAT a braising pan or a Dutch oven, and then add the oil and heat it until it shimmers. Add the onion and cook over low to medium heat until translucent, about 5 minutes. Then raise the heat to medium-high, add the meat, and brown on all sides, about 25 minutes.

ADD the vermouth and vinegar, and turn the heat up slightly for a minute or two to evaporate the fumes. Add the tomatoes and lower the heat.

CRUSH the juniper berries in a mortar and pestle, or put them in a plastic bag and crush them with a hammer or meat pounder. Pound the crushed berries with the anchovies and rosemary needles to make a coarse paste. Add this to the pot.

Coarse sea salt and freshly ground black pepper, to taste

1 to 2 cups water

SPRINKLE salt to taste and a generous grinding of black pepper over the meat, and add 1 cup of the water. Cover and cook over very low heat for 1½ to 2 hours, or until the meat is very tender. Check the pot periodically to see if you need to add more water to prevent the stew from sticking or burning. If you are cooking it in a good heavy pot and can set the burner to a very low temperature, it probably won't be necessary.

WHEN the meat is done, remove it with a slotted spoon and keep it warm. Cook the tomato broth until it is reduced to a thick sauce (about one third of its previous volume), about 10 minutes. If you are serving the stew immediately, defat the sauce with a spoon. Otherwise, refrigerate the meat and the sauce separately overnight, and remove the hardened fat with a knife the next day. Return the meat to the sauce, reheat it gently, and serve.

HEATING THE PAN BEFORE ADDING THE OIL

Because the heat closes the pores of the metal, which means that food proteins can't get caught in it, preheating the pan before you heat the oil goes a long way toward preventing food from sticking. And because the pan's heat thins the oil, allowing it to cover more surface, you use less oil when cooking in a preheated pan.

Put the pan on the heat, and heat it over medium heat until the sides of the pan feel hot to a quick touch. (Hot, not smoking!) Add the oil to the hot pan and let it heat for a few seconds, until it thins, shimmers, and smells fragrant, or until a drop of water or shred of food makes it sizzle. Now add the food to be cooked.

Learning to heat the pan first was a significant step forward in my own cooking development, and it went a long way toward pleasing the dishwasher in my life. Pans that I'd formerly disdained as being too prone to sticking suddenly became my favorites, and the foods I cooked tasted better because they had a chance to develop a good outer crust.

CHARCOAL-GRILLED BUTTERFLIED LEG OF LAMB, TURKISH STYLE

SERVES 8

EASY TO PREPARE AND GUARANTEED to wow your guests, this festive grill meal has an exotic yet friendly flavor. Get your butcher to bone, butterfly, and trim the lamb to make one fairly even slab, or grab your sharpest knives and do it yourself. Start marinating the lamb in the morning of the night you plan to grill. If you can't charcoal-grill, try this under a broiler, setting the pan as close to the heating element as possible.

Try this with Grilled Side Vegetables (page 184) for a whole grilled meal.

This marinade is also good with other meats to be grilled, such as butterflied whole chickens, cubes of lamb on skewers, or (as one of the testers reported) ground lamb "lamburgers."

One 5- to 7-pound leg of lamb, boned and butterflied

Turkish marinade

¼ cup whole-milk plain yogurt (or sheep's-milk yogurt if you can get it)

¼ cup olive-y and peppery olive oil

10 cloves garlic, peeled and finely minced

2 tablespoons Turkish chili paste (available in Middle Eastern groceries) or 2 teaspoons hot paprika mixed with 2 tablespoons tomato paste

Juice of 1 lemon, plus the squeezed lemon cut into wedges

2 teaspoons fresh or dried mint leaves

2 teaspoons fresh thyme leaves

PLACE the butterflied lamb in a flat pan such as a roasting pan. Mix all the marinade ingredients together, and spread it on both sides of the lamb. Cover with plastic wrap, and refrigerate for at least 3 hours and preferably for 6 to 8 hours. Bring to room temperature before grilling.

PREPARE and clean the grill and grate, if necessary. Lightly oil the grate. Light the charcoal and let it burn until it is gray and ashed over. Distribute the hot coals in two layers in half the grill area and in a lower single layer in the other half. Cover the grill for 5 to 10 minutes to distribute the heat. Then carefully place the slab of lamb over the highest heat (the double layer of coals) to sear it. Cover and cook for 10 minutes. Check the meat—it will probably be ready to turn. It should have small char marks and a cooked aroma. After turning it, cook the meat for another 10 to 15 minutes on the lower heat. When the meat is pinkish in the center, remove it from the grill, let it rest for 10 minutes, then slice and serve.

BUTTERFLIED WHOLE CHICKEN UNDER A BRICK, TURKISH STYLE

The Turkish marinade (page 172) works very well with chicken, too. To butterfly a chicken, cut along both sides of the backbone with poultry shears or a sharp knife, and remove the backbone. Lay the chicken flat on a cutting board, and make small cuts along the shoulder and thigh to allow the chicken to lie flat. Cover with the marinade. Loosen the skin of the breast with your fingers by putting your hand between skin and meat, gradually pulling them apart. Use a small spatula or your fingers to apply marinade under the skin.

Wrap a brick or a cast-iron frying pan with aluminum foil, and place it on the bird to keep it flat on the grill, skin side down.

Follow the grilling instructions for the lamb, adjusting the timing to ensure that the chicken is cooked through without any traces of pink, 25 to 30 minutes in all. The timing will depend on the size of the bird and the heat of the fire. Carefully cut into the leg to determine doneness—if there is any trace of pink, keep cooking until done.

NEI NOSTRI OLIVETA
SI PRATICA L'ANTICA
COLTURA TRADIZIONALE

Imbottigliato
L. il   22-11-00

Da consumarsi
preferibilmente
entro il   22-05-02

battglian   122H

NON DISPERDERE NELL'AMBIENTE

MARINATED LAMB CHOPS WITH THYME AND OREGANO

SERVES 4

MARINATING MEAT AND POULTRY in olive oil, wine, and herbs turns up the flavor volume every time. I'm so glad that even the largest chain supermarkets now sell little plastic boxes of fresh herbs—their intense fragrance makes such a difference. If you can get lean little loin or rib lamb chops, you'll find their delicate flavor goes well with this preparation method. If all you can find are large shoulder chops, just cut off all the visible fat. If you have the time, marinating for at least an hour will yield the best results. Serve the chops on a mound of fresh baby spinach that has been dressed with balsamic vinegar and a fruity olive oil, or with mashed potatoes (page 188) or soft polenta (page 186).

¼ cup dry red wine

Juice of 1 lemon

1 shallot, finely chopped

3 cloves garlic, peeled and finely chopped

3 tablespoons chopped fresh thyme leaves

1 tablespoon chopped fresh oregano leaves

½ cup fruity and fragrant olive oil

2 pounds loin lamb chops

Coarse sea salt and freshly ground black pepper, to taste

MIX the wine, lemon juice, shallot, and garlic together in a blender, a glass jar, or a mortar. Add the thyme and oregano, crushing the leaves with the pestle if using. Then slowly add the olive oil, using the blender or mortar to roughly emulsify it. If using a jar, just shake the mixture well.

ARRANGE the lamb chops in a shallow nonreactive dish, and pour the marinade over them. Turn the meat once or twice to make sure it is coated, and let it sit in the marinade at room temperature for up to 1 hour; if you are marinading them for a longer period, cover and refrigerate. Bring to room temperature before cooking.

HEAT a grill pan, an outdoor charcoal or gas grill, or a heavy cast-iron frying pan until very hot. If using a pan on the stove, sprinkle the hot pan surface with a spoonful of coarse sea salt. Pick up each chop and let any excess marinade drain back into the dish. Lay the chops on the grill or pan and cook each side rapidly over high heat, 4 to 5 minutes per side, until the outside is browned and crisp and the interior is only slightly pink (or to taste). Grind fresh pepper over the meat before serving.

Vegetables
and side dishes

OVEN-ROASTED ASPARAGUS

SERVES 4

ASPARAGUS GAIN a depth of flavor from the intense heat of the oven in this preparation. This is magnified if you use a cast-iron frying pan because it holds the heat.

Oven-roasted asparagus can be the basis for a wonderful spring pasta dish: *Pasta with Oven-Roasted Asparagus and Cheese.* Instead of roasting the asparagus whole, cut them on the diagonal into 1-inch pieces, which will roast in 5 to 8 minutes. While the asparagus pieces roast, bring a large pot of salted water to a boil and cook a pound of pasta. (I like gemelli, because they are approximately the same size and shape as the cut asparagus.) After draining the cooked pasta, mix in the roasted asparagus pieces, their juices, some lemon zest, and olive oil. Generously grate Parmesan cheese over all.

1 pound fresh asparagus

2 tablespoons fruity and fragrant olive oil or lemon-infused olive oil

Coarse sea salt and freshly ground black pepper, to taste

Fresh lemon zest *or* freshly grated Parmesan cheese (optional)

I often roast asparagus at the same time that I am preparing Flash-Roasted Salmon (page 150), using two frying pans and both oven shelves for an almost-instant dinner. With a basket of good bread and a salad, I can have dinner on the table less than 15 minutes after entering the kitchen!

PREHEAT the oven to 500°F, and preheat a cast-iron frying pan or a roasting pan in the oven.

WASH and drain the asparagus, snapping or cutting off any woody ends. Carefully remove the hot frying pan from the oven, and put a little of the olive oil in the pan; it should thin immediately from the heat of the pan. Place the asparagus on top of the oil, and pour the rest of the oil over the asparagus. Toss or shake the pan until all the stalks are coated with oil, and put the pan back in the hot oven. Roast for 10 to 15 minutes, shaking the pan occasionally to make sure the asparagus aren't sticking. After 10 minutes, remove a stalk and see if it is done to your liking (cooking times will vary according to the thickness of the stalks and their freshness). The goal is crisp-tender asparagus with slight char marks.

WHEN the asparagus are done, remove them promptly with tongs, leaving the oil behind in the pan. Serve, grating fresh lemon zest or cheese over the top if desired.

OLIVE OIL–BATHED SPRING VEGETABLES

SERVES 4

THIS RECIPE IS ADAPTED from one in Georgeanne Brennan's book, *Savoring France*. Georgeanne says that in France, baby artichokes and asparagus come into season at the same time, and so are natural candidates for cooking together. Since it's often difficult to find tender baby artichokes in New England, I make this dish with frozen artichoke hearts and the season's first asparagus. To turn this into a whole meal, serve the vegetables over potatoes, couscous, or rice, along with a salad or a soup, and serve a wedge of cheese and some fresh fruit for dessert.

1 pound fresh asparagus

2 to 3 tablespoons olive-y and peppery olive oil

2 cloves garlic, peeled and chopped

One 9-ounce package frozen artichoke hearts, thawed

1 tablespoon fresh thyme leaves *or* 1 teaspoon dried thyme

2 bay leaves

Coarse sea salt and freshly ground black pepper, to taste

Freshly grated Parmesan cheese

TRIM the woody ends off the asparagus and wash the stalks. Cut the stalks into 1-inch lengths.

IN a wide shallow sauté pan or frying pan, heat the oil and gently cook the garlic over medium-low heat until it begins to color slightly and smell wonderful. Add the asparagus and artichoke hearts to the pan, and stir in the thyme and bay leaves. Continue to cook and stir for a minute or two until all the vegetables are coated with olive oil. Cover, and cook over low heat for another 10 minutes, or until the asparagus and artichokes are cooked to crisp tenderness. Remove and discard the bay leaves. Season with salt and pepper.

SERVE, immediately, with a generous grating of cheese over each serving.

CARAMELIZED CAULIFLOWER

SERVES 4

AN ARTICLE BY AMANDA HESSER in *The New York Times* spurred me to start browning thin slices of raw cauliflower, and the resulting flavor got me hooked. This dish has been the surprise hit of several dinner parties. Cookbook author Kathy Gunst uses the same technique for broccoli and says it converts even broccoli-haters into enthusiasts. Note that you really do have to slice the cauliflower thin and cook it slowly until it browns; otherwise, it won't taste the way it should. This is another dish for which the pan you use makes a difference; a nonstick pan won't work here. Try a black cast-iron skillet (as large as you've got), or a dark hard-anodized aluminum sauté pan such as those made by Calphalon.

Equally appealing at room temperature, this cauliflower can be prepared hours ahead of time. Leave it in the oven with only the pilot light on; or if you have an electric oven, preheat it to 200°F, then turn it off and let the dish sit in the oven, undisturbed.

To make *Sicilian-Style Caramelized Cauliflower* with sweet and sour flavors, add a good handful of raisins, a whole bunch of fresh flat-leaf parsley, finely chopped, and up to ¾ cup finely grated olive oil–fried bread, along with an anchovy that has been pounded to a paste. Toss well with the caramelized cauliflower and let sit for a few hours for the flavors to develop. Serve at room temperature.

1 head firm white cauliflower

¼ cup fruity and fragrant olive oil, plus more to drizzle if desired

Coarse sea salt and freshly ground black pepper, to taste

AFTER washing and draining the cauliflower, slice off the stem so that the whole head sits flat on a cutting board. Using a very sharp large knife, such as an 8- or 10-inch chef's knife, thinly slice the cauliflower from top to base into ⅛-inch-thick pieces, trying to keep each slice whole (the sharper the knife, the easier this is to do). Thin slices matter because if the cauliflower is too thick, it won't cook through.

HEAT a heavy pan over medium heat, and when the sides are hot to the touch, add the oil. After about a minute, when the oil is hot and fragrant, add whole slices of cauliflower, making sure each lies flat in the pan. (Depending on the size of your pan, it may take two or three refills to brown all of the cauliflower.) Cook each slice until it is browned in patches on both sides and is fork-tender, 10 to 15 minutes. As pieces finish cooking, remove them to a serving platter with tongs or a slotted spatula, leaving as much oil as possible in the pan.

SPRINKLE with salt and pepper to taste, and serve. Pass a cruet of oil to drizzle over the cauliflower if desired.

WHITE BEAN PUREE WITH SAGE AND GARLIC

SERVES 6 TO 8

MAKING THIS WHITE BEAN PUREE with dried rather than canned beans will be a flavor revelation—I promise! This classic of Italian cooking gets a slightly American twist with the use of navy beans instead of harder-to-find cannellini (white kidney) beans. (Note, however, that you can buy dried cannellini beans from specialty grocers such as Corti Brothers.) Be sure to soak the beans at room temperature for at least 4 hours, or overnight, and discard the soaking water.

Fresh sage leaves also make a big difference in the flavor. If you can't find any, you can use fresh rosemary sprigs or, as a last resort, whole dried sage leaves. Please don't use ground dried sage—the dish will taste bitter. Alternatively, you can chop a bunch of parsley with 1 or 2 cloves of garlic, sauté the mixture in a little olive oil, and add it to the beans just before you puree them.

This recipe yields about 3 cups of puree—enough for a side dish for 6 to 8 people, or for a great many more when served in small bowls as a first course, or thickly spread on garlic-rubbed grilled bread as an appetizer (think of it as Italian hummus). Save some puree to make a Grilled Portobello, White Bean, and Arugula Sandwich (page 75)—an inspired lunch or light supper. I especially like to serve White Bean Puree as a side dish with roast lamb—I think the flavors marry well. The vegetarians in my family make a meal of White Bean Puree with lots of salad and good bread.

To turn this into *White Bean Soup with Sage and Garlic,* increase the amount of water by 2 to 3 cups to make a thinner puree; if you like, puree only a portion of the beans and leave the rest whole. Garnish the soup with snippets of fresh sage leaves.

1 pound dried navy beans or cannellini (white kidney beans)

4 fresh sage leaves

4 fat cloves garlic, peeled

3 tablespoons plus ½ cup leafy green and grassy olive oil

2 teaspoons sea salt

Freshly ground black pepper to taste

SOAK the dried beans in cold water to cover for at least 4 hours, or as long as overnight. (Or put the dried beans in a large saucepan, add water to cover, and bring to a boil; set aside, covered, for 1 hour.) Drain the beans and rinse them well.

CHOP 4 sage leaves and the garlic. Heat a heavy pot or Dutch oven over medium-low heat; when it is hot, add the 3 tablespoons olive oil and heat to a shimmer. Then gently sauté the garlic and sage. Add the drained beans, stir them around in the aromatic oil for about 3 to 5 minutes, and add enough cold water to cover by a depth of 1 inch. Cover the pot and bring to a boil.

WHEN the water is boiling, remove the cover, turn the heat to medium-low, and add the salt. Let the beans simmer gently for 1½ to 2 hours, or until tender and melting, with nearly all of the water evaporated. (The timing will vary according to the dryness and age of the beans.)

USING an immersion blender, a stand blender, or a food processor, puree the cooked beans to a smooth paste, adding the ½ cup olive oil as it purees. Taste, and add additional salt and freshly ground pepper as needed.

SERVE warm or at room temperature.

EGGPLANT PUREE WITH VANILLA-INFUSED OLIVE OIL

SERVES 4

I FIRST TASTED THIS DISH in a restaurant in Bodrum, Turkey, and I fell in love with it. Who knew that vanilla would be a good match with eggplant? You can cook the whole eggplant any way you like—on a grill, in the oven, or in a microwave. Microwaving is the fastest. With warmed pita, some fast-cooking red lentils, and a green salad, Eggplant Puree with Vanilla-Infused Olive Oil can be a whole meal.

1 large eggplant *or* 2 small Japanese eggplants

Coarse sea salt and freshly ground black pepper, to taste

Vanilla-Infused Olive Oil (recipe follows)

WASH the eggplant and prick it all over with a fork. Set it on several pieces of paper towel and bake in a microwave oven on full power for 10 to 15 minutes, or until collapsed and soft. (Or bake it on a baking sheet in a conventional oven at 375°F for about 45 minutes.)

REMOVE the eggplant from the oven and set it aside until cool enough to handle. Then pull off and discard the skin. Scrape out the flesh of the eggplant, avoiding the seeds if possible. Place the flesh in a food processor, and process until smooth. Season with salt and pepper to taste. Drizzle the Vanilla-Infused Olive Oil over the puree, and serve at room temperature.

VANILLA-INFUSED DESSERT OIL

Vanilla-Infused Olive Oil is also splendid as a dessert ingredient—drizzled over sliced berries or thinly sliced oranges, for example. I like to put sliced fresh strawberries in a wineglass and drizzle vanilla olive oil over them, then garnish with a sprig of mint. It's a wonderfully refreshing dessert.

VANILLA-INFUSED OLIVE OIL

MAKES ¼ CUP

1 whole vanilla bean, preferably oily and pliable

¼ cup fruity and fragrant olive oil

1 teaspoon very good pure vanilla extract, if needed

YOU CAN MAKE this successfully with olive oil that has little flavor, because the vanilla will take up the slack. Even better, though, is to make it with a great fruity oil and let the fruit of the vanilla tree duke it out with the fruit of the olive tree. If you have a good dark, oily vanilla bean and you don't overheat the oil, you won't need the vanilla extract. Taste for yourself and see. Include the extract as a backup in case the bean is less than perfect, that is, dry and cracked.

SPLIT the vanilla bean along the seam with a small sharp knife, and using the point, scrape out the seeds.

PUT the oil in a small heavy saucepan and add the vanilla bean and the seeds. Begin to gently heat the oil. Be careful, because too high a heat will kill the flavor. If you have a deep-fat thermometer, you are aiming for 180°F. Cook for no more than 3 minutes over low heat, swirling the pan so that the seeds do not scorch or burn. Remove the pan from the heat and pour the contents into another container to cool. When cool, add the vanilla extract if needed.

POUR the oil, seeds, and bean into a sterile jar. Use within a week.

GRILLED SIDE VEGETABLES

SERVES 4

TRY THIS WITH Charcoal-Grilled Butterflied Leg of Lamb (page 172). Other good candidates for grilling by this method include zucchini sliced lengthwise into ¼- to ½-inch-thick slices, radicchio sliced in half lengthwise, garnet yams cut into long slices about ½-inch thick, wedges of seeded green, yellow, and red peppers, and asparagus spears. This recipe is written for an outdoor grill, but you can also grill vegetables on a grill pan on top of the stove, although the smoky flavor will be missing.

2 large eggplants *or* 4 small Japanese eggplants

4 tomatoes, cut into wedges

⅓ cup fruity and fragrant olive oil

Coarse sea salt and freshly ground black pepper, to taste

Lemon wedges

HEAT an outdoor grill.

SLICE the eggplants into long ½-inch-thick strips just before you are ready to cook them, to avoid any bitterness. When the grill is hot, quickly brush all the vegetable pieces on both sides with a little of the olive oil and place them on the grill.

WHEN the eggplant is brown on one side and when the tomatoes are wrinkled, use long-handled tongs to turn to cook on the other side; this will take 3 to 4 minutes per side. Remove from the grill when done, and set on a platter to cool.

DRIZZLE the olive oil over the vegetables, and sprinkle with salt and pepper to taste. Place lemon wedges on the plate, and serve.

STOVETOP GRILL PANS

A ridged grill pan lets you have the look and some of the flavor of an outdoor grill. I recommend two different brands: The least expensive is a ridged cast-iron pan such as one available at Kmart under the Martha Stewart label (see page 51 for instructions on curing a new cast-iron pan). More expensive but easier on the wrist, because it's lighter in weight, is Calphalon's ridged anodized aluminum grill pan. With either pan, heat the pan until the edges are hot to the touch, and then lay on it sliced vegetables that you've coated with olive oil, or meat, poultry, or fish that has been brushed with oil or marinated.

BAKED CHERRY TOMATOES PAOLA

SERVES 4

PAOLA DI MAURO, A GREAT COOK whom I visited outside Rome, taught me how she makes this wonderful dish. It's one of those exemplary Italian dishes that rests completely on the quality of simple ingredients—sweet ripe cherry tomatoes, good homemade coarse bread crumbs from slow-risen bread, flaky sea salt, and luscious fruity olive oil. Happily, we can get, grow, or make all of these ingredients in the United States! (I've also tried this dish with small "grape" tomatoes and it works, although it takes longer to cut such small tomatoes in half and arrange them.) If you have a *cazuela* or a shallow wide ceramic casserole, this is a good dish to bake and serve it in. This is also a fine dish for a buffet, since it's good at room temperature as well as hot from the oven.

4 tablespoons fruity and fragrant olive oil

1 pound cherry tomatoes, washed and drained

2 to 3 slices stale or toasted country bread, crusts cut off, processed or hand-grated to make coarse crumbs

1 teaspoon coarse sea salt

Freshly ground black pepper, to taste

PREHEAT the oven to 350°F.

OIL a round or oval baking pan with 1 tablespoon of the olive oil. Cut the tomatoes in half along their circumference and arrange them, cut side up, in a spiral starting from the outside of the pan and working toward the center. Pour the bread crumbs over the tomatoes so that the tops are covered; then scatter the salt and pepper over all. Drizzle the remaining 3 tablespoons olive oil over everything.

BAKE for 20 to 30 minutes, or until the crumbs are golden brown and fragrant and the tomatoes are fragrant and bursting with intense flavor. Serve hot or at room temperature.

POLENTA

SERVES 6 TO 8

POLENTA IS ITALIAN CORNMEAL mush. It's as comforting as mashed potatoes but is even more versatile, since you can grill or pan-fry it as well as serve it fresh and soft. Polenta is also like mashed potatoes because it's great to use under something that has lots of juice or gravy, such as a stew or braise. I experienced an immersion course in polenta when I visited the Friuli region of northern Italy, because we were served it at lunch and dinner every day for a week. When I came back home and wanted to make it for my family, I found there was no better polenta-making teacher than Lidia Bastianich, who is originally from that area. Her book *Lidia's Italian Table* has exemplary directions. This is my adaptation of her no-lump cold-water method using American (fine) cornmeal.

At the end of the recipe you'll find directions for making pan-fried and grilled polenta. (I love pan-fried polenta for breakfast, drizzled with strong chestnut honey or—most un-Italian—with pure dark Vermont maple syrup.)

8 cups cold water

2 bay leaves

1 teaspoon coarse sea salt, or more to taste

1 tablespoon fruity and fragrant olive oil

1½ cups cornmeal

CHOOSE a large wide, deep pot such as a Dutch oven or other braising pan. Fill the pan with 4 cups of the cold water, and add the bay leaves, salt, and olive oil. Add the cornmeal and whisk it in. Turn on the heat under the pan and bring the mixture to a boil, whisking or stirring almost constantly. At the same time, bring a kettle or saucepan with the remaining 4 cups water to a boil.

ONCE the polenta has come to a boil, lower the heat and keep stirring or whisking—if not constantly, then pretty often. Be careful: the polenta will erupt, volcano-like, every couple of seconds, and it can burn (that's why a deep pot is such a good idea). As the mixture thickens and becomes hard to stir, it's time to add more boiling water. Add about a cup's worth, and continue stirring and cooking over medium heat. I find that I usually end up adding a total of 2 cups boiling water. When the polenta is again nice and thick, after 20 to 25 minutes in all, beat it with a wooden spoon until it begins to look shiny. This is key; otherwise, the polenta will taste underdone. Continue to cook for another 4 to 5 minutes to maximize the flavor. Remove the bay leaves and scrape the polenta into a bowl or platter.

LET the polenta rest for 10 minutes before serving, and serve it with wet spoons.

(IF you are reserving some for pan-fried or grilled polenta, spread that amount in an oiled shallow baking dish so it is about 1 inch deep—no deeper. Cover the dish with plastic wrap and refrigerate.)

CORN AND BASIL POLENTA

In corn season, boil 4 to 6 ears of corn and shave the cooked kernels into the hot polenta. A shower of about 1 cup finely chopped fresh basil, a generous grating of Parmesan, and a drizzle of great oil make this a memorable American variation on an Italian classic.

Variations

PAN-FRIED POLENTA: Cut the cooled polenta into squares or triangles and remove them from the pan piece by piece. Heat about 1 teaspoon fruity and fragrant olive oil in a preheated frying pan, add the polenta pieces, and cook until golden and crisp, 2 to 3 minutes per side.

GRILLED POLENTA: Cut the cooled polenta into squares or triangles and remove them from the pan piece by piece. Brush each piece with fruity and fragrant olive oil, and cook on a charcoal grill or under a hot broiler, turning to grill both sides, until crisp on the outside and creamy within, 2 to 3 minutes per side.

OLIVE OIL AND ROSEMARY MASHED POTATOES

SERVES 4 TO 6

IT CAN BE A REVELATION to make mashed potatoes with olive oil instead of butter—the result is much lighter and more digestible. I use skim milk, but if you prefer a richer flavor, you can certainly substitute whole milk or cream. Infusing the potato water with a sprig of rosemary imparts a lovely flavor to the potatoes, but you can omit it if you prefer. If your rosemary is fresh, it will not shed more than a couple of its needles into the water; if it's a bit old, you'll need to scoop out the potatoes from the pot and leave the needles behind in the water. I prefer to use an old-fashioned potato masher (a series of flat metal loops mounted perpendicular to a wooden handle) because it means I can push the potatoes against the hot pot bottom to cook off any excess moisture. This makes the potatoes better able to absorb the oil and milk.

1 thick sprig fresh rosemary

2 quarts salted water

2 pounds (6 to 8) Russet or Yukon Gold potatoes

¼ cup skim milk

3 tablespoons olive-y and peppery olive oil

Coarse sea salt and freshly ground black pepper, to taste

ADD the rosemary sprig to the salted water in a large pot, and bring it to a boil while you peel and quarter the potatoes. Put the potato pieces in the boiling water, making sure they are covered with water. Bring back to a boil and cook until soft, about 15 minutes.

HEAT the milk in a small saucepan, or in the microwave for 30 seconds. (If your potato pot has a flat cover, you can gently heat the milk in a metal or Pyrex measuring cup by setting the cup on top of the cover as the potatoes heat.)

WHEN they are cooked through, drain the potatoes and discard the rosemary. Return the potatoes to the dry but still hot pot. Using a potato masher, immediately mash the potatoes to a paste (the key to fluffy potatoes is to mash them while hot). Add the olive oil and milk, beating with a wooden spoon as you do so. Taste, and add salt and pepper. Serve hot.

TARRAGON POTATO SALAD

SERVES 4

AROMATIC AND REFRESHING, this potato salad uses homemade mustard mayonnaise as a base. To make it even more flavorful, you can add a tablespoon of chopped capers or caperberries. In any case, fresh tarragon is a necessity—look for it in the produce section of your grocery store.

If you prefer, you can eliminate the mustard and capers, and add fresh basil instead of the tarragon—it produces an entirely different tasting potato salad. With this version, you'll probably want to drizzle a little leafy green and grassy olive oil over the potatoes.

1½ to 2 pounds new potatoes, scrubbed, peeled, and cut into wedges

2 tablespoons chopped fresh tarragon leaves

½ cup Mustard Mayonnaise (page 67) or ½ cup commercial mayonnaise mixed with 1 table-spoon grainy mustard

2 large shallots, chopped (about ¼ cup)

Coarse sea salt and freshly ground black pepper, to taste

½ to 1 teaspoon chopped capers or caperberries (optional)

COOK the potatoes in a generous amount of boiling salted water for about 15 minutes or until tender. Immediately drain and place them in a large mixing bowl. Toss right away with all of the remaining ingredients, so that the warm potatoes will absorb the flavors of the oil and herbs.

SERVE at room temperature.

POTATO GRATIN

SERVES 4 TO 6

WE ALWAYS CALL THIS "French Potatoes" at our house, because it was one of our favorite dishes when we lived in France. Over the years we've made it simpler and simpler; unlike the traditional French dish, we don't precook the potatoes in milk, nor do we use crème fraîche or butter. Try it this way and see if it doesn't become a staple at your house.

8 or 9 Russet potatoes

2 to 3 tablespoons leafy green and grassy olive oil

1 teaspoon coarse sea salt

1 cup milk

½ cup heavy cream

Freshly ground black pepper, to taste

½ cup freshly grated Parmesan cheese (optional)

PREHEAT the oven to 400°F, and set a rack in the upper half of the oven.

WASH and dry the potatoes. Using a mandoline or the thinnest slicing blade of a food processor, or by hand with a sharp knife, slice the potatoes as thin as possible.

OIL a shallow glass or ceramic gratin dish or casserole, spreading about 1 tablespoon of the olive oil along the bottom and sides. Pour in the potato slices, fanning out any clumps. Sprinkle with the salt, and pour the remaining olive oil over the potatoes. Using your hands or a wooden spoon, gently mix the potatoes to coat them all with a film of oil.

POUR the milk and cream over the top. The dish should be no more than half filled with liquid; otherwise it may boil over and you will have a very messy oven to clean. If your dish is too full, move everything to a larger dish or set the dish on a rimmed cookie sheet lined with aluminum foil. Generously grind pepper over all, and sprinkle on the cheese if using.

BAKE, uncovered, for 45 to 60 minutes, or until the edges of the potatoes are brown and crunchy and all the potatoes are cooked through. The liquid will have disappeared.

SERVE hot.

OLIVE OIL–GLAZED GREEN BEANS

SERVES 4

THIS TRADITIONAL TURKISH technique for cooking vegetables is a great tool in any vegetable-cooking arsenal, as the combination of oil and water produces a legume that is glazed with its own starch, sugars, and juices. It works well with zucchini too. Olive oil–glazed vegetables are good hot or at room temperature.

¼ cup leafy green and grassy olive oil

1 onion, finely chopped

1 pound green beans, ends trimmed, cut into ½-inch pieces

½ teaspoon fine sea salt

Freshly ground black pepper, to taste

½ teaspoon sugar

½ cup cold water

1 tomato, finely diced, for garnish

HEAT a sauté pan over medium heat, and then add the olive oil and heat it. Add the onion and lower the heat. Slowly simmer until the onions are beginning to be wilted and translucent, about 3 minutes.

ADD the beans, salt, pepper, and sugar, and stir to combine. Then add the water and cook, uncovered, over medium-low heat until all the water is absorbed, about 30 minutes, depending on the freshness of the beans and their size.

SERVE hot or at room temperature, garnished with the chopped tomato.

BRAISED GREENS WITH GARLIC

SERVES 4

THIS SIMPLE METHOD of cooking greens works for a wide variety of leafy vegetables, from relatively delicate stemmed greens such as spinach and arugula to sturdy central-rib greens such as chard and kale. There are only two things you need to know: Stemmed greens cook much more rapidly than do ribbed greens, and ribbed greens are often improved if you add ½ cup or so of chicken stock to the pot after they're sautéed, to further tenderize and cook them down. In addition to using such greens as a side vegetable, consider the Tuscan appetizer *Bruschetta with Braised Greens:* Serve the cooked greens on grilled bread rubbed with garlic, sprinkling them with coarse sea salt and drizzling lightly with a little hot broth and fragrant olive oil.

1 pound greens

3 cloves garlic

¼ cup leafy green and grassy olive oil

½ cup chicken stock, if using ribbed greens

Coarse sea salt and freshly ground black pepper, to taste

Freshly grated Parmesan cheese (optional)

REMOVE the stems or ribs from the greens, and if the leaves are very large (such as kale or chard), cut them crosswise into ribbons an inch wide or less. Wash extremely well. Drain. Smash and chop the garlic.

HEAT a large, wide pan, such as a sauté pan or Dutch oven, over medium-high heat. Add the oil, and heat it until it thins and is fragrant but not smoking. Lower the heat to medium-low and add the garlic, stirring it for a few seconds. Then add the greens with the water that is still clinging to the leaves. If your pot is large enough, toss the greens in the oil. Cover at once, and shake the pan a little to move the greens around (especially useful if you haven't been able to stir the greens).

IF you are cooking stemmed greens, steam them in the oil for 3 to 4 minutes. Remove the cover and cook off any liquid that remains.

IF you are cooking ribbed greens, steam them in the oil for 5 minutes and then add the chicken stock. Cover and cook for another 5 minutes over medium-high heat. Uncover the pan and cook off most of the liquid.

SEASON the greens with salt and pepper, and sprinkle with Parmesan if desired, before serving.

PUREED SPINACH WITH RICOTTA

SERVES 2 TO 4

I FIND THIS SO DELICIOUS, I can eat it with a spoon as if it were dessert.

1 recipe Braised Greens with Garlic (page 192) made with spinach, cooled slightly

½ cup whole-milk ricotta cheese

½ cup freshly grated Parmesan cheese

Coarse sea salt and freshly ground black pepper, to taste

½ teaspoon freshly grated nutmeg

DRAIN and press on the cooked spinach over a bowl to make it fairly dry, reserving the liquid. Put the drained spinach in the bowl of a food processor and add all the other ingredients. Process until completely smooth. If too dry, add some of the reserved spinach water. Reheat gently if necessary, and serve.

SWEET
TARALLE
(CIAMBELLE)

MAKES 30 TO 40
COOKIE RINGS

YOU MAY BE FAMILIAR with savory taralle, those fennel-flavored dough rings that are so addictive with wine. These are their sweet counterparts, equally delicious with a dessert wine or with espresso or tea. Not too sweet, their crunch and flavor make for a unique light dessert. You could sift confectioners' sugar over them if you want them to look slightly more elegant.

½ cup delicate and mild olive oil

½ cup dry vermouth

¼ cup sugar

About 1½ cups unbleached all-purpose flour

PREHEAT the oven to 350°F. Line a cookie sheet with parchment paper.

IN a medium bowl, mix the olive oil and vermouth together. Add the sugar and then gradually add the flour while you mix (you may not need all of the flour, or you may need a bit more). Knead the dough slightly until blended and smooth—it should be moist and easy to roll but not sticky. Keep in mind that you want to use as little flour as possible.

PINCH off about a tablespoon's worth of dough and roll it into a snake that's 4 to 5 inches long and the diameter of a fat pencil. Form it into a ring and twist the ends together. Lay it on the parchment-lined sheet, and repeat with the remaining dough, keeping the rings about ½ inch apart.

BAKE for 30 to 35 minutes, or until fragrant and dark golden brown (these taste significantly better if not undercooked). Cool on wire racks, and store in an airtight tin.

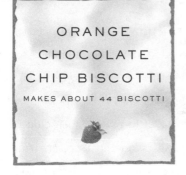

ORANGE CHOCOLATE CHIP BISCOTTI

MAKES ABOUT 44 BISCOTTI

I BELIEVE THAT adding chocolate almost always improves a dessert, and these cookies are no exception. Biscotti keep very well, so send some off to that college student or use them to keep the cookie jar stocked.

6 tablespoons delicate and mild olive oil or orange olive oil

1 cup sugar

2 eggs

Grated zest of 1 orange

⅓ cup fresh orange juice

1 cup semisweet chocolate chips

4 to 5 cups unbleached all-purpose flour

1½ teaspoons baking powder

PREHEAT the oven to 350°F. Line 2 baking sheets with parchment paper.

MIX the olive oil, sugar, eggs, orange zest, and orange juice together in a large bowl. Add the chocolate chips. In another bowl, mix 3½ cups of the flour with the baking powder. Add the dry mixture to the wet one and mix until just barely blended. The dough should be soft and wet and able to be patted into shape. If it's like a batter, add more flour in ½-cup increments.

SCRAPE the dough onto a floured board, and divide it into three parts (this is easiest with a plastic or metal "bench knife" or a large hard rubber or plastic spatula). Roll each part in a little flour, and then form it into a 12-inch-long log. Lay the logs on the parchment, leaving a few inches between them. Pat the logs flat with your hands so that they end up 2 to 3 inches wide.

BAKE for 20 to 25 minutes, or until lightly browned and fragrant. Remove the baking sheets but keep the oven on.

ALLOW the loaves to cool slightly on the sheets. Then, using a sharp knife, cut them into ½-inch-wide slices on a diagonal to form long thin cookies. (If they get too cool, they tend to crumble when you slice them. If this happens, put them back in the oven for a few minutes to reheat.) Arrange these slices, cut side up, on parchment-lined baking sheets. Bake again for 12 to 15 minutes, turning them over halfway through, until both surfaces are lightly browned. If you like your biscotti very crunchy, cook until medium-dark; if you like a more crumbly cookie, cook only until they just begin to color.

COOL on wire racks and store in airtight tins.

SLICING THE DOUGH

There's a paradox with cutting the dough logs into slices—they slice fairly well when warm, but not at room temperature. Best of all is to slice the dough after an overnight rest in the refrigerator.

You can also freeze the logs, well wrapped, and then slice off biscotti to bake as needed.

PARCHMENT PAPER

Parchment paper helps ensure that a cake comes out of the pan perfectly, and that cookies and biscotti slide right off the baking sheet when they're done. Good-quality baking parchment, such as that available by mail from the King Arthur Baker's Catalogue, is so heavy that you can reuse the sheets a number of times. Supermarket parchment, in contrast, is a lighter gauge and usually can be used just once. If you don't have access to parchment paper, waxed paper is a mediocre substitute, but it's still more effective for protecting some baked goods than merely greasing the pan. Precut parchment paper rounds, scaled to 8- and 9-inch cake pans, are extremely convenient; I find these in kitchen stores and even in some hardware stores with good housewares departments.

BUTTERMILK LEMON-ALMOND CAKE WITH STRAWBERRY COULIS

SERVES 10 TO 12

I MAKE THIS CAKE in a standard springform pan and serve it in wedges with the sauce. On more festive occasions, I split the cooled cake with a serrated knife and fill it with whipped cream and berries. For a practically cholesterol-free cake, you can substitute Egg Beaters for the eggs.

If you have access to self-rising cake flour, you can just use 2 cups of that in place of the cake flour, salt, and baking soda.

2 cups cake flour

⅛ teaspoon sea salt

¾ teaspoon baking soda

1¼ cups sugar

6 tablespoons delicate and mild olive oil

3 eggs

2 tablespoons fresh lemon juice

1 teaspoon almond extract

1 cup buttermilk

Strawberry Coulis (recipe follows)

Whipped cream (optional)

PREHEAT the oven to 350°F. Lightly rub a 9-inch springform pan with olive oil.

WHISK the flour, salt, baking soda, and sugar together in a mixing bowl. In another large bowl, beat the olive oil and the eggs together until well blended. Add the lemon juice and almond extract.

ALTERNATING, add the dry ingredients and the buttermilk to the oil/egg mixture, starting and ending with the flour. Mix only until the batter is blended—don't overmix.

SCRAPE the batter into the prepared pan and bake for 50 to 60 minutes, or until fragrant, golden, and done in the center. Cool in the pan for about 15 minutes, and then remove the sides and finish cooling on a wire rack.

TO serve, spoon a generous amount of Strawberry Coulis on each plate, and place a wedge of cake on top. If you like, top with a dollop of whipped cream.

STRAWBERRY COULIS

MAKES 2 CUPS

2 cups fresh or frozen strawberries, thawed

Grated zest and juice of
1 lemon

1 tablespoon sugar, or more
if needed

1 tablespoon grappa, brandy,
or Triple Sec

THE FRENCH CALL A thin sauce of sieved fruits or tomatoes a *coulis*. Unsieved, this coulis is thinned with a liqueur to add flavor and to dilute the consistency.

WHIRL all the ingredients together in a blender or food processor. Taste, and add more sugar if required. Don't make this too sweet, though, because a slight acidity is a good contrast to the cake.

THE *coulis* will keep, covered and refrigerated, for up to a week.

WHY FLOUR MEASUREMENTS ARE APPROXIMATE

I once took a class at the Cambridge (Massachusetts) School of Culinary Arts with Carol Field, the great Italian baking expert, who lives in San Francisco. She was demonstrating a recipe from one of her books, and as she measured out the flour, she said: "When I'm at home, I know that this measure for flour is absolutely correct. But when I'm on the East Coast, I always hold some flour back, since the humidity is different here." Flour does change from batch to batch, and it's profoundly affected by the weather and the time of year (winter on the East Coast is dry, while summer is wet). Always add flour gradually, and don't assume that you'll need all the flour the recipe specifies.

LAVENDER-INFUSED PEAR CLAFOUTIS

SERVES 4 TO 6

TRADITIONAL CLAFOUTIS is made with cherries, but this winter version uses rock-hard pears and precooks them into softness in delicate olive oil. Infusing the milk with lavender flowers adds an ineffable flavor and scent to this easy, homey dessert.

In summer, you can use sliced peeled peaches or nectarines. Blanch the fruit in boiling water for a minute or two, or until the skin splits. Immediately chill the fruit in a bowl of ice water, and then peel off the skin. If the fruit is unripe, cook as directed below until soft and juicy.

Make sure the lavender you use is pesticide-free.

1 cup whole milk

1 tablespoon dried lavender buds (see Resources)

1 tablespoon delicate and mild olive oil or Vanilla-Infused Olive Oil (see page 183)

2 unripe winter pears, such as Bosc or hard green Anjou, cored and coarsely diced

2 eggs

1 tablespoon cornstarch

⅓ cup sugar

Pinch of sea salt

Grated zest of 1 lemon

Confectioners' sugar, for garnish

PREHEAT the oven to 375°F.

HEAT the milk just to a boil, remove from the heat, and add the lavender buds. Set aside to steep.

CHOOSE an ovenproof frying pan or a braising pan with a cover. Heat the pan on the stove until warm to the touch, and then add the oil and heat just until it is fragrant and shimmery. Reduce the heat and add the pears, stirring to coat them with oil. Cover the pan and let the pears cook until tender, 10 to 15 minutes. Remove from the heat and set aside.

USING a wire sieve, strain the lavender buds from the milk, pressing on them with a wooden spoon to extract all their flavor; discard the buds and reserve the milk.

BEAT the eggs, lavender-infused milk, cornstarch, sugar, salt, and lemon zest together in a bowl, and pour over the cooked pears in their pan.

BAKE, uncovered, for about 40 minutes or until the custard is set. Let cool to room temperature. Dust with confectioners' sugar and serve from the pan, cut into wedges.

TORTA DI NOCI

SERVES 10 TO 12

BASED ON A TRADITIONAL Italian Passover cake, this walnut sponge cake's keeping power is increased by adding olive oil, which helps the cake to stay moist. For Passover, substitute potato starch for the flour.

2 tablespoons delicate and mild olive oil

2½ cups walnuts

1½ cups sugar

6 eggs, separated

⅛ teaspoon sea salt

Grated zest of 1 orange

1 teaspoon vanilla extract

2 teaspoons ground cinnamon

½ teaspoon nutmeg, freshly grated if possible

Confectioners' sugar, for garnish

PREHEAT the oven to 325°F. Use 1 tablespoon of the olive oil to grease a 10-inch springform pan; flour the pan.

USING a food processor, grind the nuts with 1 cup of the sugar until they make a coarse flour. Add the egg yolks and process briefly.

IN a large bowl, beat the egg whites with the salt and remaining ½ cup sugar until they are stiff. Spoon one third of the whites into the yolk mixture in the processor. Add the orange zest, remaining 1 tablespoon olive oil, vanilla, cinnamon, and nutmeg. Process until the mixture is smooth and light. Scrape it into another large bowl, and fold in the remaining egg whites.

POUR the batter into the prepared pan, and bake for 1 hour. If the cake is at all wet in the center, bake for up to another 15 minutes, checking every 5 minutes. The cake should be springy and dry.

COOL the cake completely in the pan on a wire rack. Then remove the springform sides. Sprinkle with confectioners' sugar before serving.

APPLE-CHERRY CARDAMOM STRUDEL

SEREVS 12 TO 14

MY MOTHER USED TO describe her grand-mother's strudel as being so big and so thin that she rolled it on a huge linen tablecloth. In this strudel, I paste 12 sheets of filo dough together to make a 30-inch square of dough to fill and roll. Unlike my great-grandmother, I use olive oil instead of melted butter to paint the strudel leaves. I particularly like The Fillo Factory's organic filo; they also make filo of spelt and whole wheat. You'll need a pastry brush for painting the sheets of dough with oil.

Don't be daunted by this recipe—it's really pretty easy. Just remember to thaw the frozen filo overnight in the refrigerator, then bring it to room temperature, still in the box, for an hour or two.

For the filling

½ cup dried sour cherries

2 tablespoons kirschwasser (cherry-flavored liqueur) or dark rum

3 pounds cooking apples (I use Cortlands), washed, cored, peeled, and quartered

1 tablespoon fresh orange or lemon juice

½ cup sugar

¼ teaspoon sea salt

1 teaspoon ground cardamom

1 cup almond meal (see page 205) or unflavored bread crumbs

3 teaspoons grated orange zest

SOAK the dried cherries in the kirschwasser for 20 to 30 minutes. If the cherries are very dry, combine them in a small saucepan and heat the two together before setting aside to soak.

USING a food processor or a hand grater, shred the apple quarters and place them in a bowl. Immediately sprinkle with the orange juice to prevent browning. Mix in the sugar, salt, cardamom, almond meal, and orange zest. Drain the cherries and add them to the apple mixture. Set aside while you assemble the pastry. (Do not prepare the apple mixture ahead of time; if it sits too long, it will get too watery. If that happens, drain the apple mixture in a colander before using it.)

PREHEAT the oven to 375°F. Grease a cookie sheet, and line it with greased parchment paper if desired.

LAY a large sheet of parchment paper or cloth on a large work surface, such as a kitchen island or kitchen table, to cover an area 30 x 30 inches in size. Take out the first sheet of filo from the package; reroll the rest and keep the dough

For the pastry

12 sheets filo (phyllo) dough, defrosted and covered according to the manufacturer's directions

½ cup delicate and mild olive oil

1 cup almond meal (see Note)

Confectioners' sugar, for garnish

covered with a tea towel, waxed paper, or plastic wrap. Lay the first sheet of dough with the long edge facing you. Using a pastry brush, paint the whole sheet with olive oil. Lay the second sheet of filo next to the first sheet, again with the long edge facing you, with a 2-inch overlap on the short edges. Paint this sheet with oil. Now you have a long skinny rectangle.

REPEAT with the next two sheets, placing them so that the long edges overlap the long edges of the first two sheets by 2 inches, and so that their own short edges overlap by 2 inches. Now you have a large rectangle that's twice as long and twice as wide as a single filo sheet.

REPEAT this process with the next 2 sheets, adding them to the rectangle to make a square. Every sheet should be coated with oil, and you should be able to see 6 connected sheets in front of you, forming a 30-inch square.

DO the same thing all over again to form a second layer on top of the first, so that you end up with a two-layer 30-inch square of filo that is painted with olive oil.

SPRINKLE the almond meal over the first third of the dough, leaving an empty 2-inch border on the bottom and sides. Using a spoon, place the apple filling on the almond meal, leaving a 3-inch border along the whole long side. Fold in the two side edges of the dough, using the parchment or cloth to help you handle the fragile dough. Now, again using the parchment or cloth, start rolling the dough around the filling, pulling the paper away as you roll to prevent it from rolling into the strudel. Keep rolling until all the dough is wrapped around the filling. Paint the strudel with olive oil. Roll the strudel on the prepared baking sheet so it is seam side down, bending the ends to form a horseshoe shape (since the roll will be longer than the baking sheet). Don't worry if the strudel cracks when you curve it—once you slice it, these cracks will not be apparent.

BAKE the strudel for 1 hour or until golden and crisp. Let it cool on the pan. Then carefully remove it from the pan, using a long spatula, and dust it well with confectioners' sugar. Cut into slices and serve at room temperature.

Note: You can make your own almond meal, as described in the sidebar on page 205, for the filling. Leftover strudel can be wrapped in plastic wrap and refrigerated. Before serving, bake it, uncovered, at 400°F for about 10 minutes to recrisp the pastry.

INSPIRED BY THE WAY the Aztec flavored chocolate, and by the film *Chocolat,* this cake is hot by virtue of spices, not temperature. Actually, the peppers add a mild and pleasant edge rather than any real heat; they amplify the earthiness of the chocolate's flavor. I've tried this cake with ground dried ancho chiles, with Spanish sweet paprika, and with tiny pellets of urfa pepper from Turkey (available from Zingerman's). It's good with all three, although the urfa adds the smokiest notes. After trying the cake with differing amounts of pepper, I've written the recipe conservatively; if you love smoke and heat with chocolate, feel free to double the amount of chile. Note that this cake bakes in a small springform pan, available in specialty cookware stores. The cake will rise above the pan as it bakes and then deflate as it cools.

In this recipe, the vodka does not add flavor directly; rather, it releases flavors that would otherwise be hidden. If you want to substitute water, you can—there will be a subtle difference in flavor.

8 ounces semisweet chocolate (I use Callebaut)

4½ tablespoons fruity and fragrant olive oil

2 tablespoons honey

1 teaspoon Turkish urfa pepper, mild chile powder (preferably ancho), or sweet paprika

½ teaspoon fine sea salt

¼ cup sugar

½ cup almond meal (see page 205)

5 eggs, at room temperature, separated

½ teaspoon ground cinnamon

1 tablespoon vodka

1 teaspoon vanilla extract

PREHEAT the oven to 375°F, with a rack in the center of the oven. Grease a 7-inch springform pan, and line it with a greased parchment round if you wish. Set it aside.

MELT the chocolage in a double boiler over low heat (or in a glass dish in a microwave oven for 3 minutes on full power, checking every minute). Stir in the olive oil, honey, hot pepper, salt, sugar, and almond meal. Let cool, and then add the egg yolks, stirring to blend. Add the cinnamon, vodka, and vanilla, and stir again briefly.

BEAT the egg whites in a large bowl until stiff, firm, and glossy. Stir one third of the beaten egg whites into the chocolate mixture to lighten it. Then pour this mixture into the remaining beaten egg whites, and fold them together.

Garnish

Confectioners' sugar

Unsweetened whipped cream

SCRAPE the batter into the prepared cake pan (the pan will be nearly filled), and bake for 30 minutes. The cake will rise over the level of the pan like a soufflé.

COOL the cake in the pan on a rack (it will deflate) for about 15 minutes. Then run a knife around the edges of the pan, remove the sides of the pan, and sift confectioners' sugar over the cake. Serve warm or at room temperature (never cold), with whipped cream.

ALMOND MEAL

Almond meal can be found in the refrigerated section of health-food stores. You can also create your own by grinding blanched almonds, in pulses, in a food processor along with ¼ cup sugar. (The sugar helps absorb the nut oil and improves the texture.) Just remember when you proceed with the recipe that you've already incorporated that ¼ cup sugar.

LEMON ALMOND POLENTA TORTA WITH BEATEN RICOTTA CREAM

SERVES 10 TO 12

INTENSELY LEMONY, with a homey cornmeal taste, this modest cake is fast and easy to put together in a food processor. Serve it for breakfast or with afternoon coffee or tea, or in thin wedges with Beaten Ricotta Cream for dessert. If you prefer a sweeter cake (or if your lemon is very sour), you can add up to ½ cup more sugar—I've tried it both ways and find I like the cake less sweet, particularly if I'm serving it with the ricotta cream. You can also serve berries (blueberries are especially good) alongside the cream, if you wish.

¼ teaspoon sea salt

½ cup cornmeal

2 teaspoons baking powder

1¼ cups blanched almonds

1 to 1½ cups sugar

1 large lemon, well washed

½ cup fruity and fragrant olive oil plus a little more for oiling the pan

½ cup milk

2 eggs

½ teaspoon almond extract

Confectioners' sugar, for garnish

Beaten Ricotta Cream (recipe follows)

PREHEAT the oven to 350°F. Oil a 9-inch round cake pan, line it with a parchment round, and then grease the paper as well.

MIX together the salt, cornmeal, and baking powder, and set it aside.

IN a food processor, grind the almonds with the sugar to make a slightly coarse flour; leave it in the processor.

CUT the lemon into quarters and carefully pick out all the seeds with the point of a knife. Add the lemon pieces to the processor and process until reduced to a coarse puree. Add the olive oil, milk, eggs, and almond extract, and process for a minute or two to combine well. Add the cornmeal mixture and pulse just briefly to combine.

POUR the batter into the prepared pan, and bake for 55 to 60 minutes, or until golden, fragrant, and slightly moist in the center.

COOL the cake in the pan on a rack. Then run a knife around the edge of the cake, invert it onto a cake plate, and sift confectioners' sugar over the top.

SERVE with the Beaten Ricotta Cream.

BEATEN RICOTTA CREAM

MAKES 1 CUP

1 cup whole-milk ricotta cheese

½ cup sugar

1 tablespoon vanilla extract

BEAT all the ingredients together in a food processor. This will keep in the refrigerator for a few days, covered.

LEMON-LIME
PAN DI SPAGNA

SERVES 10 TO 12

ADAPTED FROM Michele Scicolone's butter-based Torta di Arancia, this is an Italian version of sponge cake—not too rich, light in texture, and full of flavor. Limoncello, a lemon liqueur from Amalfi, is a wonderful summer drink. You can order it from Corti Brothers (see Resources if you can't find it at your liquor store). If you don't have limoncello, you can use any lemon- or orange-flavored alcoholic drink such as lemon rum or Grand Marnier. Lemon-Lime Pan di Spagna is delicious with coffee or tea, and is a great summer dessert with fresh blueberries or raspberries. On more festive or celebratory occasions, you can split the cooled cake with a serrated knife and top one layer with a thick layer of purchased lemon curd. Put the other layer on top, and sift confectioners' sugar over the whole, decorating the top with a circle of berries.

1⅓ cups unbleached all-purpose flour

1 cup sugar

½ teaspoon sea salt

4 eggs, separated

Grated zest of 1 lime

2 tablespoons fresh lime juice

2 tablespoons limoncello, other lemon liquor, or Grand Marnier

⅓ cup fruity and fragrant olive oil

1 teaspoon almond extract

PREHEAT the oven to 325°F. Set out an un-greased 10-inch springform pan.

PUT the flour, ⅔ cup of the sugar, and the salt in a mixing bowl. In the bowl of a stand mixer fitted with the flat beater, mix together the egg yolks, lime zest, lime juice, limoncello, olive oil, and almond extract. Beat until the mixture is pale yellow and smooth. Add the flour mixture and beat until just blended.

IN another bowl, beat the egg whites until soft peaks begin to form. Add the remaining ⅓ cup sugar as you finish beating the whites until stiff.

BEAT one third of the beaten whites into the batter mixture to lighten it. Using a rubber spatula, fold in the rest of the beaten whites by hand.

POUR the batter into the ungreased pan, and bake on the middle shelf of the oven until dry in the center, 45 to 50 minutes. Cool the cake in the pan on a rack. When it is cool, run a knife around the edge to loosen the cake, and then remove the sides of the springform.

ORANGE, ALMOND, AND CARAWAY SEED CAKE

SERVES 10 TO 12

FOOD-WORLD FRIENDS kept telling me about a wonderful breakfast cake served in Italy at the Capezzana estate, so I had to come up with my own version. Here it is, one of the great breakfast cakes of all times, although it can also be served as a homey dessert with a dessert wine or coffee. It's most intensely orange-flavored when you use Boyajian's orange oil, available at fine groceries, Williams-Sonoma, or directly from Boyajian (see Resources), but this cake is also perfectly good with grated orange or tangerine zest. Even if you normally never sift your dry ingredients, do so here—it makes a difference in the finished cake. I make sifting easy by dumping all the dry ingredients into a bowl-size fine-mesh sieve and shaking them into a mixing bowl. This is one of the easiest and most forgiving cakes I bake, and it's a great favorite.

2 cups unbleached all-purpose flour

1¼ cups sugar

¼ teaspoon fine sea salt

1 teaspoon baking powder

1 teaspoon baking soda

3 large eggs, beaten

1½ cups whole milk

½ cup fruity and fragrant olive oil plus more to oil the pan

¼ teaspoon orange oil *or* grated zest of 1 orange

1 teaspoon pure vanilla extract

½ cup sliced almonds

1 tablespoon caraway seeds

Confectioners' sugar, for garnish

PREHEAT the oven to 350°F. Oil a Bundt pan with olive oil.

IN a large bowl, sift together the flour, sugar, salt, baking powder, and baking soda. Make a well in the center of the dry ingredients and add the eggs, milk, olive oil, orange oil, and vanilla.

USING a whisk, beat the wet ingredients together in the center of the bowl, gradually drawing in some of the dry mixture as you beat. Continue until all the ingredients are blended. Add the almonds and caraway seeds, and mix lightly with a spatula or a wooden spoon.

POUR the batter into the prepared pan and bake for 55 to 60 minutes, or until the cake is cooked through and golden brown. Cool the cake in the pan on a rack. Then run a knife around the edge and invert it onto a serving plate. When it is completely cool, dust the cake with confectioners' sugar.

GINGERED CARROT CAKE WITH FIGS

SERVES 8 TO 10

THIS HAS BEEN A FAVORITE rich birthday cake in our household for years, and the birthday child has always insisted on eating more of it for breakfast the next day. Thanks to the olive oil, it's a very good keeper, and it also freezes very well, un-iced. For a really big cake, this recipe can be doubled and baked in a Bundt pan for 1½ hours or as a layer cake in two 8- or 9-inch round cake pans for 1 hour. Depending on how much ginger flavor you want, you can use either freshly grated ginger root, for a strong flavor note, or dried ground ginger, for a much milder taste.

6 dried figs, stems removed

½ cup walnuts

1 cup plus 2 tablespoons sugar

¾ cup delicate and mild olive oil

2 eggs

1¼ cups unbleached all-purpose flour

1 teaspoon baking powder

1 teaspoon baking soda

¼ teaspoon sea salt

1 teaspoon ground cinnamon

2 teaspoons freshly grated ginger root *or* 1 teaspoon ground dried ginger (see headnote)

½ teaspoon freshly grated nutmeg

½ teaspoon ground allspice

1½ cups grated carrots (about 2 large carrots)

Cream Cheese Frosting (recipe follows)

PREHEAT the oven to 350°F. Grease a single 9½-inch round cake pan with olive oil, and line the bottom with a round of parchment paper; grease the paper.

IF you are making this cake by hand or in a stand mixer, finely chop the figs and walnuts. (If making this in a food processor, this step is unnecessary, as the processor will do the chopping.)

IN a mixing bowl, the bowl of a stand mixer, or a food processor, beat the sugar, olive oil, and eggs together. In another bowl, combine the flour, baking powder, baking soda, salt, cinnamon, dried ginger if using, nutmeg, and allspice. Sift the flour mixture over the egg mixture, blending briefly until just combined. Add the figs, nuts, grated carrots, and grated ginger root if using, and stir (or pulse) to blend.

POUR the batter into the prepared pan and bake for 1 hour, or until fragrant, brown, and dry in the middle. Cool in the pan on a rack. Then run a knife around the edge and invert the cake onto a serving plate. Frost with Cream Cheese Frosting.

CREAM CHEESE FROSTING

MAKES ENOUGH FROSTING FOR 1 SINGLE-LAYER CAKE

4 ounces cream cheese

2 tablespoons unsalted butter

1 cup confectioners' sugar

1 teaspoon vanilla extract

Grated zest of 1 lemon or orange

THIS IS a standard cream cheese frosting, with the addition of a little citrus zest for added flavor. If you wish, you can reserve some of it and tint that portion orange to pipe into tiny carrot decorations.

HAVE all the ingredients at room temperature. Place the ingredients in the bowl of a food processor, and process until creamy and smooth.

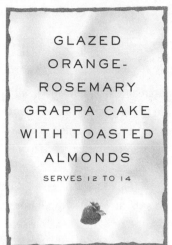

GLAZED ORANGE-ROSEMARY GRAPPA CAKE WITH TOASTED ALMONDS

SERVES 12 TO 14

THIS LARGE FESTIVE CAKE will feed a crowd in style and will stay fresh a long time, thanks to the olive oil. If you don't want to use grappa, you can use dry vermouth or vodka instead; although the liquor contributes some flavor of its own, it's used mostly as a vehicle for infusing the cake and glaze with the rosemary flavor.

½ cup grappa, dry vermouth, or vodka

1 fat sprig fresh rosemary

3 teaspoons baking powder

3 cups almond meal (see page 205)

3 oranges, organic if possible, washed, quartered, and seeded

6 eggs

½ cup delicate and mild olive oil

1½ cups sugar

1 cup orange marmalade

¼ cup water

½ cup whole blanched almonds, toasted (see page 61) and finely chopped

PREHEAT the oven to 350°F. Oil the bottom of an 11-inch springform pan, line it with a parchment round, and oil the parchment as well.

HEAT the grappa in a small heavy saucepan to just below boiling. Add the rosemary sprig, making sure it has maximum contact with the liquor, and cover the pot. Remove it from the heat and let it steep for 15 to 20 minutes. Then remove and discard the rosemary.

USING a spoon or a whisk, mix the baking powder with the almond meal in a small bowl.

PLACE the orange quarters in the bowl of a food processor and puree, skin and all.

IN a mixing bowl, beat together the eggs, olive oil, and sugar. Add the almond meal mixture and the orange puree. Then add ¼ cup of the rosemary-infused grappa and mix well.

POUR the batter into the prepared pan and bake on the middle shelf of the oven for 1½ hours or until the cake is deep golden and fragrant and a cake tester comes out clean.

COOL the cake in its pan on a wire rack. When the cake is completely cool, run a knife around the edges and then remove the sides of the pan. Place the cake on a dish or rack so you can glaze it.

CAREFUL!

Watch the grappa closely when you're heating it—you don't want it to boil. Keep the pot lid handy, and if the alcohol combusts, quickly clamp the lid on the pot to smother the flames.

TO make the glaze, mix the marmalade, the remaining ¼ cup rosemary-infused grappa, and the water in a small heavy saucepan. Bring this mixture just to a boil, stirring. Reduce the heat and cook it down by about a third, or until it seems slightly thickened, 3 to 5 minutes. Strain this glaze through a sieve to remove the orange shreds, pressing down with a wooden spoon to extract all the flavor. Discard the shreds and ladle the glaze onto the cake, allowing it to drip down the sides. Scatter the chopped toasted almonds over the top of the cake.

RESOURCES

Retailers of Olive Oil, Other
Ingredients, and Accessories

Aidells Sausage Company
(877-AIDELLS, www.aidells.com)

Classical Wines
(inq@classicalwines.com)
A specialty importer of fine wines; they also
import some extraordinary olive oils.

A Cook's Wares
(800-915-9788, www.cookswares.com)
Specialty catalog that sells Vann's spices,
olive oils, knives, pots and pans, and other
cooking equipment.

Corti Brothers
(800-509-3663)
An extraordinary source for a wide range of
foodstuffs, including olive oils, bottarga,
saba, dried beans, anchovies, capers, and
other Italian and non-Italian specialty ingredients, including limoncello. An extremely
informative newsletter that describes ingredients and new products is available free;
call for a subscription.

Dean and DeLuca
(800-221-7714, www.deandeluca.com)
The celebrated New York store—their mail-
order catalog features a select group of olive
oils, spices, equipment, and much more.

DeMedici Imports
(845-651-4400)
Imports and sells a carefully selected and
outstanding collection of fine olive oils; ask
for their catalog.

Esperya
(877-907-2525, www.esperya.com)
Internet source for an extraordinary selection of highest-quality Italian ingredients
(including Sicilian belly tuna, capers from
Pantelleria, great Italian cheeses, chestnut
honey) and olive oils, arranged by regions of
Italy. Click on the American flag to read the
site in English, get prices in dollars, and get
delivery details. They also have a call-back
system if you want to talk with them
directly, and they send an informative and
free e-mail newsletter to subscribers.

Global Food Market
(fax 818-879-0462,
www.globalfoodmarket.com)
Sells a variety of ethnic ingredients including
peeled fava beans and pomegranate
molasses, at reasonable prices.

Gourmet Oil Co.
(jane@nywines)
A specialty importer of a select group of
extraordinary olive oils, most of which are
associated with the wines they carry.

Katz and Co.
(707-254-1866, www.katzandco.com)
Very good selection of fine California olive
oils, plus accessories like pouring spouts and
dipping bowls. Ask for their catalog.

King Arthur Flour Company Store
(800-827-6836)
Sells pizza stones and peels, pearl sugar, and
other hard-to-find equipment and
foodstuffs.

Market Hall Foods
(888-952-4005)
The retail source for all of the outstanding
oils from Manicaretti Imports.

Nomads
(www.nomads.com)
A website that specializes in goods from
Morocco, including an olive oil they import
and sell under their own label.

O&Co., or Oliviers & Co.

(212-973-1472, www.oliviersandco.com)
The American wing of a French company,
they currently have two retail stores in New
York City that feature an extraordinary
range of olive oils from all over the
Mediterranean, extracted and bottled to
their own specifications, as well as other
olive products.

Olive Merchant

(www.olivemerchant.com)
Extremely knowledgeable Internet source
for a great and discerning selection of fine
olive oils. They also make up gift baskets of
oils and related goods like olive oil soaps.

The Olive Oil Club

(800-665-2975, www.oliveoilclub.com)
A monthly (or every other month) delivery
of a different olive oil on a subscription
basis, carefully chosen for quality and variety. Some of the oils they carry are
unavailable elsewhere in the U.S.

Penzey's

(800-741-7787, www.penzeys.com)
Sells juniper berries, herbes de provence
blend, and just about any spice you can
think of.

Rogers International

(www.rogersintl.com)
Carries a unique and thoughtful selection of
olive oils.

Shamra

(800-880-6062, www.shamra.com)
Source for a wide variety of Mediterranean
and Arabic foodstuffs, as well as music and
housewares.

Simpson and Vail

(800-282-TEAS, www.svtea.com)
Sells great olive oils on their website; their
olive oils are not presently featured in their
catalog.

The Spanish Table

(206-682-2827, www.tablespan.com)
Excellent source for a wide array of Spanish
and Portuguese products and foodstuffs, as
well as music, cookware, etc.

Spirit of Provence

(www.spiritofprovence.com)
Internet source for great French olive oils
from Provence, as well as other Provençal
specialties; based in the U.S.

Strictly Olive Oil

(408-372-6682)
Betty Pustarfi is a great resource for information, tastings, and olive oil sales.

Teitel Brothers

(800-850-7055, www.teitelbros.com)
An Italian specialty market on Arthur
Avenue in the Bronx. In addition to the
pleasures of shopping in their store, you can
mail- or phone order hard-to-find ingredients, or shop via the Internet.

Tienda

(888-472-1022, www.tienda.com)
U.S.–based Internet and mail-order source
for Spanish foodstuffs, *cazuelas,* etc. Catalog
available.

Trader Joe's

(www.traderjoe.com)
A chain of discount gourmet food stores;
their website can direct you to their nearest
location. They sell a wide variety of products
under their own label, including a number
of olive oils.

Zingerman's

(888-636-8162, www.Zingermans.com)
This celebrated store in Ann Arbor,
Michigan, is available to us all via mail order
and the Internet. It's a source for an especially discerning selection of fine olive oils,
specialty ingredients like urfa pepper and
fennel pollen, good-tasting real breads (with
a breads-of-the-month club!), and more.
Catalog available.

Olive Oil Producers Who Sell Direct to Consumers

Because the Internet has made it possible for even small regional food producers to sell directly to consumers, some of these extra virgin olive oils are available only on the Internet. However, some of the producers below also sell their oils through distributors or through retail stores. In any case, you can get more information from their websites or by telephone.

Blauel Olive Oil, an organic oil from the Mani in Greece, is sold under a number of different brand names, including Greek Gold. It is also available direct from the producer at sales@blauel.gr.

Calaveras Olive Oil (California): 209-785-1000.

Carpineto Olive Oil (Italy): www.carpineto.com.

Darien Cheese. A specialty store in Darien, Connecticut, owned by Ken Skovron. His own blends of California oils are sold under the brand name "Corsica," and, along with other outstanding oils he carries, are available by mail and phone order (203-655-4344).

DaVero Olive Oils: www.Davero.com.

Elea Olive Oil (Greece): www.eleaoliveoil.com.

Eleni Olive Oil (Greece): www.elenigourmet.com.

Frantoio Proprietor's Select and **Frantoio California Unfiltered:** www.frantoio.com.

Gallo Olive Oil and **Victor Guedes Olive Oil** (Portugal): Triunfo Imports is the retail mail-order source (973-491-0399).

Kotinos Olive Oil (Greece): www.kotinos.com.

Laleli Olive Oils (Turkey): www.zeytinim.com.

L'Oulibo Cuvée Olive Oils (France): export@deelen.com.

McEvoy Olive Oils (California): www.mcevoyranch.com.

O Olive Oils are available in stores and at www.ooliveoil.com.

Olio del Le Colline di Santa Cruz (California) is available from Valancia Creek Farm (831-662-2345).

Olive Farm Olive Oils (Turkey): www.olivefarm.com (available only via the Internet but shipped from the Pacific Northwest). They also offer some Turkish spices, table olives, and housewares.

Pons Olive Oil and **Mas Portel Olive Oil** (Spain): www.casaponsusa.com.

Podere Pornanino Olive Oil (Italy): www.chiantionline.com.

Primoli Olive Oils, including a line of Italian regional specialty oils: www.minervausa.com.

Rasna Olive Oil: www.rasna.com.

Romeu Olive Oil (Portugal): www.olivetree.cc.

Sciabica Olive Oils: www.sciabica.com.

St. Helena Olive Oil Co: 800-939-9880.

St. Pierre Olive Oils (California) are available from John Addleman (797-585-9955).

Terroirs de Provence: www.terroirsdeprovence.com. Click on the English flag to read the site in English.

Wente Vineyards "Oro Fino" (California): 925-456-2300.

Zeytinim: www.zeytinim.com.

Other Websites of Interest

California Olive Oil Council: www.cooc.com.

International Olive Oil Council: www.internationaloliveoil.org

www.olivesource.com.
www.theolivepress.com.

BIBLIOGRAPHY

Bastianich, Lidia Matticchio. *Lidia's Italian Table.* William Morrow, 1998.

Bianchi, Anne. *Zuppa!* Ecco Press, 1996.

Brennan, Georgeanne. *Savoring France.* Time/Life, Weldon Owen, 1999.

Brettschneider, Dean and Lauraine Jacobs. *Baker: Best of International Baking from Australia and New Zealand Professionals.* Tandem Press, 2001.

Bugialli, Giuliano. *Foods of Sicily and Sardinia.* Rizzoli, 1996.

Casas, Penelope. *The Foods and Wines of Spain.* Alfred A. Knopf, 1982.

Davidson, Alan. *The Oxford Companion to Food.* Oxford University Press, 1999.

DeMori, Lori et al. *Italy Anywhere.* Viking/Penguin, 2000.

Ehrlich, Elizabeth. *Miriam's Kitchen.* Viking/Penguin, 1997.

Field, Carol. *In Nonna's Kitchen.* HarperCollins, 1997.

Gray, Patience. *Honey From a Weed.* Harper & Row, 1986.

Hazan, Marcella. *More Classic Italian Cooking.* Alfred A. Knopf, 1978.

International Olive Oil Council. *World Olive Encyclopedia.* IOOC, 1996.

———. *Olive Oil and Health.* IOOC, 1997.

———. *The Olive Tree, the Oil, the Olive.* IOOC, 1998.

Jenkins, Nancy Harmon. *Flavors of Puglia.* Broadway Books, 1997.

Kasper, Lynne Rossetto. *The Italian Country Table.* Scribner, 1999.

Klein, Maggie Blyth. *The Feast of the Olive.* Chronicle Books, 1983.

Knickerbocker, Peggy. *Olive Oil: From Tree to Table.* Chronicle Books, 1997.

Kochilas, Diane. *The Glorious Food of Greece.* William Morrow, 2001.

Kremezi, Aglaia. *The Foods of the Greek Islands.* Houghton Mifflin, 2000.

La Place, Viana and Evan Kleiman. *Cucina Rustica.* William Morrow, 1990.

Marks, Gil. *The World of Jewish Desserts.* Simon & Schuster, 2000.

Midgley, John. *The Goodness of Olive Oil.* Random House, 1992.

Olney, Richard. *Simple French Food.* Atheneum, 1975.

Plotkin, Fred. *La Terra Fortunata.* Random House, 2001.

———. *Recipes from Paradise.* Little, Brown, 1997.

Rosenblum, Mort. *Olives: The Life and Lore of a Noble Fruit.* North Point Press, 1996.

Rubinstein, Nela. *Nela's Cookbook.* Alfred A. Knopf, 1983.

Schwartz, Arthur. *Naples at Table.* HarperCollins, 1998.

Scicolone, Michele. *A Fresh Taste of Italy.* Broadway Books, 1997.

Selvaggio, Piero. *The Valentino Cookbook.* Villard, 2001.

Viazzi, Alfredo. *Alfredo Viazzi's Cucina e Nostalgia.* Random House, 1979.

Werle, Loukie. *Saffron, Garlic and Olives.* Fisher Books, 1999.

Wolfert, Paula. *The Cooking of the Eastern Mediterranean.* HarperCollins, 1994.

———. *Paula Wolfert's World of Food.* Harper and Row, 1988.

METRIC EQUIVALENTS

Liquid and Dry Measure Equivalents

CUSTOMARY	METRIC
¼ teaspoon	1.25 milliliters
½ teaspoon	2.5 milliliters
1 teaspoon	5 milliliters
1 tablespoon	15 milliliters
1 fluid ounce	30 milliliters
¼ cup	60 milliliters
⅛ cup	80 milliliters
½ cup	120 milliliters
1 cup	240 milliliters
1 pint (*2 cups*)	480 milliliters
1 quart (*4 cups, 32 ounces*)	960 milliliters (*.96 liter*)
1 gallon (*4 quarts*)	3.84 liters
1 ounce (*by weight*)	28 grams
¼ pound (*4 ounces*)	114 grams
1 pound (*16 ounces*)	454 grams
2.2 pounds	1 kilogram (*1,000 grams*)

Sweet Italian, Penne with Spinach and, 132–33
sauté pans, 53–54
Scallops, Seared, on Chickpea Crepes, 158–59
sea salt, coarse, 57–58
sensual cues, 50
Shrimp, Spaghetti with Rosemary-Infused Grappa, Chestnut Honey and, 142–43
side dishes, *see* vegetables and side dishes
Sinolea method, 7, 9
Sirloin Steak, Seared, on Bed of Watercress with Parmesan Shavings, 95
soil, 4, 5
soups, 102–11
  Beet, Cold, 110–11
  Celery, with Feta, Toasted Walnuts, and Apple, Iced, 109
  Chickpea, with *Cavolo Nero*, 104–5
  Fava Bean, 102–3
  Gazpacho, 107
  Ginger-Pea, Fresh, with Truffle Oil, Iced, 108
  Green Split Pea, with Chicken-Apple Sausage, **2**, 106
  pouring oil on, 103
  White Bean, with Sage and Garlic, 180
spaghetti:
  with Bottarga di Tonno, 138
  with Fried Egg and Greens, 93
  with Parsley and Olive Oil, 138
  with Shrimp, Rosemary-Infused Grappa, and Chestnut Honey, 142–43
Spain, Spanish oils, 4–5, 6, 7, 8, 15
  tasting notes for, 41–43
Spanish-style dishes:
  Chicken Braised with Saffron, Cinnamon, and Lavender, Topped with Almonds, **5**, 166–67
  Fried Egg and Arugula Salad with Croutons, 92–93
  Gazpacho, 107
  Manchego Cheese, Red Pepper, and Anchovy Melts, 76
  Rice with Mixed Sausages, 168–69
  Tomato Toast, 77
Spareribs, Slow-Cooked Boneless, in Tomato, Rosemary, and Juniper Sauce, 170–71
spices, 60
spinach:
  Penne with Sweet Italian Sausage and, 132–33
  Pureed, with Ricotta, 193
  and Strawberry Spring Salad, 100
spoons, wooden, 55

spreads:
  Cauliflower, Pureed, with Truffle Olive Oil on Grilled Bread, 73
  Eggplant Caviar, 74
  Tapenade, 72
Spring Vegetables, Olive Oil–Bathed, **1**, 177
Steak, Seared Sirloin, on Bed of Watercress with Parmesan Shavings, 95
storing olive oil, 19–20, 26
strawberry:
  Coulis, Buttermilk Lemon-Almond Cake with, 198–99
  and Spinach Spring Salad, 100
Strudel, Apple-Cherry Cardamom, **8**, 202–3
substitutions, 52–53
sugar, 145
Summer Pasta with Raw Tomato Sauce, 144
Sweet Taralle (*Ciambelle*), 195
swordfish:
  Chioccioli with, in Tomato Sauce, 140–41
  Steaks, Yogurt-Marinated Grilled, **6**, 154

T

Tapenade, 72
Taralle, Sweet (*Ciambelle*), 195
Tarragon Potato Salad, 189
Tart, Fresh Tomato, **3**, 79
tasting notes, 30–45
tasting olive oil, 22–28
  author's process for, 23–25
  flavor categories for, 22–23, 28
  suggestions for, 26–28
tin containers for olive oil, 18
tomato(es):
  Basil, Mozzarella, and Olive Oil on Baguette, 78
  Cherry, Baked, Paola, 185
  Gazpacho, 107
  Grilled Side Vegetables, 184
  Oven-Dried, 62–63
  Oven-Dried, Cellentani Pasta with Gorgonzola and, 134–35
  Raw, Sauce, Summer Pasta with, 144
  Rosemary, and Juniper Sauce, Slow-Cooked Boneless Pork Spareribs in, 170–71
  Sauce, Chioccioli with Swordfish in, 140–41
  Smoked Mozzarella, and Basil Filling (for Piadina), 115
  Sun-Dried, Poultry Sausage with, Whole Wheat Gobbetti with Red Pepper, Kale and, 128–29
  Tart, Fresh, **3**, 79
  Toast, 77